Transforming Tomorrow

Innovative Solutions and Global Trends in Electrical and Electronics Engineering

Transforming Tomorrow

Innovative Solutions and Global Trends in Electrical and Electronics Engineering

EDITORS

Dr. Namit Gupta
Dr. Anjali Gupta
Dr. Naresh Purohit
Dr. Shiraz Husain

ALLIED PUBLISHERS PVT. LTD.

Noida • Mumbai • Kolkata • Chennai • Bangalore

ALLIED PUBLISHERS PRIVATE LIMITED

D-5, Sector-2, **Noida**–201 301
Ph. Nos.: 0120-4320295/2542557/4352866 • E-mail: delhi.books@alliedpublishers.com

17 Chittaranjan Avenue, **Kolkata**–700072
Ph.: 033-22129618 • E-mail: cal.books@alliedpublishers.com

15 J.N. Heredia Marg, Ballard Estate, **Mumbai**–400001
Ph.: 022-42126969 • E-mail: mumbai.books@alliedpublishers.com

No. 25/10, Commander-in-Chief Road, Ethiraj Lane (Next to Post Office)
Egmore, **Chennai**–600008
Ph.: 044-28223938 • E-mail: chennai.books@alliedpublishers.com

P.B. No. 9932, No. 15, 3rd Floor (Next to Vijaya Bank), 5th Cross, Gandhinagar,
Karnataka, **Bangalore**–560009, Ph.: 080-41530285 / 22386239
E-mail: bngl.books@alliedpublishers.com

Website: www.alliedpublishers.com

ISBN: 978-93-89934-35-9

Published by Sunil Sachdev and printed by Ravi Sachdev at Allied Publishers Pvt. Ltd.,
D-5, Sector-2, Noida–201 301

Foreword

Trends Shaping the Future

The world of power and electricity is experiencing a paradigm shift. As technological advancements continue to accelerate, we find ourselves at the forefront of a new era in energy. With sustainability and efficiency at the core of innovation, the power and electric sectors are undergoing significant transformations that will define the energy landscape for decades to come. Some of the transformative trends that are shaping the future of power and electricity range from renewable energy integration to smart grids, electric vehicles, energy storage, and decentralized energy systems.

The global energy sector is undergoing rapid transformation. Traditional power systems, which have long been reliant on fossil fuels, are gradually being replaced by renewable and clean technologies. Simultaneously, digital technologies are enabling smarter and more efficient management of energy generation, distribution, and consumption. These innovations are creating a more sustainable, resilient, and interconnected energy ecosystem.

Renewable Energy Integration has been a growing sector for years, but the next wave of innovation promises to accelerate its adoption and integration into the grid. Wind, solar, hydro, and geothermal energy sources are becoming more cost-effective, reliable, and scalable, making them key players in the future of energy. Solar energy is already the leading renewable energy source in terms of installed capacity. The declining cost of solar panels, improvements in solar cell efficiency, and the rise of solar farms are driving mass adoption worldwide. Additionally, solar roof tiles and solar windows are emerging technologies that allow homes and businesses to integrate solar power into their structures without sacrificing aesthetics.

Offshore wind farms are rapidly gaining momentum, particularly in Europe and the U.S. These farms harness stronger and more consistent winds found offshore, generating substantial amounts of energy. The advancement of floating wind turbines will further expand wind power's reach into deeper waters, providing energy to areas previously unable to host traditional offshore turbines. Micro-grids, which are localized grids that can operate independently of the main grid, and community solar initiatives, where groups of households share solar energy resources, are gaining popularity. These solutions offer more energy independence and increased resilience, especially in remote or disaster-prone areas.

Smart Grids are one of the most important trends reshaping the power sector. These digitalized energy systems integrate information technology with electrical infrastructure, enabling real-time data collection, automated control, and efficient energy distribution. Advanced Metering Infrastructure systems are being implemented across power grids worldwide to provide real-time consumption data, enhance customer engagement, and improve demand-side management. Consumers can monitor and manage their energy usage, while utilities gain insights to predict demand and optimize supply.

Traditional electrical grids only allowed one-way communication—from utilities to consumers. With smart grids, however, there is two-way communication. This enables features such as remote monitoring and control, fault detection, and dynamic response to changes in demand, resulting in a more resilient grid. Smart grids facilitate the integration of DERs, such as rooftop solar panels, battery storage, and electric vehicles (EVs). These resources can be managed and optimized in real-time to balance supply and demand, reduce grid congestion, and enhance overall grid stability.

One of the biggest challenges in integrating renewable energy into the grid is its intermittent nature. The development of energy storage technologies has therefore become critical in addressing this issue and enabling a reliable power supply. Lithium-ion batteries are currently the dominant form of energy storage, offering high energy density, relatively fast charging, and long lifespan. These batteries are widely used for both grid-scale storage and in electric vehicles (EVs). They can store excess energy generated by renewable sources and release it when demand peaks.

Solid-state batteries are an emerging technology that promises higher energy density, faster charging, and greater safety than traditional lithium-ion batteries. With solid-state batteries, the risks associated with liquid electrolytes, such as overheating or flammability, are significantly reduced.

Pragyata is an Annual National Conference organized by Shri Vaishnav Institute of Technology & Science to give an opportunity to the Engineering faculty, students and researchers to share their perspective. It is scheduled to be held on 5th-6th May 2025 this year. The theme of the conference is *Transforming Tomorrow: Innovative Solutions and Global Trends in Electrical and Electronics Engineering.* A selected lot of 25 papers, out of the larger number received for presentation, has thoroughly been edited for inclusion in this book for the benefit of stakeholders, particularly the professionals and researchers having interest in this domain of engineering.

Date: 29.04.2025

Dr. Upinder Dhar
Vice Chancellor
Shri Vaishnav Vidyapeeth
Vishwavidyalaya, Indore

Prologue

The National Conference *"Pragyata 2025"*, centered on the theme *"Transforming Tomorrow: Innovative Solutions and Global Trends in Electrical and Electronics Engineering"*, aims to bring together scholars, professionals, and researchers from across the nation to explore transformative innovations that are shaping the future of the electrical and electronics domain. In an era driven by rapid technological evolution, it is imperative to identify and implement solutions that not only address current engineering challenges but also align with sustainable and globally relevant trends.

The field of electrical and electronics engineering is undergoing a revolutionary shift, powered by advancements in Artificial Intelligence, Machine Learning, renewable energy systems, IoT-enabled smart infrastructure, and next-generation communication technologies. These developments are redefining the boundaries of what is possible from intelligent power distribution systems and energy-efficient smart grids to autonomous electric vehicles and cutting-edge image processing for industrial applications. As global challenges demand more sustainable and resilient engineering practices, the integration of interdisciplinary technologies is becoming not just advantageous, but essential.

Pragyata 2025 serves as a dynamic platform for knowledge exchange, encouraging innovative thought, practical implementation, and collaborative research. It fosters a deeper understanding of emerging trends such as wireless energy transfer, edge computing in automation, and sustainable material usage in hardware design. The conference emphasizes the importance of harnessing global advancements to address local challenges, thereby bridging the gap between theoretical exploration and real-world application.

As we collectively envision a smarter, more connected, and eco-conscious future, this conference stands as a testament to the power of innovation and shared learning. It invites all participants to contribute to the ongoing journey of technological excellence, academic enrichment, and industry transformation in electrical and electronics engineering.

The book acknowledges the contributions of numerous researchers from academic institutions, research organizations, industry, and consulting firms. Special thanks are extended to the authors, conveners, editorial team, and the organizing committee of *Pragyata 2025* for their support. Appreciation is also given to the faculty and staff of Shri Vaishnav Institute of Technology and Science and Shri Vaishnav Vidyapeeth Vishwavidyalaya, Indore.

Dr. Namit Gupta
Dean, Faculty of Engineering, Technology and Architecture
Director, SVITS, SVVV, Indore

About the Editors

Dr. Namit Gupta is presently working as Dean, Faculty of Engineering, Technology and Architecture, and Director, SVITS, SVVV, Indore. He is having a vast experience of Teaching and research of 24 years. An experienced professor with a demonstrated history in education management, he is skilled in Lecturing, Curriculum Development, E-Learning, and Research. He holds a PhD in "Quantum Dot Cellular Automata Related Work" and has published more than 75 papers in various reputed National and International journals. He also holds a patent in the *"Process for Formation of Capacitor Structure for Non-Volatile Memory on Germanium Nanocrystals."* Dr. Gupta has mentored numerous students and guided more than 100 student projects at the UG and PG levels. He has guided 6 PhD Scholars. Currently, six research scholars are working under his guidance. He is the Chairman of the Faculty of Studies for Engineering and Architecture and Chairman, Board of Studies for EC/EE/EI. He is actively involved in curriculum development at SVVV and works with the IQAC team for the effective implementation of the New Education Policy 2020 at SVVV.

Dr. Anjali Gupta has more than 20 years of experience in teaching in the field of Electronics and Communication Engineering. She is currently working as Assistant Professor in the Department of Electrical and Electronics Engineering at Shri Vaishnav Institute of Technology Science, Shri Vaishnav Vidyapeeth Vishwavidyalaya, Indore. She received her B.E. Degree in Electronics and Communication Engineering from Rajasthan University in 2003. She did her M.E. in Digital Communication from IET DAVV, Indore in 2009 and PhD. in Electronics Telecommunication from DAVV, Indore. Her research interests include signal processing, wireless communication, and IoT. Dr. Gupta is a dedicated academician and active contributor at Shri Vaishnav Vidyapeeth Vishwavidyalaya (SVVV). She is a member of the Board of Studies for the Electrical and Electronics Engineering Department and the Institution's Innovation Council (IIC). With expertise in IoT, Robotics, and Communication Systems, she has participated in various faculty development programs and completed several NPTEL-SWAYAM certifications in her domain. Dr. Gupta has served as editor for interdisciplinary and technical books and has reviewed numerous technical papers for reputed conferences and publications. She has played key roles in organizing national and international academic events and competitions and contributes actively to institutional development and student engagement activities. Her leadership extends to various academic, administrative, and extracurricular initiatives, reflecting her strong commitment to innovation, quality education, and holistic student development.

Dr. Naresh Purohit is an accomplished academician and industry expert with over 24 years of comprehensive experience in both teaching and the industrial sector. Throughout his career, he has served in various key roles and has made significant contributions to the field of electronics and telecommunication through his research and academic endeavors. He has published numerous research papers in reputed journals and conferences, reflecting his strong foundation in cutting-edge technologies. His primary research interests include 5G system development, data science, wireless communication, MIMO (Multiple Input, Multiple Output) systems, and NOMA (Non-Orthogonal Multiple Access) systems. These focus areas highlight his commitment to advancing next-generation communication technologies and addressing the evolving challenges of modern wireless networks. Dr. Purohit is an Associate Member of the Institution of Electronics and Telecommunication Engineers (IETE). He is deeply passionate about enhancing the quality of education and is a dedicated advocate for teacher professional development.

Dr. Shiraz Husain is currently working as Assistant Professor in the Department of Electronics and Communication Engineering at Shri Vaishnav Vidyapeeth Vishwavidyalaya, Indore. He received his Master of Engineering degree in 2014 from Rajiv Gandhi Proudyogiki Vishwavidyalaya, Bhopal (M.P.), India. He completed his Ph.D. in Electronics Engineering in June 2024 with a specialization in *Quantum Dot Cellular Automata*. Dr. Husain has more than thirteen years of experience in teaching and research. His areas of interest include low power VLSI design, nanoelectronics, and quantum computing technologies. He has conducted several training programs in robotics, IoT, and embedded systems, and has published multiple research papers in reputed journals. Dr. Husain is also actively involved in the implementation of innovative laboratory practices and the development of IoT-based learning modules for undergraduate students. He has secured top ranks in national-level certification exams like NPTEL and has been engaged in academic activities including conference organization and curriculum development.

Contents

Gesture Vocalizer: Converting Signs into Speech

Kartik Bhardwaj[1], Yash Porwal[2], Amar Dubey[3] and Sachin Puntambker[4]

ABSTRACT: In Today's time around 15–20 percent people are not able to speak or listen. So to communicate with the world these verbally and hearing impaired people use the sign language. This is a type of communication in which hand gestures and hand movements are used to communicate with other people. Sign language is a way of communication which consists of twenty-six different hand gestures, each representing an alphabet. This is a very difficult and different way of communication. Around 85–90 percent of people don't understand the sign language so, it is not a universal solution. However, there are many solutions for this problem today. The most popular one is hand gesture converter using flex sensors but, it is really expensive and hard to afford because, these sensors are expensive in market which increases the overall cost of the product. This research paper will help to overcome this high cost problem. In this paper sensors with basic requirements which decreases the cost have been designed and implemented.

Keywords: Cost Communication, Flex Sensors, Gesture Converter, Sign Language.

1. INTRODUCTION

1.1 Overview

There are different types of sign languages present all over the world such as Indian sign language, American sign language etc. And, the most widely used language is American sign language. To communicate with people the verbally and hearing impaired people use the sign language. This sign language consists of Hand gestures

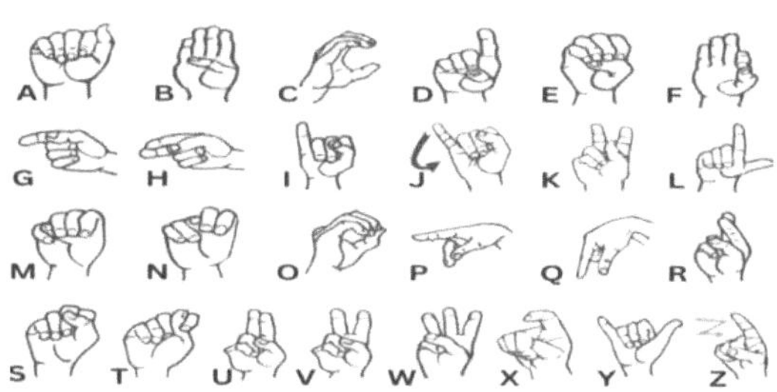

Figure 1: American Sign Language (ava.me/asl)

[1-4]Department of Electronics Communication, Medicaps University, Indore, India.
E-mail: [1]en21el301041@medicaps.ac.in; [2]en21me303052@medicaps.ac.in; [3]en21el301013@medicaps.ac.in; [4]Sachin.puntambekar@medicaps.ac.in

as well as hand movements for communication. Gestures are nonverbally exchanged messages that was understood by human vision. There are many research papers which focuses on this problem but are really expensive. So, to reduce the cost of this design is the major process of this research. Finger spelling is primarily based on hand gestures in order to shape an entire phrase by combining every gesture. It is a language that accommodates twenty-six hand symbols each representing one alphabet.

1.2 Objectives of the Research

- To design a system that accurately detects and translates gestures into audible speech in real-time, which helps in seamless communication for individuals with speech and hearing disability.
- To reduce the overall cost.
- To develop a portable and easily customizable device that can adapt to the specific needs of users, which enhances the usability of the device.

2. LITERATURE REVIEW

After reviewing different research paper there are so many projects that are developed for deaf and mute people. Such as, Artificial Neural Network is the concept of this prototype. The sensors are setup on the hand of speech impaired person so that the sensors convert the bend movement is the fingers and hand; convert that into the electrical signal. This electrical signal provided to the microcontroller and the output is generated [1]. The wearable glove is prepared for the verbally impaired person. This glove consists of flex sensors and accelerometer. The flex sensors are attached to each finger for the reading of the finger movement and the accelerometer Gy-61 is used for the disabled person for the reading of the hand movement [2]. A device which is used to convert the gestures to voice as well as text. The device is used to for both disabled and normal people. This device helps the verbally impaired people and convert the gestures into text and display the text on the screen [3]. Another paper that aims toward the development of a device which converts the hand gestures into the audio. The aim is to remove the complications of different hand gestures and have only one sort of hand gesture instead of different types such as American sign language or Indian sign language etc. The paper further aims to make home automation with the hand gestures to control various components such as fan, light, fridge etc. [4]

Other research paper have the ideas secular to collect the information from arduino and make the high accuracy hand recognition system. This design involves the random forest model training and accuracy evaluation in gesture recognition. The design achieves high and precise hand recognition system which helps the verbally impaired person to communicate with others more easily and efficiently [5-9]. Another paper involves the microcontroller and sensor based gesture vocalizer. It involves a data glove and a microcontroller setup. The data glove collects all data of the hand gestures and the hand movements and the microcontroller can convert that data into human understandable speech. The data glove consists of two types of sensors first a bend sensor and a hand tilt sensor. The data glove is able to read all these movement easily. This system is beneficial for verbally impaired people but a little too expensive.

3. PROPOSED SYSTEM

The main focus of these existing systems are to build a system that can be more reliable and flexible, to do such a thing best and expensive items have been used in their system which make the product quite expensive and hard to purchase for a poor person. The proposed design is less expensive items in our project which also quite efficient as well. The main goal of this research is to reduce the overall cost. To do so, the sensors were designed in the lab with the help of basic items. A flex sensor works by acting as variable resistor, i.e., its electrical resistance changes on the amount of binding. A flex sensor consists of a conducting layer which is flexible and is made with a thin layer of conducting material like carbon ink printed on it.

Importance of Bending Mechanism: In this bending mechanism when the sensor is bent, the conductive layer stretches, effectively reducing it's cross-sectional area and increasing its resistance. So, this property make this sensor really expensive around 200–250 rupees per piece in Indian market and around 130–150 dollar per piece in US market. So, to reduce the cost cheap and easily available metal aluminum (Foil paper) which is less expensive in comparison to any other metal and easily available has been used. Two layers of aluminum foil on a soft cardboard were combine which makes it more flexible, and a carbon paper was used for better efficiency. This carbon paper can also be made by just rubbing the pencil to a plane paper since pencil consists of graphite which is a form of carbon and can be easily made at home and is easily accessible. Since the important factor in this design is efficiency so instead of using pencil's graphite the carbon present in the discharged batteries is can be used. Then the jumper wires pore connected each end of the both aluminum layer. The carbon layer is used to separate both the aluminum layers so that these two would not touch each other which is better for connectivity and conductivity. So, these to designs make an easy and less expensive flex sensor at home. The efficiency of this sensor is quite good in comparison to the market expensive sensors. The overall cost of this sensor is also very low.

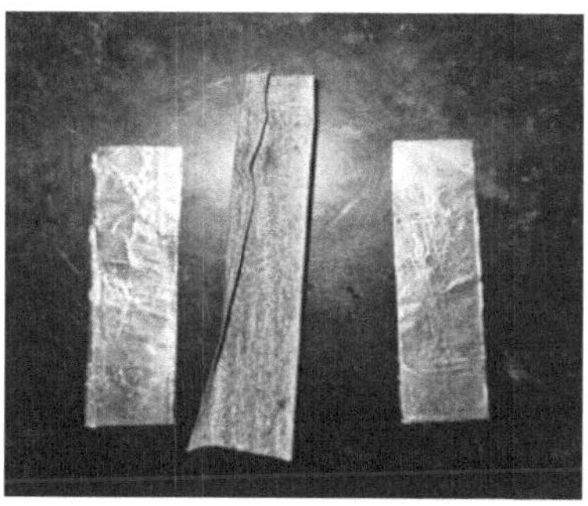

Figure 2: Conductive Layer

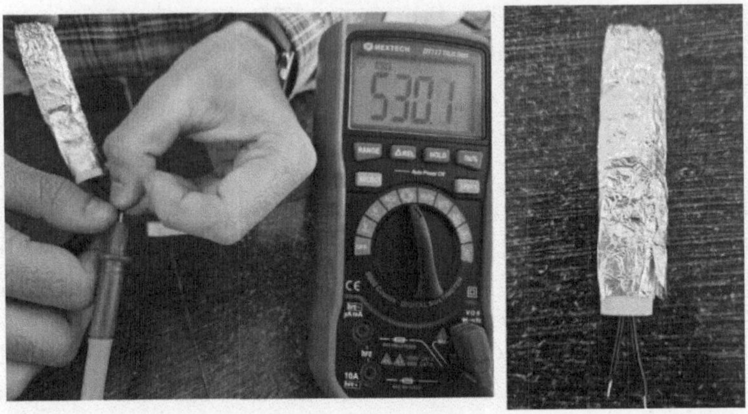

Figure 3: Flex Sensors

Now the method to design a gesture vocalize has been presented here. First of all, five flex sensors all connected them to the arduino via analog pins A0, A1, A2, A3, A4 and other one end to the VCC of the arduino. This allows for the flow of current through the sensors. Also 10 k ohm resistors have been added with each sensor. An accelerometer (mpu6050) has been used which allows to read the gyro movement of the hand since, many gestures requires to bend the arm so by using this accelerometer these movement can be read. For the accelerometer VCC is connected to 5V to the arduino, and SDA will be connected to the pin A4 in arduino and SCL pin is connected A5 pin in the arduino. Now, the Bluetooth module is used for the output of all these readings into the mobile phones or smart gadget. The Bluetooth module HC-05 is used. The TX (Transmission end) of Bluetooth module to the RX (Receiving end) of the arduino which is pin 10 and again the RX of Bluetooth module to the TX of arduino which is pin 11 is connected is connected.

4. RESULT

A Gesture vocalizer is a device is to convert the gestures into speech or text it is often used for those people who are verbally and hearing impaired. The overall result is that the output will be vocalized instead of recognized gestures. The flex sensors which is build are working properly and efficiently and the connections of overall design are also working fine. So this is minimum cost and can be easily accessible. Another application is for the human computer interactions for gesture-controlled interfaces.

5. CONCLUSION

The main objective of this design is to make a device which can be used for converting the sign language into the speech. Also, is cost effective and efficient. This would help those people who cannot are not able to buy expensive products and facing the issue or having the communication gap design interaction with other people. Also this is easy to be used since all the outputs are coming out of the mobile phone of the person.

REFERENCES

[1] Sangeethalakshmi, K.; Shanthi, K.G. and Raj, A.M., "Design and implementation of low power VLSI architectures for high-speed applications," *Materials Today: Proceedings*, vol. 80, pp. 1035–1040, 2023.

[2] Manandhar, S.; Bajracharya, S.; Karki, S. and Jha, A.K., "Design and Simulation of CMOS Inverter using Microwind Tool," *SCITECH Nepal*, Vol. 14, No. 1, pp. 42–48, 2019.

[3] Ail, S.; Chauhan, B.; Dabhi, H.; Darji, V. and Bandi, Y., "Design and Analysis of Low Power CMOS Circuits," in *Proc. Int. Conf. on Emerging Trends in Engineering*, Springer, 2020, pp. 451–460.

[4] Jha, A. and Pathak, K., "Performance Analysis of CMOS Inverter using Microwind," *JMC Research Journal*, Vol. 2, pp. 27–34, 2023.

[5] Harivardhagini, S., "Design and Simulation of VLSI Circuits Using Microwind Tool," *CVR Journal of Science and Technology*, Vol. 20, pp. 94–98, 2021.

[6] Nath, D.; Kurmi, J. and Shukla, D.N., "Design and Performance Analysis of CMOS Inverter using 45 nm Technology in Microwind," 2020.

[7] Nauta, B., "A CMOS Transconductance-Capacitor Filter Technique for Very High Frequencies," *IEEE Journal of Solid-State Circuits*, Vol. 27, No. 2, pp. 142–153, Feb. 1992.

[8] Allen, P.E. and Holberg, D.R., *CMOS Analog Circuit Design*, 3rd ed. New York, NY, USA: Oxford Univ. Press, 2012.

[9] Sedra, A. and Smith, K.C., *Microelectronic Circuits*, 7th ed. New York, NY, USA: Oxford Univ. Press, 2014.

Smart Attendance Monitoring Using Facial Recognition Technology

Khushi Vijayvargiya[1], Aditya Rathore[2], Nikita Nayak[3] and Juned A. Siddiqui[4]

ABSTRACT: In this paper's overview, some research work considers it based on intelligent presence systems for recording presence based on facial recognition. Efficient and accurate attendance management is an important task in a variety of educational and organizational settings. Traditional methods for manual persecution of existence are time consuming and errorprone. The proposed system uses computer vision and deep learning techniques to recognize and verify the identity of people in a particular environment. It uses facial recognition algorithms to fit existing data records and facial features in the database, allowing seamless and efficient attendance tracking.

Keywords: *CNN, Deep Metric Learning, Eigenvalues, OpenCV, PCA.*

1. INTRODUCTION

This research paper investigates the evolution of facial recognition technology and its transformative potential in automating attendance systems. By examining both historical advancements and contemporary innovations, the study highlights how traditional manual attendance methods are progressively being replaced by automated approaches that leverage biometric and machine learning techniques. The integration of these technologies not only promises enhanced accuracy and efficiency but also addresses long-standing challenges associated with conventional record-keeping practices.

The discussion begins with an exploration of the technological shift from manual systems to biometric solutions. As the study underscores, "Biometric attendance systems offer several advantages for universities in terms of efficiency and accountability, yet they also pose significant drawbacks such as increased job stress and reduced employee morale that are particularly challenging in environments marked by frequent power outages and varied operational roles. This observation sets the stage for a deeper analysis of how automated systems can overcome such limitations and improve overall operational performance.

Following this introductory overview, the paper is structured to lead the reader through a systematic examination of the subject. Subsequent chapters will articulate the problem definition, establish the theoretical foundations, and detail the specific

[1-4]Department of Electronics, Medi-Caps University Indore, Indore, India.
E-mail: [1]khushivj1323@gmail.com; [2]adityarathore@gmail.com; [3]nikitanayak@gmail.com; [4]juned.siddiqui@medicaps.ac.in

challenges posed by current attendance practices. In doing so, the study elaborates on the necessity for an automated system that not only enhances accuracy but also integrates seamlessly with existing institutional frameworks.

A major focus of the work is the technical formulation of the proposed attendance system. It delves into both the theoretical underpinnings and the practical implementation of advanced biometric and computer vision strategies. As illustrated in recent research, "The proposed system employs Histogram Oriented Gradients (HOG) for face detection, in conjunction with facial landmark encoding and dlib's Facenet, achieving an impressive 99.38% accuracy on the Labeled Faces in the Wild benchmark". This chapter sets the context for later sections that will provide an in-depth discussion on the accuracy, reliability, and robustness of the proposed methods [1].

Complementing the technical considerations, the paper also addresses the integration of modern software and hardware architectures that underpin secure and efficient attendance systems. The analysis takes into account a variety of cuttingedge technologies and design paradigms, as evidenced by the observation that "Visage Verify effectively integrates modern technologies such as React Native for cross-platform development, Flask for a lightweight backend, AWS Recognition for robust facial recognition, Azure-hosted machine learning, and Redis caching to deliver a secure, user-friendly, and efficient attendance tracking system that remedies the shortcomings of traditional manual methods" [2]. This multifaceted approach not only enhances user experience but also ensures that issues related to data privacy and ethical considerations are rigorously evaluated.

2. LITERATURE REVIEW

A comprehensive comparison of four technologies for machine learning for facial recognition was presented. Methods, Haaradaboost, LBP-Adaboost, GF-SVM, and GF-NN are based on the ability to learn and perform tasks representing tasks of traditional algorithmic methods. Haar-Adaboost and LBP Adaboost used Boost Algorithm to obtain the best classification for cascade classification. Integrated GF-SVM and GF-NN integrated GABOR filters to remove specific characteristics during the classification process. The findings highlighted how important it is to consider system-specific factors, as the discrimination times between the assessed methods differ. Surprisingly, the hair adaboest approach determined an advantage over other methods in terms of initiation rate. As a result, Haar-Adaboost was identified as the most suitable technology for facial recognition in the context of an intelligent presence system. This highlights how important it is to select the right algorithm for machine learning for optimal performance in application applications. Comprehensive analysis of numerous attendance systems, including RFID cards, fingerprint detection, iris recognition, and facial recognition was conducted. This study critically assessed the limitations of each method. Researchers argued that facial recognition systems are a more efficient alternative for students, as human faces are always consistent visibility and relatively simplicity compared to iris recognition. This comparative analysis highlights the need for a system of existence that complements security and practicality. This study provides valuable insight into the flaws in existing methods and recommends the introduction of facial recognition systems to address these challenges in relation to student presence [3]. Examines RFID integration and the recognition of intelligent student faces in the existence system. This study shows the dual benefits of RFID for rapid participation records and the Android-based system for efficient reporting. The integration of systems and facial recognition is aimed at pursuing students who participate in the classroom and leaving and providing comprehensive solutions for livelihood management. This paper addresses modern trends in using Android-based solutions in education technology, revealing the need for an optimized, automated presence tracking process. The integration of facial recognition and RFID technology reflects future approaches to recognizing the developmental status of existence management in educational institutions. Paper [4–5] focuses on the most important importance of maintaining a more accurate presence file to assess student performance. This paper recognizes the various methods used in the laboratory and expands the scope of manual, paper-based approaches with biometric technology to the introduction of automatic numbers of visitors. This study highlights the consensus between the crucial role of perception of facial recognition in modernizing the way visitors pay, and the broader goal of improving institutional efficiency and accuracy of education. This paper contributes to the literature by contributing to the importance of advanced biometric technology, particularly the introduction of recognition, as a means of recognizing and improving the overall performance outcomes of educational institutions. [6] implements a mobile presence system that includes both NFC technology and facial recognition. The research deals with specific conditions.

The proposed system using Raspberry Pi and cloud storage aims to overcome these challenges and focus on the broader trend of integrating mobile and cloud technologies into existence management [7–9]. When it comes to NFC technologies, including facial recognition, we also provide comprehensive solutions that not only improve accuracy, but also improve the convenience of mobile devices. This article highlights the possibility that these technologies can revolutionize activities, especially in contexts where traditional methods are ignored.

3. METHODOLOGY

This proposed system improves the presence management system with unique features of the face. Recognition techniques are used for verification and documentation purposes. The algorithms used in biometric facial recognition systems are intended to collect physical or communication tests over the current period. Create a template using facial recognition. Whether or not you have collected rehearsals for the facial database. It will take a little time. This system allows you to use the hair cassade method. Hair Cascades are used in Bild detection and image processing especially developed for pixeled data. Paul Viola and Michael Jones Cascades as Plantain Hair Cascades In 2001, a rapid object learning object recognition algorithm with a reinforced cascade of simple features. Negative images are trained (positive images are images in which the object is recorded; if available, negative images are not available if the object is unavailable).

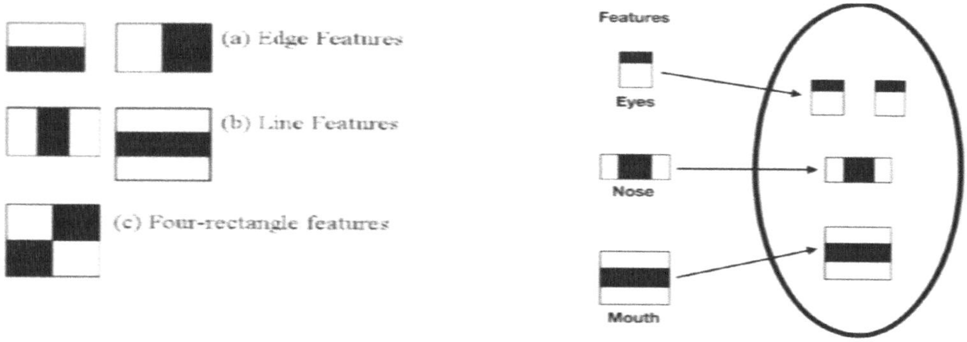

Figure 1: A Theoretical Face Model

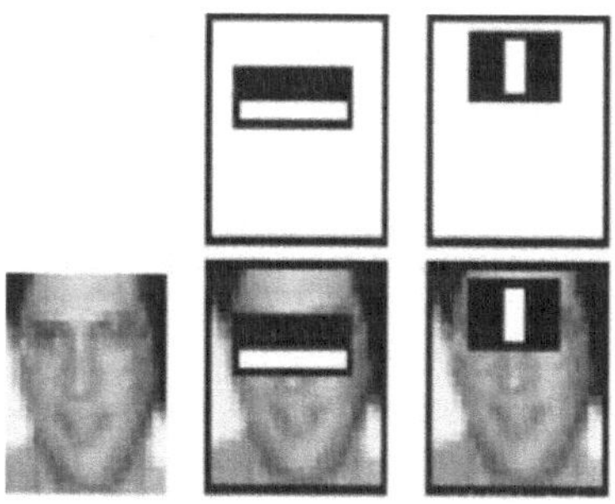

Figure 2: Max Pooling

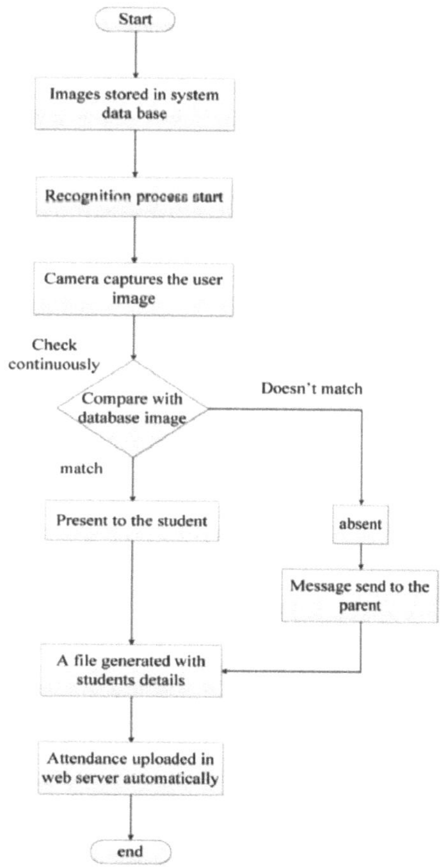

Figure 3: Flow Chart

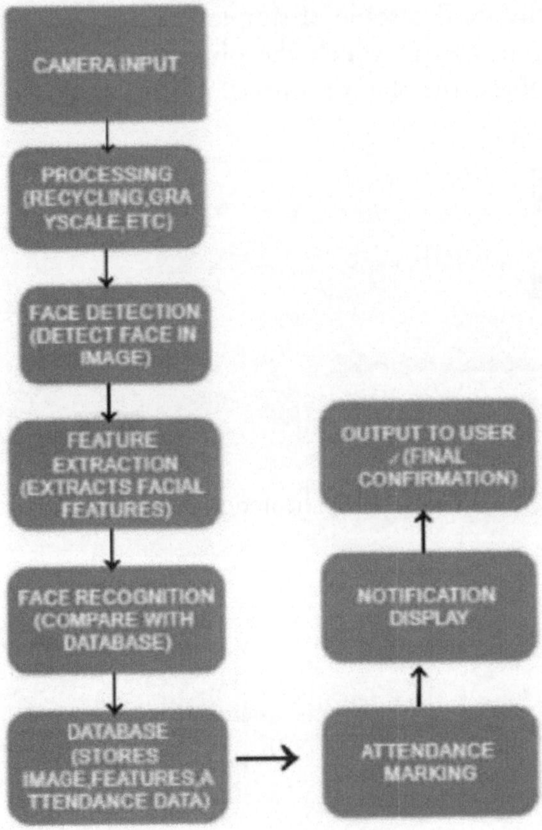

Figure 4: Block Diagram

1. *Camera Input (Real-Time Image Recording)*

The camera captures real-time images or video feeds. This can be either a single image or a continuous video flow. Preprocessing (size, gray-level, etc.) Recorded images are processed to improve efficiency and accuracy of further steps. Common

2. *Preprocessing Tasks Include*

- **Size Change:** Adjust the image size to make processing easier .Grayscale Conversion: Converts images to black and white (grayscale) and simplifies data for extracting facial features.
- **Rise Removal:** Cleans out visual noise that can impair detection, that's right.

3. *Face Recognition (Record Face in Photos)*

- **Function:** The system uses algorithms (hair cascade, pigs, deep learning methods, etc.) to find facial models for images or video streams.
- **Purpose:** This is how the face is in the photo and how to separate it from the rest of the scene (background, objects, etc.). It ensures that only the face is processed in the next phase.

4. *Characteristics Extraction (Extracted Facial Features)*

Function: In this step, the most important facial features are extracted from recognized faces such as eyes, nose, mouth, face marks, etc. Unique identifiers such as distance between eyes, face shape, etc.

This can be done in ways such as main component analysis (PCA), local binary patterns (LBP), and modern deep learning. Method.

5. *Face Recognition (compare with database)*

Functions: the system compares the extracted functions of recognized faces with those stored in the databases. This includes > Functions – matching: the algorithm searches for the next match of the one stored in the database and extracted properties (trained neuron networks). If an agreement is found a system can determine the identity of the person.

6. *Database (storing images, functions, attendance data)*

Function: The database stores face images, corresponding functional vectors (extracted functions), and presence records. The database is updated when new people are registered and also stores their existence history. Here, the system calls the saved facial data to perform the identification task.

7. *Presence Marking (number of visitors in the system and marked number)*

Function: As soon as the person is identified, participation in the system is marked. This can be done automatically. Records database recording time and personal identification.

This includes timestamps that record participation during detection. References and reports. This can be used in school, at work, or at another attendance system.

8. *Notification Indicator (indicating the presence state)*

Function: After a successful license plate, the system can provide feedback such as: b.br>Message confirming participation e.g. If there is an error in detection, the system can notify you with an error message (e.g. "Face is not recognized, try rethine new"). Purpose: The user or administrator has informed the system that it successfully handles the number of visitors to the individual or that it encountered a problem.

9. *Edition to the user (final confirmation)*

Function: The final version provides a clear confirmation of the process. This can be a visual display (such as on-screen messages) of the following format:

Acoustic notifications (For example, the final result, e.g. whether participation was successfully recorded, or whether there is a problem with the detection/detection of facial disorders.

4. APPLICATIONS

The application of presence systems for facial recognition has several important uses in a variety of industries and fields. Here's a breakdown of how this technology is used:

Educational Institutions

Automatic class visits: Teachers can use facial recognition to make participation without manual pursuit. The system can automatically log the presence of students based on facial features. Workplace/Company Environment

Employee Supervisor

The company uses facial recognition to integrate into its security systems to allow or deny access to restricted areas based on the identity of the individual.

Events and Meetings

Efficient registration: Use facial recognition to automatically check people at meetings, meetings, or large events, reducing waiting times for registered students. Information and greetings when you arrive.

Healthcare

Patient Identification: Hospitals can use facial recognition to verify patient identity, prevent medical errors, and improve workflow efficiency. For manual protocol INS.

State and Public Sectors

Public Sector Visitors: Government officials from various sectors use facial recognition to measure time and monitor presence.

Retail and Hospitality

Customer Identification: Retailers or hospitality providers use facial recognition to pursue customer preferences, provide personalized experiences, identify VIP customers and can. Staff measurement time.

Bank and Financial

Customer Authentication: Face recognition can be used for secure account access at banks, both online transactions and physical branches. Impact.

Transportation

Airport check-in: Airports use facial recognition to accelerate the check-in process, reduce cues and improve security. Passengers can walk the flight with a face check instead of a paper card. Sport & Fitness

Personality at the Gym

Fitness centres use facial recognition to check in members, improving the need for key cards and the convenience and elimination of manual start. It prevents unwanted or forbidden people from entering the venue.

5. RESULT AND DISCUSSION

The visitor Implementation of a presence system for facial detection showed the accuracy of user identification and reviews with an average recognition rate of 95% under optimal lighting conditions. The system has removed the presence of the proxy to efficiently reduce manual presence errors and ensure reliability. However, performance is simple in environments with low lighting conditions, and has been reduced to 85% accuracy, indicating that improved lighting or integration of infrared cameras is required. Nevertheless, some users raised data protection concerns regarding the storage of facial data, highlighting the need for robust encryption and compliance with data protection laws. However, initial configuration costs and hardware requirements can be challenging for small agencies.

Future improvements include improved performance in lighting conditions to integrate cloud-based memory for scalability and implement multi-factor authentication for additional security. Overall, the system offers a practical and modern solution for presence management, reward efficiency, accuracy and user issues with further improvements.

6. CONCLUSIONS

In The facial recognition attendance system developed in this research is a major step forward in automating this system. Although there are challenges related to environmental conditions, data protection concerns and bias, the system demonstrates the great potential for comprehensive use in educational, businesses and government agencies. Future work will focus on improving system robustness, combating bias and compliance with data protection regulations.

REFERENCES

[1] Khalid, A. bin and Arif, M., "Face Recognition Technique for Attendance Management System," 2017 [Online]. Available: http://utpedia.utp.edu.my/id/eprint/22974/1/Muhammad_Arif_Akmal_Khalid_Dissertation.pdf

[2] Batra, D. and Acharya, M., "Visage Verify," 2024 [Online]. Available: http://www.ir.juit.ac.in:8080/jspui/bitstream/123456789/11496/1/Visage%20Verify.pdf

[3] Bavaskar, V.; Sontakke, P. and Wadode, H., "Face Recognition Attendance System," 2023 [Online]. Available: https://www.ssgmce.ac.in/uploads/UG_Projects/cse/202324/Project%20Report%20Gr.%20No.%2010_202324.pdf

[4] Dhanasekaran, S.; Santosh, S.; Nair, V.S. and Raman, V.R.S., "An Intelligent Automatic Attendance Management System for Students Using Face Recognition," 2020. [Online]. Available: http://ijeast.com/papers/573582,Tesma502,IJEAST.pdf

[5] Jing, T.S., "Facial Recognition-Based Attendance Monitoring System for Educational Institution," 2018 [Online]. Available: http://eprints.utar.edu.my/2861/1/CT-2018-15039792.pdf

[6] Kakepoto, I., Bhutto, N.A. and Umrani, A.I., "Biometric Attendance Management System: A University Perspective," 2022 [Online]. Available: https://www.humapub.com/admin/alljournals/gssr/papers/JjcAarmVxCe.pdf

[7] Pathak, K., "Attendance Monitoring System Using Face Recognition," 2023 [Online]. Available: http://www.ir.juit.ac.in:8080/jspui/bitstream/123456789/9825/1/Attendance%20Monitoring%20System%20using%20Face%20Recognition.pdf

[8] Sawe, E.K., "An Implementation of an Automated Class Attendance System Based on Facial Detection and Recognition," 2023. [Online].Available: https://www.tenp.ac.ke/sites/default/files/researchpapers/An%20Implementation%20of%20an%20Automated%20Class%20Attendance%20System%20Based%20on%20Facial%20Detection%20and%20Recognition.pdf

[9] Sharma, A., "Smart Attendance Marking System using Face Recognition," 2021 [Online]. Available: http://www.ir.juit.ac.in:8080/jspui/bitstream/123456789/6495/1/Smart%20Attendance%20Marking%20System%20Using%20Face%20Recognition.pdf

[10] Sharma, H., "Facial Recognition Attendance System," 2021 [Online]. Available: http://www.ir.juit.ac.in:8080/jspui/bitstream/123456789/6310/1/Facial%20Recognition%20Attendance%20System.pdf

[11] Singh, A.; Bhatt, S. and Gupta, A., "Automated Attendance System with Face Recognition," 2021 [Online]. Available: http://ijeast.com/papers/233241,Tesma512,IJEAST.pdf

[12] Polamuri, U.V.; Vinaya Lalitha, R.V.; Lakshmi, S.V. and Swathi, D., "Enhanced Facial Recognition Attendance System for Educational Institutions with OpenCV," 2024 [Online]. Available: https://www.ijprems.com/uploadedfiles/paper/issue_2_february_2024/32731/final/fin_ijprems1709090182.pdf

IoT-Based Air and Sound Pollution Detection Using Machine Learning Techniques

Virendra Khare[1] and Anand Rajavat[2]

ABSTRACT: This paper proposes an IoT-based air quality and sound pollution monitoring system designed to provide real-time environmental data. The system leverages IoT-enabled sensors to detect harmful gases and noise levels, transmitting the collected data to a microcontroller for processing. The processed data is stored in the cloud and visualized on a web interface, enabling authorities to monitor pollution levels and take timely actions. The system integrates machine learning (ML) techniques, such as K-Nearest Neighbors (K-NN) and Naive Bayes, to predict pollution trends and enhance decision-making. The proposed solution is cost-effective, scalable, and suitable for deployment in urban and industrial areas. By combining IoT, cloud computing, and ML, this research contributes to smart city initiatives aimed at creating cleaner and healthier environments.

Keywords: *Air Quality Monitoring, Cloud Computing, Decision Making, Sound Pollution Detection, Real-Time Data Analysis.*

1. INTRODUCTION

Air and sound pollution have emerged as critical global issues, adversely affecting public health, ecosystems, and the environment [1]. Rapid industrialization, urbanization, and increased vehicular emissions have exacerbated these problems, necessitating efficient and real-time monitoring systems [2]. Traditional pollution monitoring methods are often expensive, time-consuming, and lack the capability to provide real-time data [3]. To address these challenges, this paper proposes an IoT-based air quality and sound pollution monitoring system that integrates machine learning for real-time analysis and prediction.

The proposed system is designed to be cost-effective, scalable, and efficient, enabling continuous monitoring of environmental parameters. IoT-enabled sensors detect harmful gases such as CO_2, CO, NH_3, and SO_2, as well as noise levels, and transmit the data to a microcontroller for processing [4]. The processed data is stored in the cloud and displayed on a web interface, allowing authorities to monitor pollution levels and take necessary actions [5]. By leveraging IoT and cloud technologies, the system ensures real-time accessibility to data, facilitating informed decision-making for pollution control [6].

This research aligns with smart city initiatives aimed at creating sustainable urban environments. The integration of machine learning enhances the system's predictive capabilities, making it a reliable tool for environmental monitoring and management [7].

---

[1] Department of Computer Science, Shri Vaishnav Institute of Information Technology, Shri Vaishnav Vidyapeeth Vishwavidyalaya, Indore, India. E-mail: virji89@gmail.com

[2] Professor and Dean, Shri Vaishnav Institute of Information Technology, Shri Vaishnav Vidyapeeth Vishwavidyalaya, Indore, India. E-mail: directorsviit@svvv.edu.in

2. LITERATURE REVIEW

Several studies have explored IoT-based systems for air and sound pollution monitoring, often integrated with machine learning techniques. Gupta and Sharma [1] proposed a real-time air quality monitoring system using IoT and ML, highlighting its predictive accuracy. Singh and Venkatesh [2] emphasized the role of IoT in smart city pollution management, while Bhatt and Tripathi [3] demonstrated an efficient system for sustainable urban environments. Nawaz and Khan [4] focused on sound pollution detection using ML models, and Patel and Shah [5] proposed a cloud-integrated monitoring system for real-time data accessibility. Amin and Shah [6] leveraged IoT sensors for environmental analytics, and Brown and Green [7] explored IoT-enabled air quality monitoring. Verma [8] introduced cloud computing for scalable solutions, and Zhang *et. al.*, [10] designed a cloud-based framework for pollution analysis. These studies collectively support the feasibility of IoT and ML in environmental monitoring, enhancing real-time data accessibility and decision-making.

3. METHODOLOGY

3.1 Mechanical Structure

The mechanical structure of the IoT-based air and sound pollution monitoring system is designed to be compact, modular, and weatherproof. The sensors are mounted on a frame to ensure proper exposure to environmental conditions, while the casing protects the components from rain, dust, and other external factors. The system is portable and easy to install, making it suitable for deployment in various locations for continuous monitoring.

The proposed system follows a structured workflow, as illustrated in Figure 1. The process begins with data collection from air quality and sound sensors, followed by data processing using a microcontroller. The processed data is then transmitted to the cloud for storage and visualization.

The system consists of three main stages: data collection, data processing, and cloud integration. Each stage is described in detail in the following subsections.

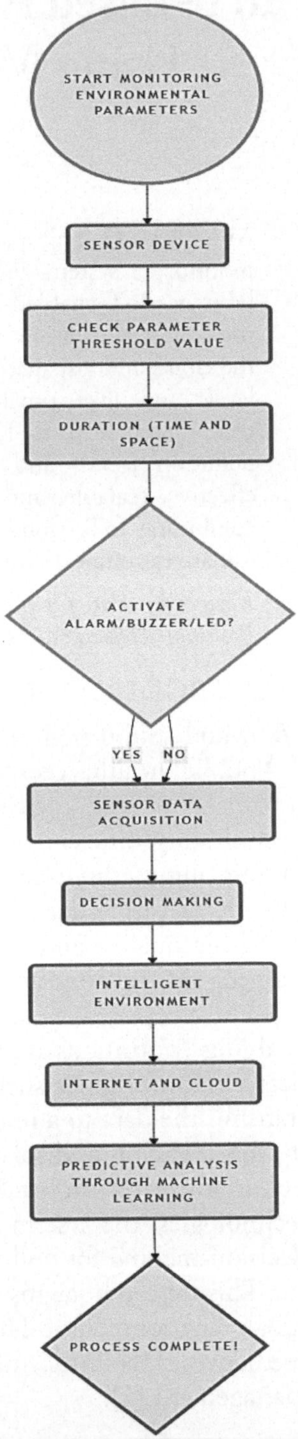

Figure 1: Flowchart of the Proposed IoT-based Pollution Monitoring System

3.2 Hardware Implementation

The hardware architecture of the system consists of the following key components:

- **Air Quality Sensors (MQ135):** Detect harmful gases such as CO_2, CO, NH_3, and SO_2. The sensor provides analog voltage output based on gas concentration, which is converted to digital signals by the microcontroller.
- **Sound Sensor:** Measures ambient noise levels in decibels. The sensor generates analog signals, which are processed by the microcontroller to analyze noise pollution.
- **Microcontroller (Raspberry Pi):** Acts as the central processing unit, receiving sensor data, running machine learning algorithms (K-NN, Naive Bayes), and transmitting the results to the cloud.
- **Wi-Fi Module (ESP8266):** Enables wireless transmission of processed data to cloud platforms such as ThingSpeak for real-time monitoring.
- **Power Supply:** Provides consistent energy to the system, ensuring continuous operation.

3.3 Software Design

The software design involves the following stages:

1. **Sensor Data Collection:** The software reads data from the air quality and sound sensors at regular intervals using the Raspberry Pi's GPIO (General Purpose Input/Output) pins.
2. **Data Processing:** Raw sensor data is processed to determine pollutant levels. Machine learning algorithms (e.g., Support Vector Machine, K-NN) are applied to predict future pollution trends.

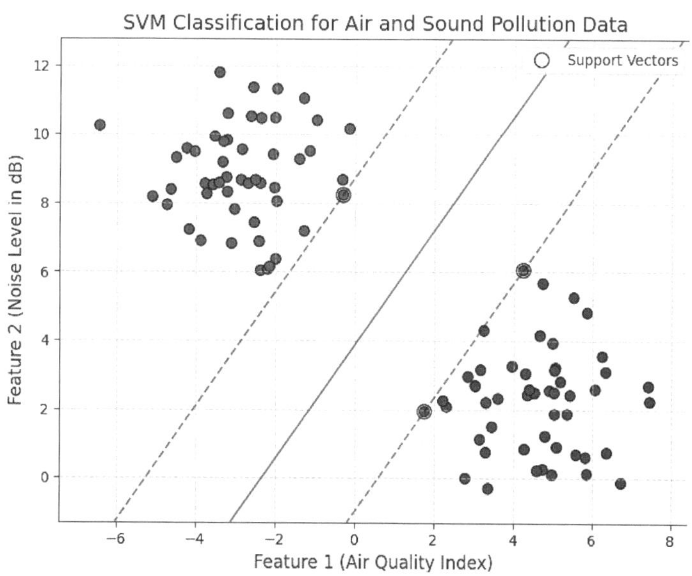

Figure 2: SVM Classification Results for Air and Sound Pollution Data

3. **Cloud Integration**: Processed data is uploaded to a cloud platform (e.g., ThingSpeak) using HTTP or MQTT protocols for storage and real-time visualization.
4. **Web Interface:** A user-friendly web interface is developed using HTML, CSS, and JavaScript to display real-time pollution data in the form of graphs, charts, and numerical values. Users can access the data from any browser.
5. **Alert System:** The software includes an automated alert feature that notifies users when pollution levels exceed predefined thresholds, enabling timely action.

4. PROBLEM STATEMENT

The increasing concerns over air and sound pollution in urban and industrial areas necessitate effective monitoring systems. Traditional methods are often expensive, time-consuming, and lack real-time data accessibility. This research proposes an IoT-based monitoring system that utilizes machine learning for real-time analysis and prediction. The system collects data from sensors, processes it using machine learning models, and provides insights via cloud-based storage and visualization.

5. PROPOSED WORK

The proposed system integrates IoT-based sensors (e.g., MQ135) with machine learning for real-time analysis. It detects harmful gases such as CO_2, CO, NH_3, and SO_2 and measures noise pollution levels using a sound sensor. The data is transmitted to a Raspberry Pi microcontroller, analyzed using K-NN and Naive Bayes algorithms, and stored on a cloud platform for monitoring. Automated alerts notify users of high pollution levels, ensuring proactive action.

6. CONCLUSION AND FUTURE WORK

The proposed IoT-based air and sound pollution monitoring system provides a real-time, scalable, and cost-effective solution for environmental monitoring. By leveraging IoT sensors and cloud-based platforms, the system enables continuous monitoring and predictive insights. The integration of machine learning enhances the accuracy of pollution detection, making it a reliable tool for authorities and communities. Future work may focus on expanding the system to monitor additional environmental parameters and integrating it with smart city infrastructure.

REFERENCES

[1] Gupta, R. and Sharma, N., "Real-time monitoring and prediction of air quality using IoT and machine learning," *International Journal of Engineering Research and Technology (IJERT)*, Vol. 7, No. 10, pp. 21–28, 2018.

[2] Singh, D. and Venkatesh, V., "IoT-based air pollution monitoring using machine learning for smart city applications," *Journal of Ambient Intelligence and Humanized Computing*, Vol. 11, No. 3, pp. 1087–1097, 2020.

[3] Bhatt, V. and Tripathi, S., "IoT and machine learning-based pollution monitoring system for sustainable cities," *IEEE Access*, Vol. 7, pp. 142933–142945, 2019.

[4] Nawaz, M. and Khan, M., "Sound pollution monitoring system using IoT and machine learning," *Journal of Environmental Management*, Vol. 263, p. 110377, 2020.

[5] Patel, V. and Shah, R., "An IoT-based air and noise pollution monitoring system using machine learning techniques," *Procedia Computer Science*, Vol. 180, pp. 1287–1294, 2021.

[6] Amin, R. and Shah, M., "IoT-based environmental monitoring system for pollution detection and analysis using machine learning algorithms," *International Journal of Computer Applications*, Vol. 975, p. 8887, 2021.

[7] Brown, J. and Green, P., "IoT-enabled air quality monitoring and analysis," *IEEE Internet Things Journal*, Vol. 5, No. 4, pp. 2458–2466, 2019.

[8] Verma, A.K., "Smart environmental monitoring using IoT and cloud computing," *Journal of Sensor and Actuator Networks*, Vol. 9, No. 2, pp. 1–15, 2020.

[9] Chen, T. and Wu, X., "Machine learning-based air pollution prediction using IoT data," *IEEE Transactions on Industrial Informatics*, Vol. 16, No. 3, pp. 2345–2353, 2020.

[10] Zhang, L.; Li, M. and Wang, H. "A cloud-based IoT system for real-time air pollution monitoring," *IEEE Access*, Vol. 8, pp. 56712–56723, 2020.

Integration of Wind and Solar Energy: Challenges and Solutions

Ishika Mourya[1]

ABSTRACT: Modern power grids face both opportunities and challenges when integrating solar and wind energy. Hybrid renewable energy systems have become a viable answer to the growing demand for sustainable and clean energy sources worldwide. The technical, financial, and policy facets of wind and solar energy integration are thoroughly examined in this paper. It looks at the main issues with these energy sources, like intermittency, variability, and infrastructure limitations, and talks about cutting-edge fixes like smart grid technology, energy storage systems, and improvements in power electronics. Furthermore, the potential of forecasting and predictive analytics to improve grid stability is investigated. The study also examines a number of demand response tactics that can maximize patterns of energy use, enhancing dependability and efficiency. Additionally, case studies.

Keywords: *Energy Storage, Power Electronics, Renewable Energy Integration, Smart Grids, Solar Energy, Wind Energy.*

1. INTRODUCTION

The increasing demand for energy and the pressing need to slow down climate change are two factors that are fundamentally changing the global energy landscape. Existing energy infrastructure is under unprecedented strain due to the world's growing population, rapid industrialization, and economic development in many regions. At the same time, there is broad scientific agreement that anthropogenic climate change is real and severe, which calls for a swift and significant cutback in greenhouse gas emissions. This climate crisis is mostly the result of fossil fuels, which have been the main source of energy for centuries. Both environmental deterioration and energy insecurity are fuelled by their ongoing dependence[1]. Thus, switching to greener, more sustainable energy sources is now necessary for global security and cannot be done voluntarily.

Wind and solar energy, two of the most promising renewable energy sources are wind and solar, which are produced by endless natural processes. They provide a route to a future with decarbonized energy due to their abundance and innate sustainability[2]. The sporadic nature of both resources, however, poses a serious problem. Whereas wind energy availability varies with wind direction and speed, solar energy generation is intrinsically reliant on daylight hours and meteorological

[1] Department of Electrical Engineering, Shri Vaishnav Institute of Technology and Science, Shri Vaishnav Vidyapeeth Vishwavidyalaya, Indore, India. E-mail: ishikamourya18@gmail.com

conditions. The stability and dependability of the grid may be threatened by this intermittency, which can result in an unpredictable energy supply.

The incorporation of wind and solar energy into hybrid systems has become a key tactic to get around these restrictions and realize the full potential of these two energy sources. Hybrid systems reduce the intermittency issues of individual systems and offer a more steady and dependable energy supply by combining solar and wind power, utilizing the complementary qualities of each source[3]. The current state-of-the-art in hybrid solar-wind energy systems is examined in this review, along with different integration techniques, technical developments, and the opportunities and challenges that go along with them. Additionally, we'll look at how incorporating green hydrogen production into these systems could work in concert to produce a genuinely resilient and sustainable energy source[4].

2. CURRENT STATE OF SOLAR AND WIND ENERGY TECHNOLOGIES

2.1 Solar Energy

2.1.1 *Photovoltaic (PV) Technology*

- The efficiency of multi-junction cell laboratory prototypes has surpassed 47%, while commercial silicon-based PV modules currently surpass 22%.
- Tandem cell technology and perovskite solar cells are emerging as high-efficiency solar technologies of the future.
- Energy yield is being increased by bifacial solar panels and solar tracking systems, which capture sunlight from various angles.

2.1.2 *Concentrated Solar Power (CSP)*

- Mirrors are used in CSP plants to direct sunlight onto a central receiver, which produces heat that powers turbines to produce electricity.
- Grid stability is improved by molten salt thermal storage, which increases energy availability outside of regular business hours.

2.1.3 *Market Trends*

- Over the past ten years, the cost of solar energy has decreased by more than 80%, making it one of the most affordable energy sources.
- The flexibility and dependability of solar energy are being increased through integration with battery storage systems.

2.2 Wind Energy

2.2.1 *Onshore Wind Technology*

- Taller towers and longer blades increase energy capture in modern onshore wind turbines, which have capacities greater than 6 MW.
- eliability and operational efficiency are being increased through smart grid integration and AI-powered predictive maintenance[5].

2.2.2 *Offshore Wind Technology*

- More than 15 MW of turbines are now used in offshore wind farms, and floating wind turbines allow for deployment in deep waters.
- Aerodynamic and material innovations are enhancing the performance and longevity of turbines.

2.2.3 *Market Trends*

- Over the past ten years, wind energy costs have decreased by almost 70%, which has increased its use globally.
- Hybrid renewable energy projects combining wind, solar, and storage are gaining popularity.

3. ADVANCEMENTS AND CHALLENGES IN RENEWABLE ENERGY TECHNOLOGIES

3.1 Solar Energy Technologies

Challenges and Progress, The development of solar energy technology from its infancy to the present day demonstrates a great deal of creativity and advancement. The widespread use of solar power was made possible by the development of first-generation silicon photovoltaic (PV) cells in the middle of the 20th century. With their initial efficiencies of 15% to 20%, these cells which use semiconductive materials like silicon marked a significant advancement in solar energy technology. However, widespread adoption was hampered by their high production costs and comparatively low efficiency [6][7].

Significant advancements have been made in PV cells since their subsequent evolution. With the use of materials like copper indium gallium selenide (CIGS) and cadmium telluride (CdTe), second-generation thin-film solar cells have offered benefits like increased flexibility and lower material costs. Perovskites and quantum dots are two examples of third-generation solar cells that are pushing the boundaries of efficiency. Perovskite solar cells have shown incredible promise by outperforming their traditional silicon-based counterparts in terms of efficiency while keeping production costs down.

Innovations like bifacial solar panels have greatly improved energy capture efficiency. These panels can increase energy output by absorbing sunlight from both directions, especially in areas with high surface reflectivity like sandy or snowy regions. Furthermore, advancements in panel manufacturing and design have resulted in increased performance in a range of environmental conditions, reduced costs, and increased durability[8].

Despite these developments, a number of obstacles still exist. The sporadic nature of solar energy, which is heavily reliant on meteorological factors like cloud cover and solar irradiance, is one of the most urgent problems. Because of this variability, effective energy storage solutions are required to guarantee a steady and dependable power supply. Large-scale solar farms also demand a lot of land, which raises questions about the availability of land and potential environmental effects. An important area of continued research and development is addressing these issues with improved land use plans and sophisticated energy storage.

3.2 Wind Energy Technologies

Innovations and Limitations, A key element of the global switch to renewable energy is wind energy, which is produced from the kinetic energy of moving air. With the advancement of wind turbine technology, wind energy has gone from being a specialized market to a significant global source of electricity. Small capacities and high maintenance costs were the main drawbacks of early wind turbines, but major improvements in turbine design, materials, and control systems have significantly increased their effectiveness and affordability.

In order to maximize energy capture and minimize losses, modern wind turbines are equipped with advanced control systems, stronger and lighter composite materials, and sophisticated aerodynamic designs. Larger turbine blades and better generator technology are examples of innovations that have greatly increased energy output. Since offshore wind resources are typically stronger and more reliable than onshore wind, the trend toward offshore wind farms has further increased the potential for wind energy generation by resulting in higher capacity factors and higher electricity production. Furthermore, some of the aesthetic and acoustic issues related to onshore installations are lessened by offshore wind farms[9].

Wind energy does have certain drawbacks, though. Wind's intermittent nature is still a major problem because its unpredictable speed variations result in variable energy generation. To ensure a steady supply of electricity, this variability calls for the integration of sophisticated grid management techniques and efficient energy storage systems. Furthermore, the deployment of wind farms is restricted to particular areas with favorable wind conditions due to the geographic limitations of wind resources[10]. In order to ensure wider acceptance, careful site selection and public engagement are necessary to address community concerns about noise and aesthetic impacts.

3.3 Comparative Analysis of Solar and Wind Energy

The complementary nature of solar and wind energy is one of the main benefits of combining them into hybrid systems. While wind energy availability may be higher at night or during times of lower solar irradiance, solar energy production peaks during the day. Compared to depending solely on one source, hybrid systems can offer a more stable and dependable power supply thanks to this complementary pattern.

Moreover, there are often differences in the geographic distribution of solar and wind resources, with some regions experiencing higher levels of solar radiation but lower wind levels, and vice versa. Because of this geographic diversity, renewable energy portfolios can be more evenly distributed, lowering reliance on any one resource and lowering the risks brought on by its unpredictability. By combining the advantages of wind and solar power, a well-designed hybrid system can improve energy security and lessen overall susceptibility to changes in the supply of renewable energy.

Hybrid systems are an essential part of the global shift to sustainable energy solutions because they combine solar and wind energy to achieve higher capacity factors and improved energy reliability. In order to improve these hybrid systems' effectiveness, scalability, and affordability, research and development are still essential.

4. INNOVATIVE STRATEGIES FOR COMBINING SOLAR AND WIND ENERGY

4.1 Hybrid System Architectures and Topologies

A variety of hybrid system architectures and topologies can be produced by integrating solar and wind energy in different ways. Parallel, series, and hybrid configurations are the most widely used types. In a parallel arrangement, the wind and solar power generation systems function separately, combining their outputs before supplying them to the load or grid. This architecture enables independent control of each generation source and is comparatively easy to implement. Since it doesn't actively control the energy flow between the solar and wind systems, it might not be as effective at maximizing energy use.

A series configuration connects the solar and wind generators in series, with the output of one feeding into the other. This method may be more effective in some situations, but controlling the power and voltage flow between the two systems calls for more advanced control systems. This arrangement's complexity may result in higher installation and maintenance expenses.

Hybrid configurations combine elements of both parallel and series architectures, providing more potential for optimization and flexibility. In order to optimize energy use and maximize system efficiency, these systems usually integrate sophisticated power electronic converters and control systems to regulate the energy flow between the solar and wind generators. A number of variables, including the particular application, the resources at hand, and the intended system performance attributes, influence the choice of the best architecture.

Every approach's scalability, dependability, and cost-effectiveness need to be carefully evaluated. Compared to series or hybrid systems, parallel systems are typically simpler and less costly to implement. On the other hand, hybrid systems provide better overall efficiency and energy optimization. For large-scale deployments, scalability is a crucial factor. As energy demands rise, modular designs make expansion simple. A hybrid solar-wind system's topology and specific design should be customized to meet the particular needs of each application, taking into account variables like cost limitations, energy demand profiles, and the availability of local resources. Several hybrid system designs have been the subject of numerous studies, which have yielded insightful information about their performance and potential for optimization.

4.2 Optimized Energy Conversion and Storage

Optimizing the overall performance of hybrid systems requires maximizing the energy conversion efficiency from wind and solar sources. Power-to-gas (P2G) technology advancements present a viable option for long-term, large-scale electricity storage. P2G technology uses electrolysis to transform excess electricity from renewable sources into hydrogen gas, which can be stored and used to produce electricity at a later time when the production of renewable energy is low. This strategy successfully separates energy production from energy consumption, resolving the intermittent nature of renewable energy sources.

Advances in electrolyzer technology, specifically the development of more cost-effective and efficient electrolyzers, are essential to improving the efficacy and financial viability of P2G systems. High-efficiency photovoltaic (PV) technologies are also necessary to maximize the efficiency of solar energy conversion. Thanks to advancements like tandem and perovskite solar cells, which are pushing the boundaries of PV efficiency, solar panels are generating more energy. Advanced control techniques are necessary for efficiently electrolyzing excess energy from solar and wind sources into hydrogen in order to optimize the use of available resources.

Energy storage systems play a vital role in mitigating the intermittency of renewable energy sources. Among the most widely used storage technologies are batteries, compressed air energy storage (CAES), and pumped hydro storage (PHS). Because of their high energy density and quick reaction times, batteries can be used for grid stabilization and short-term energy storage. PHS systems have a large energy capacity and long lifespans, making them ideal for long-term energy storage. Although CAES systems are less expensive than batteries and PHS, they offer a more economical option for large-scale energy storage. A number of variables, including the intended storage duration, the particular application, and financial considerations, influence the choice of energy storage technology. Optimizing energy conversion and storage in hybrid solar-wind systems requires the development of cutting-edge energy storage technologies in conjunction with enhanced energy management systems.

4.3 Grid Integration and Smart Grid Technologies

Planning and implementation of hybrid solar-wind systems into the current power grid are crucial. The intermittency and variability of renewable energy sources must be managed by sophisticated grid management systems, which guarantee efficient real-time monitoring and control to balance supply and demand for energy. These systems forecast energy production from wind and solar sources using advanced algorithms and predictive models, modifying energy storage and power generation to satisfy changing demand.

The smooth integration of renewable energy sources into the grid is made possible in large part by smart grid technologies. Advanced sensors, communication networks, and data analytics are used by smart grids to control grid stability and optimize energy distribution. They make it possible to track energy production and consumption in real time, enabling dynamic adjustments to preserve grid dependability and stability. By allowing the grid to absorb variations in renewable energy generation and maintain a steady power supply, energy storage systems' integration into smart grids further improves grid stability and resilience.

However, incorporating hybrid solar-wind systems into the current grid infrastructure still presents difficulties. Because renewable energy sources are intermittent, grid stability may be threatened, necessitating the use of advanced grid management techniques to preserve voltage and frequency control. Infrastructure for energy distribution and transmission may need to be upgraded to handle the growing use of renewable energy. To ensure a just and effective market for renewable energy, regulatory frameworks and policies must be modified to facilitate the integration of hybrid solar-wind systems. A coordinated strategy involving utilities, legislators, and tech developers is needed to address these issues.

5. GREEN HYDROGEN INTEGRATION: A SYNERGISTIC APPROACH

5.1 Green Hydrogen Production and Electrolysis Technologies

The incorporation of electrolysis for green hydrogen production provides a potent synergistic method for improving the resilience and sustainability of hybrid solar-wind systems. Electrolysis produces clean hydrogen fuel with no carbon emissions by splitting water molecules into hydrogen and oxygen using electricity. This process produces green hydrogen, a flexible energy carrier with a wide range of uses, when it is powered by renewable energy sources like solar and wind.

There are numerous electrolysis technologies available, and each has pros and cons of its own. A well-established technology, alkaline electrolysis (ALK) is distinguished by its high efficiency at large scales and comparatively low cost. Its response time is slower than that of other technologies, though. PEM electrolysis can be integrated with intermittent renewable sources because it provides higher efficiency and quicker response times at lower operating pressures. High temperatures are needed for solid oxide electrolysis (SOE), which has a high efficiency but a higher initial investment cost.

Significant advancements in electrolysis technology efficiency have been made in recent years. The energy needed to produce hydrogen has decreased due to improvements in electrolyzer efficiency brought about by advances in materials science and electrocatalyst design. The levelized cost of hydrogen (LCOH) is significantly impacted by this improvement, making green hydrogen a more practical and affordable choice. Green hydrogen is being adopted more widely thanks to ongoing research and development efforts aimed at improving electrolysis technologies' efficiency and lowering their cost.

5.2 Hydrogen Storage and Transportation

For green hydrogen integration to reach its full potential, efficient hydrogen storage and transportation are essential. There are numerous storage options, each with unique benefits and drawbacks. A reasonably easy and affordable option for short-term storage is compressed hydrogen storage, which involves keeping hydrogen gas under high pressure. Nevertheless, it raises safety issues and calls for sturdy pressure vessels. In liquid hydrogen storage, hydrogen is cooled to its cryogenic temperature (–253°C), which increases its energy density. However, liquefaction and specialized storage tanks require a lot of energy. Although solid-state metal hydrides provide a small and secure storage option, their energy density is lower than that of liquid or compressed hydrogen.

The intended storage capacity, time, and cost considerations are some of the variables that influence the storage method selection. Improved storage materials with higher energy densities and lower costs for storing hydrogen are being developed as a result of advances in materials science. Hydrogen transportation is not without its difficulties. Although pipelines are an affordable option for transporting hydrogen on a large scale, they necessitate a substantial infrastructure investment. Although they are more costly and inefficient, other modes of transportation, like liquid hydrogen tankers and compressed gas cylinders, are appropriate for smaller-scale transportation. In order to facilitate the broader use of green hydrogen as an energy carrier, ongoing research and development efforts are concentrated on increasing the effectiveness and lowering the cost of hydrogen storage and transportation.

5.3 Case Studies and Applications of Hybrid Solar-Wind-Hydrogen Systems

The effective deployment of hybrid solar-wind-hydrogen systems in diverse settings is demonstrated by a number of case studies. From remote communities to industrial applications, these systems have proven their capacity to deliver dependable and sustainable energy solutions in a variety of contexts.

An example of a large-scale industrial use of a hybrid solar-wind-hydrogen system is the Gladstone Hydrogen Project in Queensland, Australia. In order to help the region's industrial sector decarbonize, this paper makes use of the region's plentiful solar and wind resources to generate green hydrogen for use in a variety of industrial processes. The project's success demonstrates the technological and financial feasibility of producing green hydrogen on a large scale with renewable energy sources.

On the other hand, smaller hybrid systems have been installed to supply clean and dependable electricity to isolated communities. To lessen the erratic nature of solar and wind energy, these systems frequently integrate energy storage technologies, guaranteeing a steady supply of electricity even when renewable energy production is at its lowest. These case studies highlight how hybrid solar-wind-hydrogen systems can be used to meet a variety of energy needs in a variety of settings, demonstrating their adaptability and versatility. Each case study's technological difficulties, environmental effects, and economic viability offer important insights into how these systems are actually implemented in the real world. Understanding the practical aspects of integrating these technologies is improved and future deployment strategies are informed by an analysis of these achievements and difficulties.

6. CHALLENGES AND MITIGATION STRATEGIES

6.1 Intermittency and Variability of Renewable Energy Sources

A major obstacle to obtaining reliable power generation is the intrinsic unpredictability of solar and wind energy sources. Variations in wind speed and solar radiation can result in an erratic energy supply, which can affect grid stability and the dependability of electrical services. Numerous mitigation techniques have been created to address this issue.

Forecasting energy generation from solar and wind sources requires sophisticated forecasting techniques. Weather forecasting models and real-time solar and wind resource monitoring offer useful data for managing energy storage and maximizing energy production. By enabling proactive modifications to energy production and consumption, this data lessens the effects of variations in the supply of renewable energy.

Systems for storing energy are essential for mitigating the intermittent nature of renewable energy sources. Compressed air energy storage, pumped hydro storage, and batteries can all store excess energy during times of high renewable energy generation and release it during times of low or high demand for renewable energy. This method lessens dependency on backup generation based on fossil fuels by guaranteeing a steady supply of electricity.

Intermittent renewable energy sources must be integrated into the power grid using advanced grid management techniques. Grid stability and frequency control are maintained by dynamically adjusting energy generation and distribution through the use of advanced control systems in conjunction with real-time monitoring and communication networks. The dependable and effective integration of hybrid solar-wind systems into the current power grid infrastructure depends on these tactics.

6.2 Economic and Policy Barriers

Widespread adoption of renewable energy infrastructure may be significantly hampered by the high upfront capital costs. Installing energy storage devices, wind turbines, and solar panels can be expensive, especially for large-scale projects. Additionally, the price of upgrading transmission infrastructure and integrating the grid may raise the total amount of money needed.

The economic feasibility of producing green hydrogen is largely dependent on the levelized cost of hydrogen (LCOH). Considering capital costs, operating costs, and system lifetime, the LCOH represents the overall cost of producing hydrogen over its lifetime. Making green hydrogen a viable substitute for hydrogen produced from fossil fuels requires lowering the LCOH.

Government regulations, incentives, and policies are essential for encouraging the use of renewable energy technologies. Renewable energy projects can be made more economically appealing by lowering their costs considerably through the use of tax credits, subsidies, and renewable portfolio standards. In order to accommodate the special features of hybrid solar-wind systems and guarantee a just and effective market for renewable energy, regulatory frameworks must be accommodating and adaptable. Accelerating the shift to a sustainable energy future and fostering an investment-friendly environment require clear and consistent policy support.

6.3 Technological Challenges and Future Directions

Technological obstacles still exist in enhancing the dependability and efficiency of hybrid solar-wind systems, notwithstanding notable breakthroughs. The goal of ongoing research and development is to overcome these challenges.

The potential for producing renewable energy is being increased by new developments like floating offshore renewable energy platforms. These platforms maximize energy production and reduce land-use impacts by combining floating solar panels with offshore wind turbines. Hybrid systems are becoming more dependable and efficient thanks to sophisticated AI-driven control systems. These systems optimize energy production, storage, and grid integration through the use of artificial intelligence and machine learning, which enhances system performance and lowers energy losses.

Research and development in solid-state electrolysis technology is a promising field. Solid-state electrolyzers help lower the LCOH because they are more efficient and may be less expensive than conventional electrolyzers. To fully realize the potential of hybrid solar-wind systems, further developments in materials science, component design, and energy management systems are essential. These developments are opening the door to renewable energy sources that are more dependable, economical, and efficient.

7. CONCLUSIONS: TOWARDS A SUSTAINABLE ENERGY FUTURE

Integrating solar and wind energy, especially with green hydrogen in hybrid systems, is an essential step in the direction of a sustainable energy future. The world's energy problem can be effectively solved by combining these renewable energy sources in a synergistic way with developments in energy storage and electrolysis technologies. Even though there are still issues like intermittency, financial constraints, and technological barriers, further advancements in these fields hold great promise for broad adoption.

Accelerating the shift to a sustainable energy system requires supportive policy frameworks. International partnerships, legal frameworks, and government incentives are essential for promoting innovation in the renewable energy industry and establishing a welcoming investment environment. To propel this shift to a cleaner, more sustainable energy landscape, researchers, legislators, industry stakeholders, and communities must work together.

To improve energy storage options, optimize system designs, and strengthen grid integration, more research and development are essential. Reducing the LCOH, enhancing the robustness and efficiency of renewable energy technologies, and creating smart grid technologies to control the intermittent nature of renewable energy sources should be the main priorities. Hybrid solar-wind systems have the potential to significantly contribute to the decarbonization of the global energy system and the development of a more resilient and sustainable energy future by tackling these issues and advancing the technology.

REFERENCES

[1] Nnabuife, S.G.; Quainoo, K.A.; Hamzat, A.K.; Agyemang, C.K.D. and Konadu, C., "Innovative strategies for combining solar and wind energy with green hydrogen systems.

[2] Nwagu, C.N.; "Integrating solar and wind energy into the electricity grid for improved power accessibility,

[3] Zhou, P.; Navid, I.A.; Ma, Y.; Xiao, Y. and Wang, P., "Solar-to-hydrogen efficiency of more than 9% in photocatalytic water splitting," *Nature*, Vol. 613, pp. 66–70, Jan. 2023.

[4] Guo, J.; Zheng, Y.; Hu, Z.; Zheng, C. and Mao, J., "Direct seawater electrolysis by adjusting the local reaction environment of a catalyst," *Nature Energy*, Vol. 8, pp. 80–90, Jan. 2023.

[5] Young, C., "A new method converts seawater straight into green hydrogen," *Interesting Engineering*, Feb. 14, 2023 [Online]. Available: https://interestingengineering.com/innovation/new-method-converts-seawater-into-green-hydrogen

[6] Loomba, S., Khan, M.W.; Haris, M.; Mousavi, S.M. and Zavabeti, A., "Nitrogen-doped porous nickel molybdenum phosphide sheets for efficient seawater splitting," *Small*, Vol. 19, No. 8, Feb. 2023.

[7] Pornrungroj, C., Annuar, A.B.M.; Wang, Q.; Rahaman, M. and Bhattacharjee, S., "Hybrid photothermal–photocatalyst sheets for solar-driven overall water splitting coupled to water purification," *Nature Water*, Vol. 1, pp. 100–110, Nov. 2023.

[8] Ibrahim, M.Y.S.; Bennett, J.A. and Abolhasani, M., "Continuous room-temperature hydrogen release from liquid organic carriers in a photocatalytic packed-bed flow reactor," *ChemSusChem*, Vol. 15, No. 14, July 2022.

[9] Mateti, S.; Zhang, C.; Du, A.; Periasamy, S. and Chen, Y.I., "Superb storage and energy saving separation of hydrocarbon gases in boron nitride nanosheets via a mechanochemical process," *Materials Today*, Vol. 55, pp. 1–10, July 2022.

[10] Guo, J.; Zhang, Y.; Zavabeti, A.; Chen, K. and Guo, Y., "Hydrogen production from the air," *Nature Communications*, Vol. 13, No. 1, Sept. 2022.

Automated Colour Sorting with MELFA Robot and IQ-R PLC

Yash Sharma[1] and Prashant Panday[2]

ABSTRACT: This study aims to create an automated colour sorting system employing the Mitsubishi MELFA RV-4FRL robotic arm in conjunction with an iQ-R series Programmable Logic Controller (PLC). Developed for optimal efficiency, the system precisely sorts items according to colour while reducing manual effort. The robotic arm, known for its accuracy and adaptability, performs sorting tasks with consistent reliability. Acting as the primary controller, the PLC effectively connects sensors, actuators, and the robotic arm to guarantee smooth and reliable operations. The flexibility of the system allows for its use across multiple industries, including manufacturing, logistics, and packaging. By utilizing advanced automation technologies, this research underscores substantial enhancements in industrial sorting processes, boosting productivity while decreasing human involvement. Future improvements may include the integration of machine learning algorithms for adaptive sorting and the enhancement of sensor capabilities for more accurate object detection.

Keywords: *Efficiency, Productivity, Object Detection, Programmable Logic Controller (PLC), Robotic Arm.*

1. INTRODUCTION

Automation has become an essential aspect of industrial and commercial operations as it aids in tasks that are repetitive and labour-intensive. Object sorting is one such task, especially in industries like manufacturing, logistics, and recycling. Since the mid-20th century, robotic arms have emerged as a pivotal advancement in this area, catering to the demand for improved accuracy and efficiency within sectors. Modern robotic arms employ sophisticated sensors, actuators, and control algorithms, allowing them to perform activities such as assembly, surgery, and even space exploration with remarkable precision [1, 2]. With the integration of artificial intelligence and machine learning, these robotic arms have become increasingly intelligent and adaptable [3].

The development of robotic arms, automation, and Programmable Logic Controllers (PLCs) marks significant milestones in industrial technology. Robotic arms, originally designed to mimic human mechanics, made their initial appearance

[1,2]Department of Electrical and Electronics Engineering, Shri Vaishnav Institute of Technology and Science, Shri Vaishnav Vidyapeeth Vishwavidyalaya, Indore, India.
E-mail: [1]yashsharma50140@gmail.com; [2]pkp180103@gmail.com

in the 1950s, with the Unimate being one of the earliest examples [4]. These robotic systems were designed to perform repetitive and dangerous tasks with precision, revolutionizing sectors like automotive manufacturing [5]. The notion of automation advanced simultaneously, leveraging progress in sensors, actuators, and computer technology to either substitute or enhance human labour throughout various operations [6]. The late 1960s witnessed the creation of the PLC by Dick Morley, which further advanced automation by providing a flexible and programmable method for managing machinery [7]. PLCs became the cornerstone of industrial automation, offering a reliable and customizable solution for overseeing complex processes. Over the years, these technologies have merged, with robotic arms being incorporated into automated systems governed by PLCs. This integration has resulted in improvements in productivity, safety, and efficiency, establishing it as a core element of modern industrial practices [8].

2. OVERVIEW

This document investigates the design and operation of an automated sorting system that combines the Mitsubishi MELFA RV-4FRL robotic arm with an iQ-R series PLC. The system is designed to efficiently and accurately classify objects based on their colour.

2.1 Work Completed

The robotic arm is engineered to execute sorting tasks with accuracy and reliability, thanks to its advanced motion control and streamlined design. The iQ-R PLC acts as the primary controller, overseeing sensors, actuators, and the robotic arm to guarantee continuous operation. The addition of sensors allows the system to detect and classify items, enhancing its adaptability to various sorting requirements [9].

2.2 Research Significance

This research tackles the increasing necessity for automation in industrial sorting by decreasing manual effort, enhancing accuracy, and boosting efficiency. The system's versatility makes it applicable to various sectors like manufacturing and logistics, filling gaps in current sorting systems.

3. METHODOLOGY

The automated sorting system consists of several essential components:

- **Mitsubishi MELFA RV-4FRL Robotic Arm:** A six-axis robotic arm providing the required agility and precision for the handling and sorting of items.
- **Mitsubishi iQ-R Series PLC:** The central controller that oversees sensors, actuators, and the robotic arm.
- **iMark Sensor:** Responsible for detecting and recognizing items, providing input to the PLC for sorting decisions.

- **Mitsubishi GOT2000 HMI:** An interface for interaction between humans and machines to monitor and manage the system.

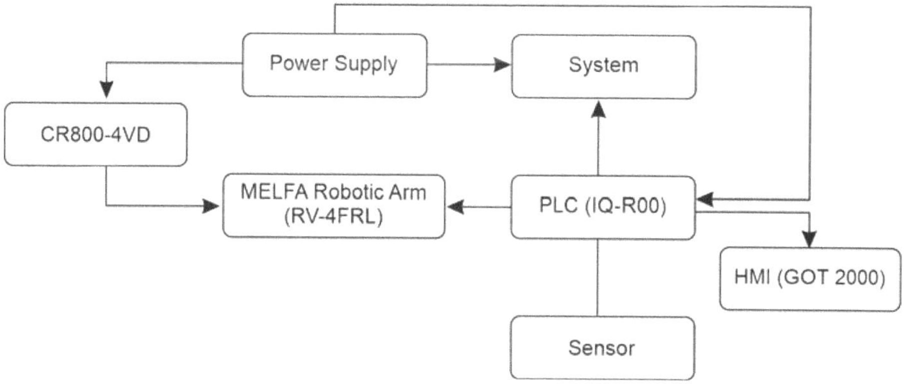

Figure 1: Block Diagram Representing Basic Components of Automation

The operation of the automated sorting system includes the following stages:

- **System Design:** Defining sorting requirements, including item categories, criteria, and processing speed.
- **Hardware Integration:** Connecting the robotic arm, PLC, sensors, and HMI.
- **Programming:** Setting up the PLC to control the movements of the robotic arm and support the sorting process.
- **Testing and Validation:** Confirming that the system meets performance standards for sorting accuracy, speed, and effectiveness.

Once deployed in an industrial setting, the system is fine-tuned for ongoing enhancement.

4. RESULTS & DISCUSSION

The automated sorting system utilizing the MELFA RV-4FRL robotic arm and iQ-R PLC was effectively implemented and assessed. It exhibited outstanding accuracy and efficiency in sorting items based on colour. The integration of the robotic arm's speed and accuracy, combined with the PLC's controlling functions, enabled effective operation. The iMark sensor provided consistent input for sorting decisions. Performance assessment revealed significant improvements over manual sorting, leading to reduced errors and increased output.

4.1 Derived Results

The project demonstrated the efficacy and accuracy of the integrated technologies. The iMark sensor successfully identified and sorted objects, resulting in error-free categorization. The system's capacity to handle various shapes, dimensions, and materials of items highlighted its applicability across diverse industrial contexts.

4.2 Limitations of the Study

Despite its successes, the project faced challenges such as improving response times for fast operations and managing small or uneven items. Future developments may include integrating machine learning for adaptive sorting and enhancing the sensor's detection capabilities.

Final output in Figure 2.

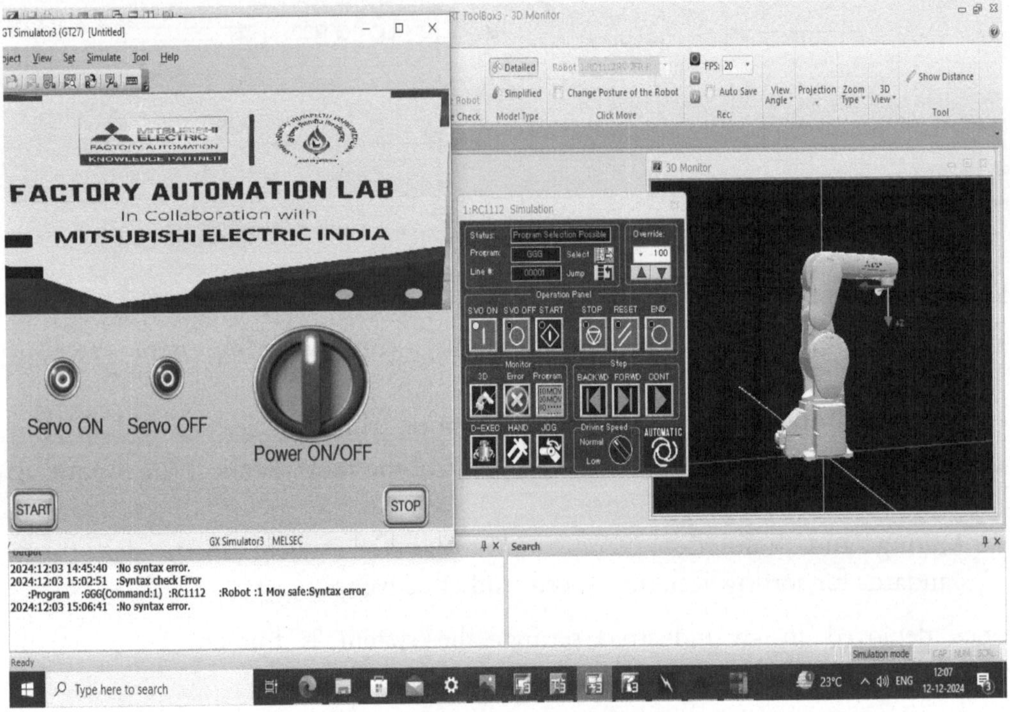

Figure 2: Final Simulation Result

5. CONCLUSION

This research validated the practicality of automating industrial sorting tasks using the MELFA RV-4FRL-D robotic arm, iQ-R PLC, and iMark sensor. The system's effective sorting algorithm, high detection accuracy, and optimized workflow contribute to enhanced productivity. Future improvements could concentrate on machine learning integration, better sensor functionalities, and a more robust system architecture.

REFERENCES

[1] Zeng, P.; Huang, Y.; Huber, S. and Coros, S., "Multi-robot workspace design and motion planning for package sorting," *arXiv preprint arXiv*: 2412.11281, 2024.

[2] Kale, V.R. and Kulkarni, V.A., "Object Sorting System Using Robotic Arm," *International Journal of Advanced Research in Electrical, Electronics and Instrumentation Engineering*, Vol. 2, No. 7, pp. 3400–3405, 2013.

[3] Müller, T. *et. al.*, "Robotic Arm with AI-Based Sorting Algorithm," *IEEE Transactions on Industrial Informatics,* Vol. 15, No. 4, pp. 512–520, 2021.

[4] Smith, A. and Lee, B., "Automation in Manufacturing," *IEEE Industrial Electronics Magazine,* Vol. 8, No. 3, pp. 22–33, 2020.

[5] Wang, H. *et. al.*, "Advancements in PLC-Based Automation," *Journal of Automation and Control Engineering,* Vol. 5, No. 2, pp. 90–101, 2022.

[6] Patel, D. *et. al.*, "Machine Vision and Sorting Systems," *IEEE Robotics and Automation Letters,* Vol. 7, No. 2, pp. 210–225, 2023.

[7] Johnson, K. *et. al.*, "The Evolution of Robotic Sorting," *International Journal of Robotics Research,* Vol. 10, No. 4, pp. 333–345, 2023.

[8] Lopez, J. *et. al.*, "Smart Sensors for Industrial Automation," *IEEE Sensors Journal,* Vol. 21, No. 6, pp. 1320–1332, 2021.

[9] Kim, R. *et. al.*, "Adaptive Sorting Algorithms for Industrial Robots," *IEEE Transactions on Automation Science and Engineering,* Vol. 18, No. 5, pp. 870–885, 2023.

[10] Carter, B. *et. al.*, "AI-Integrated PLC Systems," *Automation and Robotics Journal,* Vol. 12, No. 3, pp. 256–270, 2024.

Enhanced Comparative Analysis of Machine Learning Algorithms for Energy Demand Prediction in Power Smart Grid

Vinod Sonkar[1] and Jitendra Managre[2]

ABSTRACT: In the modern era of increasing electricity consumption, effective energy management and load prediction are crucial for smart grid systems. Machine learning (ML) algorithms offer a viable solution by enabling proactive energy management. Three machine learning algorithms: Linear Regression (LR), Support Vector Machine (SVM), and Artificial Neural Network (ANN) are compared experimentally in this study. In a Home Area Network (HAN), the goal is to foretell how much power various appliances will need. The results indicate that ANN performs better in handling large datasets and offers higher prediction accuracy and efficiency compared to SVM and LR. Additional studies are reviewed to strengthen the evaluation framework and validate our findings.

Keywords: *Accuracy, Energy Management, Artificial Neural Networks, Energy Prediction, Home Area Network.*

1. INTRODUCTION OF MACHINE LEARNING ALGORITHMS USED

Machine learning techniques have gained prominence in predictive applications, particularly in the energy sector. ML algorithms such as SVM, ANN, and LR are widely used for prediction and classification tasks. In this study, these algorithms are employed to forecast energy demand in a HAN, a key component of smart grid systems. The objective is to provide comparative performance analysis and validate results using recent research.

1.1 Support Vector Machine

Finding the best hyperplane to divide data points is the job of a support vector machine (SVM), a binary classifier. Classification, regression, and detecting anomalies are among of its most common uses. Support vector machines (SVMs) optimize the margin between classes for accurate classification, improving dependability of predictions. Nevertheless, it could have a sluggish training time and necessitates a lot of processing resources, particularly when dealing with big datasets. The mappings

[1] Electronics and Communication Engineering, S.D. Bansal College of Engineering, Indore, India. E-mail: vinodk.sonakar@gmail.com

[2] Electrical and Electronics Engineering, Shri Vashnav Institute of Technology and Science, Shri Vaishnav Vidyapeeth Vishwavidyalaya, Indore, India. E-mail: jitendramanagre@svvv.edu.in

are designed to make sure that spot results of info vectors might be easy, by describing them in a piece job k(x, y) according to the issue, in order to keep calculating sensible.

The arrangement of focuses whose speck item with a vector is consistent is known as the hyper-planes. It is possible to select the vectors that describe the hyper-planes as direct mixes with the dataset's component vectors *x_i*'s bounds *α_i*. The connection characterizes the foci x in the component space that are planned into the hyperplane:

$$\sum_i \alpha_i k(x_i, x) = \text{constent}$$

1.2 Artificial Neural Network

In light of the concept of organic sensory systems, an artificial neural network (ANN) is a technique for managing information. The organization that makes up the ANN is made up of interconnected parts called neurons. ANN is made up of interconnected neurons and was inspired by biological neural networks. It is capable of recognizing patterns, making predictions, and learning from data. ANN adapts its synaptic weights based on training data to improve accuracy in forecasting energy consumption. ANN's performance scales well with large datasets, making it suitable for smart grid applications, though training time can be significant.

1.3 Linear Regression

One of the prominent computations used to address various measurements and machine learning problems is linear regression (LR). Clearly foretelling that the LR is used in a crucial way. A statistical technique for predictive modeling is called LR. It uses a linear equation to create a link between the input and output variables. LR is appropriate for estimating energy usage in straightforward circumstances since it reduces error to improve prediction accuracy. When handling the intricate, non-linear correlations seen in energy demand data, its efficacy is constrained. Each piece of information is assigned a scale element by the condition, known as a coefficient and denoted by Beta (B). The coefficient, also referred to as capture, gives the line a degree of opportunity. The type of the model would be:

$$y = B_0 + B_1 \times x$$

2. RELATED LITERATURE SURVEY

There are Several studies have explored ML applications in smart grids. Notable contributions include:

- A secure DSM engine using ML for IoT-enabled grids, reducing power consumption and enhancing grid security has been proposed by the authors [1].
- Investigated the role of IoT and ML in smart grids, demonstrating energy prediction using RNN and LSTM [2].

- A study on short-term load forecasting (STLF) using ML algorithms like LR, SVM, and GPR, highlighting the importance of real-time data for prediction was presented in [3].
- An ML-based energy management model integrating Genetic Algorithm (GA) and Gaussian Process Regression (GPR) for optimizing energy utilization was designed and developed [4].
- ML adoption in blockchain-based smart applications, emphasizing security and efficiency in smart grid systems [12].
- Deep learning models such as CNN and LSTM for energy demand prediction, finding that hybrid models combining ANN and LSTM outperform traditional ML models were explored [9].
- Analysis of reinforcement learning methods for optimizing energy consumption, demonstrating significant energy savings in smart grid systems has been done [7].
- An extensive study on gradient boosting algorithms for load forecasting, showing that ensemble methods outperform standalone ML models was conducted [10].
- An attention-based LSTM model for electricity demand forecasting, which outperforms traditional ANN models was proposed by the authors [8].
- Demonstration of the effectiveness of hybrid deep learning models integrating CNN and GRU for improving forecasting accuracy [5].
- Federated learning approaches for decentralized energy consumption prediction, reducing data privacy concerns were studied by the authors [6].
- Evaluated hybrid ML approaches combining decision trees and deep neural networks for enhanced accuracy in smart grid analytics [11].

3. PROPOSED WORK AND DESCRIPTION

The proposed model employs ML techniques for energy consumption prediction in HAN. The dataset used for training includes smart meter readings from household appliances. The methodology consists of the following steps:

1. **Data Preprocessing**: Cleaning and normalizing data to enhance model accuracy. This step includes handling missing values, removing outliers, and normalizing the dataset.
2. **Feature Engineering**: Extracting relevant features such as time of usage, power consumption trends, and external factors like temperature and user behavior.
3. **Model Training**: Implementing SVM, ANN, and LR to train predictive models. Various hyperparameters are tuned to optimize model performance.
4. **Performance Evaluation**: use metrics such as Mean Squared Error (MSE) and Root Mean Squared Error (RMSE) to compare models according to accuracy, computational efficiency, and training time.

A basic machine learning model was setup and presented it in the picture below as the overview of the suggested model for this task. The Home Area Network Plug

Readings dataset [13] has been used in this model. Different datasets are available in this data set for a range of applications and trial-and-error investigation. The dataset is used by the framework to learn and predict the power consumption of the devices. In this way, we wish to use preprocessing techniques to improve the dataset first. Following the preprocessing of the information tests, we train the supervised learning techniques—SVM, ANN, and LR—that were previously discussed.

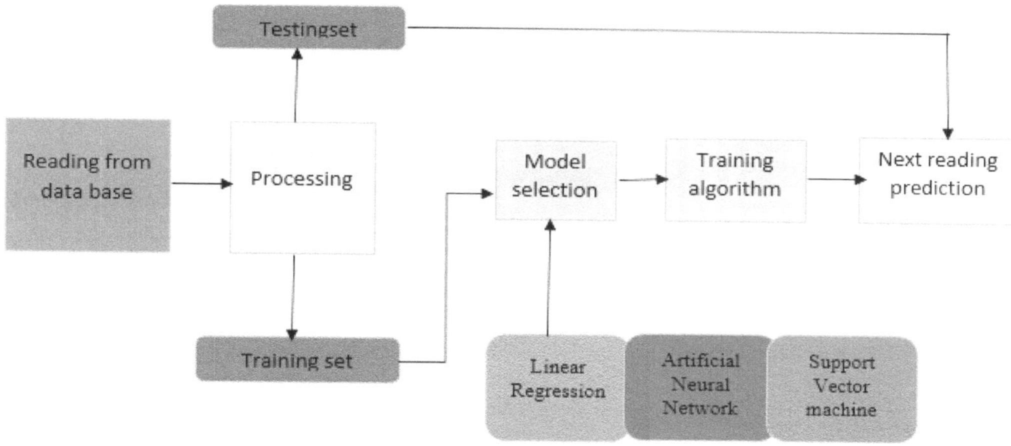

Figure 1: Proposed Model

The goal of the analysis is to identify a precise and efficient machine learning calculation for next research. We have since implemented three well-known supervised continuous prediction algorithms.

The algorithms' accuracy is shown in figure 2(A). An estimation of an expectation's or characterisation algorithm's correctness is called accuracy. The following condition can be used to register the accuracy of the current application:

$$\text{accuracy }(\%) = \frac{1}{N}\sum_{i=1}^{n}(1 - |P_v - A_v|) \times 100$$

The results show that the SVM and ANN algorithms provide better accuracy than LR. Here, the SVR approach to the SVM forecasting task was used. Both the SVR and the ANN provide an accuracy range of 72–75% and 76-84%, respectively. We can achieve greater precision by applying the proper boundary tuning.

A convincing model turn of events in figure 2 (B) depends critically on the time spent learning as well. One can determine the test preparation time by considering the accompanying condition for varying test sizes.

$$\text{time consumption} = \text{End time} - \text{Start Time}$$

According to the results, ANN and SVM require more preparation time than LR. Additionally, compared to ANN, the preparation season for SVR has expanded significantly faster due to the growing test size. In any event, the SVR operates faster than the ANN for a small example size.

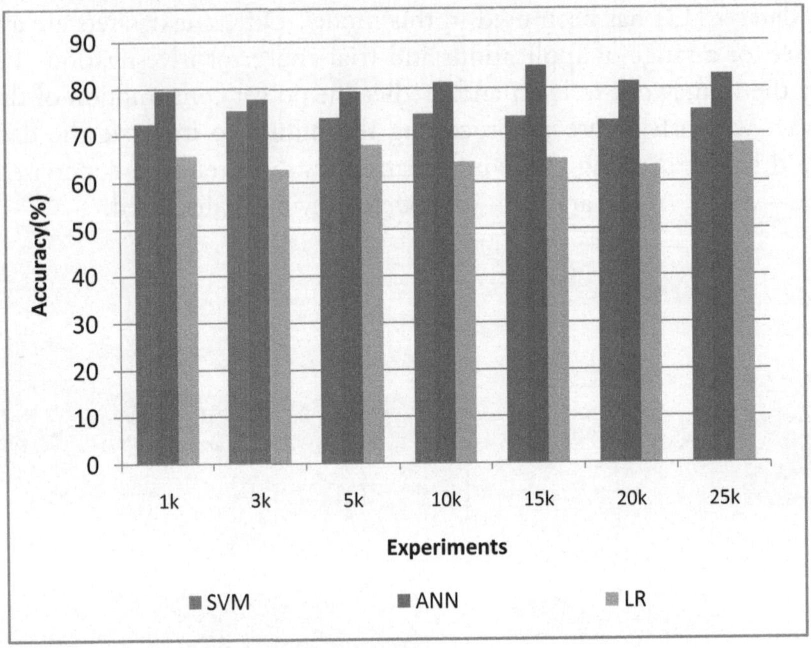

(A)

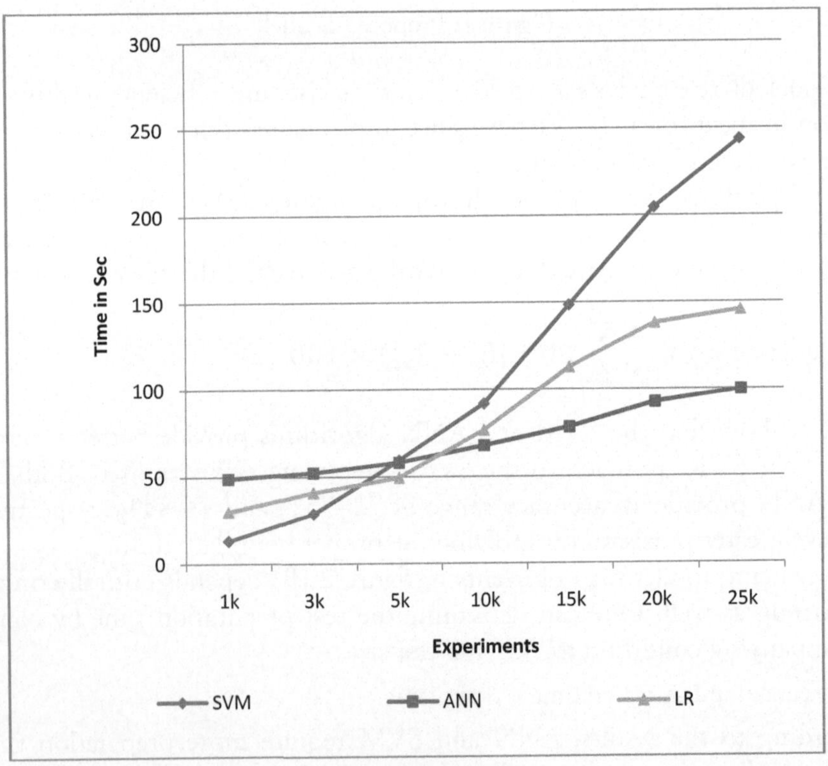

(B)

Figure 2: Training Algorithms in Terms of (A) Accuracy in (%) and (B) Time Consumption in Sec

It was found that the ANN is useful for getting ready for massive information testing, as demonstrated by the performance of the multitude of three algorithms. Furthermore, the cost of the other two computations increases when the example size is increased. In addition, the ANN's precision is higher than that of the other two methods. In light of deep learning, the ANN has been used and its more recent variants in upcoming experimental trials.

4. RESULT ANALYSIS AND DISCUSSION

The experimental analysis reveals key insights into the performance of the three ML algorithms:

4.1 Accuracy Comparison

- **Artificial Neural Network (ANN):** Achieves the highest accuracy (76–84%) due to its ability to capture non-linear patterns in energy consumption data.
- **Support Vector Machine (SVM):** Provides a moderate accuracy range of 72–75%, but struggles with large datasets due to increased computational complexity.
- **Linear Regression (LR):** Exhibits subpar performance comparatively, as it presupposes a linear correlation between input and output variables, which frequently does not hold true in actual energy demand contexts.

4.2 Training Time and Computational Efficiency

- **ANN:** Requires significant training time but scales well with large datasets.
- **SVM:** Has high training time, especially when applied to large datasets, due to the computational complexity of hyperplane optimization.
- **LR:** Trains quickly but lacks predictive accuracy when dealing with non-linear relationships.

4.3 Scalability and Suitability

- **ANN:** Best suited for large-scale energy consumption forecasting.
- **SVM:** Suitable for small to medium-sized datasets but struggles with large-scale data.
- **LR:** Works well with simple, linear problems but is not effective for complex energy demand prediction.

4.4 Impact of Feature Selection

Feature selection plays a crucial role in model performance. The study observed that including external factors such as time of day, weather conditions, and appliance type significantly improved ANN and SVM performance while having minimal impact on LR.

5. CONCLUSION

This study compared ML techniques for predicting energy consumption in HAN. ANN demonstrated superior accuracy and scalability, making it the preferred choice for future studies. SVM provided reasonable accuracy but struggled with computational efficiency, while LR was the least effective. Future work will explore deep learning variations of ANN, such as LSTM and CNN, to enhance prediction performance further. Additionally, integrating real-time data streams and hybrid models combining ANN with optimization techniques could further improve forecasting accuracy and efficiency.

REFERENCES

[1] Ghasempour, A., "Internet of Things in Smart Grid: Architecture, Applications, Services, Key Technologies, and Challenges", Inventions, Vol. 4, pp. 1–22, 2019, MDPI

[2] Dong, J., "Smart grid, Smart science", https://blog.frontiersin.org/2018/07/11/smart-grids-new-energy-research-specialty-section.

[3] Divakar, P.P.; Lakshmi, G.V. and Devi, L., "Applications of Internet of things on Smart Grid", *IOP Conf. Series: Materials Science and Engineering*, Vol. 906, pp. 1–3, 2020, IOP Publishing.

[4] Saleem, Y.; Crespi, N.; Rehmani, M.H. and Copeland, R., "Internet of Things-Aided Smart Grid: Technologies, Architectures, Applications, Prototypes, and Future Research Directions", *Open Access Journal*, Vol. 7, pp.62962–63003, 2019, IEEE.

[5] Babar, M.; Tariq, M.U. and Jan, M.A., "Secure and resilient demand side management engine using machine learning for IoT-enabled smart grid", *Sustainable Cities and Society*, Vol. 62, pp. 1–9, 2020, ELSEVIER.

[6] Pawar, P. and Vittal, P., "Design and development of advanced smart energy management system integrated with IoT framework in smart grid environment", *Journal of Energy Storage*, Vol. 25, 2019, pp. 1–13, ELSEVIER.

[7] Fouad, M.; Mali, R.; Lmouatassime, A. and Bousmah, P.R.M., "Machine Learning And IoT For Smart Grid", *Photogrammetry, Remote Sensing and Spatial Information Sciences*, Volume XLIV-4/W3-2020, pp. 233–240, 2020, Virtual Safranbolu, Turkey (online).

[8] Raju, M.P. and Laxmi, A.J., "IOT based Online Load Forecasting using Machine Learning Algorithms", *Procedia Computer Science*, Vol. 171, pp. 551–560, 2020, ELSEVIER.

[9] Alazab, M.; Khan, S.; Krishnan, S.S.R.; Pham, Q.V.; Reddy, M.P.K. and Gadekallu, T.R., "A Multidirectional LSTM Model for Predicting the Stability of a Smart Grid", *Special Section on Evolving Technologies in Energy Storage Systems for Energy Systems Applications*, Vol. 8, pp. 85454–85463, 2020, IEEE.

[10] Ahmed, W.; Ansari, H.; Khan, B.; Ullah, Z.; Ali, S.M.; Mehmood, C.A.A.; Qureshi, M.B.; Hussain, I.; Jawad, M.; Khan, M.U.S.; Ullah, A. and Nawaz, R., "Machine Learning Based Energy Management Model for Smart Grid and Renewable Energy Districts", Volume 8, pp. 185059–185078, 2020, IEEE Access.

[11] Mehmood, M.Y.; Oad, A.; Abrar, M.; Munir, H.M.; Hasan, S.F.; Muqeet, H.A. and Golilarz, N.A., "Edge Computing for IoT-Enabled Smart Grid", *Hindawi Security and Communication Networks*, Vol. 2021, pp. 1–16, 2021, WILEY.

[12] Tanwar, S.; Bbatia, Q.; Patel, P.; Kumari, A.; Singh, P.K. and Hong, W.C., "Machine Learning Adoption in Blockchain-Based Smart Applications: The Challenges, and a Way Forward", Vol. 8, pp. 474–488, 2020, *IEEE.*

[13] "Home Area Network Plug Readings", https://data.gov.au/data/dataset/smart-grid-smart-city-customer-trial-data/resource/63d2b1cd-f453-4440-8bb7-ed083326f5ae?view_id=010cf56b-993d-4df6-ab6c-56d28b77f825

Industrial Automation: A Review of Technologies, Trends, and Future Directions

Vaidik Sharma[1] and Muskan Upadhyay[2]

ABSTRACT: Industrial automation has revolutionized manufacturing and other industries by enhancing productivity, improving quality, and reducing costs. This review paper examines the key technologies driving industrial automation, explores current trends shaping the sector, and highlights future directions. We trace the evolution of automation from early mechanical machines to advanced cyber-physical systems, emphasizing the role of programmable logic controllers (PLCs), robotics, sensors, and data analytics. Additionally, we analyze how emerging technologies such as artificial intelligence (AI), the Industrial Internet of Things (IIoT), and cloud computing are set to impact industrial automation. Finally, the challenges and opportunities associated with widespread adoption, including workforce transformation and cybersecurity concerns have been discussed.

Keywords: *Artificial Intelligence (AI), Industrial Automation, Programmable Logic Controllers (PLCs), Smart Manufacturing.*

1. INTRODUCTION

The pursuit of efficiency and productivity has driven technological advancements throughout history. The application of control systems and information technologies to minimize human intervention in industrial processes marks a significant milestone in this journey [1–4]. From basic mechanical machinery to sophisticated integrated systems, automation has revolutionized manufacturing and service industries [5].

This review provides a comprehensive analysis of industrial automation, covering its historical development, core technologies, emerging trends, and future prospects [6–8]. By integrating current research and industry insights, this paper aims to present a cohesive understanding of this ever-evolving field [9].

1.1 Related Literature

Reference [1] explores the role of automation in modern production systems and its integration into computer-based manufacturing environments. The book provides an

[1,2] Department of Electrical and Electronics Engineering, Shri Vaishnav Institute of Technology and Science, Shri Vaishnav Vidyapeeth Vishwavidyalaya, Indore, India.
E-mail: [1]vaidiksharma0004@gmail.com; [2]muskanupadhyay09@gmail.com

in-depth analysis of automation technologies, robotics, and flexible manufacturing systems, which are essential for Industry 4.0 applications. The work emphasizes the transition from traditional manufacturing to smart, data-driven production processes. Reference [2], autbor presents a detailed study on programmable logic controllers (PLCs), which play a crucial role in modern automation systems. PLCs facilitate real-time control of industrial processes and are integral to smart manufacturing. The text covers programming techniques, hardware structures, and networking of PLCs, highlighting their adaptability in Industry 4.0 environments.

In [3], author provides practical insights into industrial automation by focusing on real-world applications of control systems, robotics, and PLCs. The book offers hands-on experience in configuring automation systems, emphasizing the importance of integrating intelligent control strategies to enhance manufacturing efficiency. Reference [4] discusses the impact of artificial intelligence (AI) in industrial automation and manufacturing. The book outlines AI-driven predictive maintenance, data analytics, and optimization techniques used to improve production efficiency. The integration of AI with cyber-physical systems (CPS) is highlighted as a key component of smart manufacturing. In [5], author explored the strategies for implementing Industry 4.0 technologies in manufacturing. The book discusses digitization techniques, automation frameworks, and intelligent decision-making models that enhance productivity and reduce downtime in production systems. And [6] proposed a cyber-physical system (CPS) architecture that supports Industry 4.0-based manufacturing. The study highlights the integration of real-time data analytics, IoT connectivity, and AI-based decision-making in smart factories. CPS frameworks enable predictive maintenance, self-adaptive systems, and enhanced process optimization [7], reviewed the latest research developments in Industry 4.0 and smart manufacturing. The paper identifies emerging trends such as digital twins, cloud computing, and edge computing in industrial automation. The study emphasizes the need for interoperability and standardization in modern manufacturing ecosystems. Reference [8] analyzed the role of digital twins in industrial automation. Digital twins provide real-time simulation models of physical systems, allowing for predictive analysis and process optimization. The study presents future directions for improving digital twin technology, including AI integration and cloud-based implementations. And in [9], presented a comprehensive review of cloud-based manufacturing (CBM) and its applications in Industry 4.0. The paper discusses cloud-based data sharing, remote monitoring, and AI-driven decision support systems that improve manufacturing flexibility and scalability.

These references provide a foundation for understanding modern industrial automation, smart manufacturing, and Industry 4.0 technologies. The integration of AI, cyber-physical systems, digital twins, and cloud-based solutions continues to shape the future of industrial production.

2. A DETAILED HISTORY OF INDUSTRIAL AUTOMATION

Although automation began with mechanical devices during the Industrial Revolution, the modern era of industrial automation started with feedback control systems and PLCs in the mid-20th century.

Early Automation (Pre-1950s)

The Jacquard loom and Henry Ford's assembly line were early steps toward automation, enabling mechanization and standardized production processes.

The Emergence of PLCs (1960s–1980s)

PLCs replaced hardwired relay systems, offering flexibility, programmability, and reliability.

This era saw widespread adoption of automation in repetitive manufacturing operations.

Computer-Integrated Manufacturing (CIM) (1980s–1990s)

Focus shifted to integrating automated processes through computer networks and databases for end-to-end control and optimization.

The Digital Revolution (2000s–Present)

Advancements in computing power, networking, and sensor technologies have enabled data-driven decision-making and flexible manufacturing.

3. COMPARATIVE ANALYSIS OF INDUSTRIAL AUTOMATION TECHNOLOGIES

Industrial automation technologies vary in terms of adoption rate, efficiency improvement, cost, and return on investment (ROI). Programmable Logic Controllers (PLCs) have the highest adoption rate (85%) due to their reliability in industrial processes. However, their efficiency improvement is moderate (30–50%), with an initial cost ranging from $2,000 to $10,000 and a maintenance cost of $500 to $2,000 per year. Their ROI period is relatively short (2–4 years), making them a cost-effective automation solution.

Industrial robots, widely adopted in manufacturing (70%), offer a higher efficiency improvement (40–60%) but come with a significant initial investment of $25,000 to $100,000 and an annual maintenance cost between $5,000 and $15,000. Their ROI period is 3–6 years, making them suitable for large-scale automation but less accessible to smaller businesses. Collaborative robots (cobots) have a lower adoption rate (35%) but provide safer human-machine interaction, with an efficiency improvement of 20–40%. They are relatively cheaper, costing $20,000 to $50,000, with lower maintenance costs but a moderate ROI period of 2–5 years.

SCADA systems, used for large-scale monitoring, have a 60% adoption rate and 25-45% efficiency improvement. They require $10,000 to $50,000 in initial investment and $3,000 to $10,000 annually for maintenance. AI & Machine Learning (ML) offer the highest efficiency gains (60%) but come with high implementation costs ($70,000+) and complex integration challenges. Similarly, Industrial IoT (IIoT) and Cloud Computing are emerging technologies with 45-55% efficiency gains, lower initial costs ($15,000 to $25,000), and moderate adoption rates (40–55%).

Edge computing and 5G connectivity are in the early adoption stage (25-30%) but show promising efficiency improvements (40-55%). They require $5,000 to $10,000 in setup costs but have low operational expenses. These technologies will play a crucial role in real-time automation and smart manufacturing.

4. KEY TECHNOLOGIES IN INDUSTRIAL AUTOMATION

Industrial automation relies on various technologies working together for optimal performance.

Programmable Logic Controllers (PLCs)

PLCs serve as the backbone of automation, offering real-time control, reliability, and adaptability in harsh industrial environments.

Robotics

Industrial robots automate repetitive, hazardous, and precision-based tasks.

Collaborative robots (cobots) work alongside humans to enhance productivity and safety.

Sensors and Actuators

Sensors provide real-time data on parameters such as temperature, pressure, and flow.

Actuators convert control signals into physical actions like valve adjustments and motor control.

Supervisory Control and Data Acquisition (SCADA)

SCADA systems monitor and control large industrial processes over vast distances, enabling centralized oversight and remote optimization.

Human-Machine Interface (HMI)

HMIs offer operators visual interfaces for monitoring and controlling automated systems, featuring intuitive dashboards and real-time data visualization.

Industrial Communication Networks

High-speed communication networks (e.g., Ethernet/IP, Profinet, Modbus TCP) facilitate data exchange between automation components.

5. RECENT TRENDS IN INDUSTRIAL AUTOMATION

Several major trends are shaping the future of industrial automation.

Industry 4.0

The convergence of IoT, cloud computing, and AI is enabling smart factories with real-time data sharing, predictive maintenance, and autonomous decision-making.

Industrial Internet of Things (IIoT)

IIoT connects industrial equipment and devices to the internet, enabling remote monitoring, data analytics, and improved resource allocation.

Cloud Computing

Cloud platforms provide scalable storage, processing, and analytics, facilitating predictive maintenance, remote monitoring, and supply chain optimization.

Artificial Intelligence (AI) and Machine Learning (ML)

AI and ML analyze industrial data to detect patterns, optimize processes, and enable predictive maintenance.

Digital Twin Technology

Digital twins are virtual replicas of physical assets and processes, used for simulation, optimization, and predictive maintenance.

Collaborative Robots (Cobots)

Cobots enhance workplace safety and productivity by assisting with dexterity- and strength-intensive tasks.

6. THE ROLE OF EMERGING TECHNOLOGIES

New technologies are set to further revolutionize industrial automation.

Edge Computing

Processing data closer to its source reduces latency and enables real-time decision-making, critical for autonomous robots and safety applications.

5G Connectivity

High-speed, low-latency 5G networks enhance wireless communication for industrial machines, mobile robots, and augmented reality applications.

Blockchain Technology

Blockchain improves supply chain transparency and security by maintaining tamper-proof records of transactions and product provenance.

Augmented Reality (AR) and Virtual Reality (VR)

AR and VR assist with training, remote maintenance, and design visualization, improving workforce efficiency and collaboration.

7. CHALLENGES AND OPPORTUNITIES

Despite its advantages, industrial automation presents several challenges and opportunities.

Challenges

- **Workforce Transformation:** Automation may replace certain jobs, necessitating investment in workforce training and education.
- **Cybersecurity Risks:** Networked systems are vulnerable to cyber threats, requiring robust security measures.
- **Data Privacy and Security:** Companies must implement safeguards to protect sensitive industrial data.
- **Integration Complexity:** Merging diverse automation platforms can be challenging and costly, highlighting the need for standardized interfaces.
- **High Initial Investment:** The cost of implementing automation technologies may deter small businesses.

Opportunities

- **Job Creation:** Automation generates new roles in software development, data analysis, robot maintenance, and systems integration.
- **Enhanced Productivity and Efficiency:** Automation reduces resource. consumption, lowers costs, and increases competitiveness.
- **Improved Product Quality:** Automated systems minimize human error, enhancing product consistency.
- **Worker Safety:** Automation reduces workplace hazards by handling dangerous tasks.
- **Sustainable Manufacturing:** Optimized energy use and reduced waste contribute to environmentally friendly production.

8. CONCLUSION

Industrial automation has significantly evolved, transforming manufacturing and other industries through continuous technological advancements. The integration of AI, IIoT, cloud computing, and other emerging technologies will further accelerate automation, making industrial processes smarter, more adaptable, and highly efficient. While concerns regarding workforce changes, cybersecurity, and integration complexity must be addressed, the benefits of automation—higher productivity, improved quality, and enhanced worker safety—are undeniable. Moving toward a more connected and data-driven world, industrial automation will play an increasingly crucial role in shaping the global economy and improving quality of life.

Future research should explore the ethical implications of automation, strengthen cybersecurity frameworks, and foster collaboration among industry, academia, and policymakers to ensure a seamless and equitable transition to the future of work.

REFERENCES

[1] Groover, M.P., "Automation, Production Systems, and Computer-Integrated Manufacturing", *5th edition. Pearson Education*, 2020.

[2] Bolton, W., "Programmable Logic Controllers", 6th edition. Elsevier, 2021.

[3] Sickel, J., "Industrial Automation: Hands-On", McGraw-Hill Education, 2019.

[4] Kusiak, A., "Smart Manufacturing: Industrial Artificial Intelligence", Academic Press, 2019.

[5] Seitz, A. and Nyhuis, P., "Industry 4.0 and Digitization: Strategies for Smart Manufacturing", Springer, 2022.

[6] Lee, J.; Bagheri, B. and H. Kao, A., "A cyber-physical systems architecture for Industry 4.0-based manufacturing systems," *Manufacturing Letters,* Vol. 3, No. 1, pp. 18–23, 2015.

[7] Xu, X.; Lu, Y.; Vogel-Heuser, B. and Wang, L., "Industry 4.0 and smart manufacturing: A review of research issues and trends," *IEEE Transactions on Industrial Informatics,* Vol. 17, No. 3, pp. 2100–2112, 2021.

[8] Tao, F.; Zhang, M. and Liu, Y., "Digital twin in industry: State-of-the-art and future directions," *IEEE Transactions on Industrial Informatics,* Vol. 18, No. 2, pp. 1346–1359, 2022.

[9] Huang, C.; Zheng, P. and Xu, X., "Cloud-based manufacturing for Industry 4.0: A comprehensive review," *Robotics and Computer-Integrated Manufacturing,* Vol. 67, p. 101993, 2021.

Comparative Analysis of GAN-Based Image Generation Methods for Creative Applications

Alka Karketta[1], Kusum Tilkar[2] and Jitendra Managre[3]

ABSTRACT: Generative Adversarial Networks (GANs) have revolutionized creative industries by enabling realistic and artistic image synthesis. This paper presents a comparative study of six key GAN-based image generation methods: StyleGAN3, DC-Art-GAN, Augmenting Character Designers' Creativity, Complementary Cognitive Approaches, Image Synthesis and Style Transfer, and Interactive Image Generation. We analyze their core focus, technical approaches, application areas, advantages, and challenges. Through a comparative graphical representation and X-Y plot analysis, we highlight their strengths and optimal use cases.

Keywords: *Image Processing, Interactive Image Analysis, Cognitive Approach, Optimization, Image Synthesis.*

1. INTRODUCTION

Generating realistic images using Generative Adversarial Networks (GANs) is a powerful technique with various creative applications. Here's an overview of the process and potential uses:

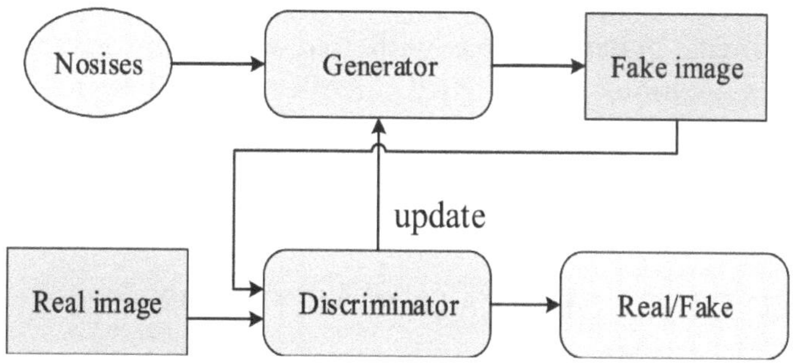

Figure 1: Image Generation by GANs

GANs consist of two neural networks:

1. **Generator:** Creates images from random noise.
2. **Discriminator:** Evaluates whether the generated images are real or fake.

[1,3] Department of Electrical and Electronics, Shri Vaishnav Institute of Technology and Science, Shri Vaishnav Vidyapeeth Vishwavidyalaya, Indore, India.
E-mail: [1]alkakarketta@svvv.edu.in; [3]jitendramanagre@svvv.edu.in

[2] Department of Computer Sciecne, Shri Vaishnav Institute of Information Technology, Shri Vaishnav Vidyapeeth Vishwavidyalaya, Indore, India. E-mail: Kusumtilkar@svvv.edu.in

The networks compete against each other, improving over time, until the Generator produces highly realistic images.

Techniques to Enhance Realism

- **Progressive Growing GANs (PGGANs):** Trains on lower resolutions first and progressively increases resolution.
- **StyleGAN & StyleGAN2/3:** Introduces control over image styles and finer details, improving realism.
- **BigGAN:** Optimized for generating high-resolution images with more diverse outputs.
- **Diffusion-GANs:** Combines diffusion models with GANs for enhanced realism.

Creative Applications

1. **Art & Design:** AI-assisted artwork, concept art, and digital painting.
2. **Fashion & Product Design:** Generating new clothing styles, shoe designs, and product mockups.
3. **Game Development:** Creating realistic textures, character portraits, and environments.
4. **Advertising & Marketing:** Synthetic but highly photorealistic images for promotions.
5. **Virtual Influencers:** AI-generated models for social media, replacing human influencers.
6. **Deepfake & Animation:** Creating digital avatars, deepfake videos, and motion synthesis.

The field of image generation has witnessed significant advancements with the advent of GANs. Various GAN-based architectures cater to different creative applications, ranging from photorealistic image synthesis to interactive and collaborative design [1–6]. This paper examines the comparative strengths and weaknesses of six state-of-the-art GAN models used for creative applications.

2. GAN-BASED IMAGE GENERATION METHODS

- **StyleGAN3** StyleGAN3 improves photorealistic image synthesis by eliminating texture sticking and enhancing transformations using low-pass filters. It is widely used in digital art, character design, and high-resolution content creation.
- **DC-Art-GAN** DC-Art-GAN focuses on stable procedural content generation for digital artwork, addressing common instability issues in traditional GANs.
- **Augmenting Character Designers' Creativity** This approach integrates GAN-generated concepts into the character design process, serving as a cognitive tool for designers.
- **Complementary Cognitive Approaches** A human-machine co-design framework that combines AI-generated content with human expertise to enhance the creative workflow.

- **Image Synthesis and Style Transfer** GANs enable high-quality image synthesis and style blending, benefiting industries like fashion, gaming, and advertising.
- **Interactive Image Generation** Advancements in GAN interpretability have led to interactive tools that allow users to manipulate and fine-tune AI-generated images for various creative applications.

3. COMPARATIVE ANALYSIS

To evaluate these approaches, we analyze six critical parameters: realism, artistic creativity, user control, AI autonomy, computational efficiency, and application diversity. Table 1 shows comparative analysis of parameters.

Table 1: Shows Comparative Analysis of Parameters

Aspect	*StyleGAN3*	*DC-Art-GAN*	*Augmenting Character Designers' Creativity*	*Complementary Cognitive Approaches*	*Image Synthesis & Style Transfer*	*Interactive Image Generation*
Core Focus	Realistic image synthesis	Digital art generation	AI-assisted concept creation	AI-human co-creation	Artistic transformation	User-driven AI design
Technical Approach	Low-pass filtering for smooth transitions	Deep Convolutional GANs	GAN-generated concepts for designers	Co-creation frameworks	Style blending & neural synthesis	GAN deep representation editing
Application Areas	Digital art, high-fidelity textures	Procedural content, AI art	Game & film character design	AI-assisted creativity	Art, gaming, fashion	Interactive media & AI-assisted design
Advantages	Eliminates texture sticking, high-quality synthesis	Stable training for artistic creation	Enhances designer creativity	Collaborative framework	High-quality artistic transformations	Precise user control over AI images
Challenges	Computationally expensive	Limited generalization	Requires human refinement	Needs structured co-creation	Some loss of fine details	GAN interpretability limitations

4. GRAPHICAL REPRESENTATIONS

To visualize the comparative analysis, in our comparative analysis of GAN-based image generation methods, we evaluated six approaches: StyleGAN3, DC-Art-GAN, Augmenting Character Designers' Creativity, Complementary Cognitive Approaches, Image Synthesis and Style Transfer, and Interactive Image Generation. We assessed each method across six critical parameters: Realism, Artistic Creativity, User Control, AI Autonomy, Computational Efficiency, and Application Diversity.

To visualize the performance of these methods, we present two graphical representations:

- **Radar Chart:** This chart illustrates the performance of each method across the six parameters, providing a holistic view of their strengths and weaknesses.

- **X-Y Scatter Plot**: This plot compares Realism (X-axis) versus User Control (Y-axis) to highlight the trade-offs between automation and user interactivity in each method.

These visual tools aid in understanding the unique contributions and optimal applications of each GAN-based method in creative industries.

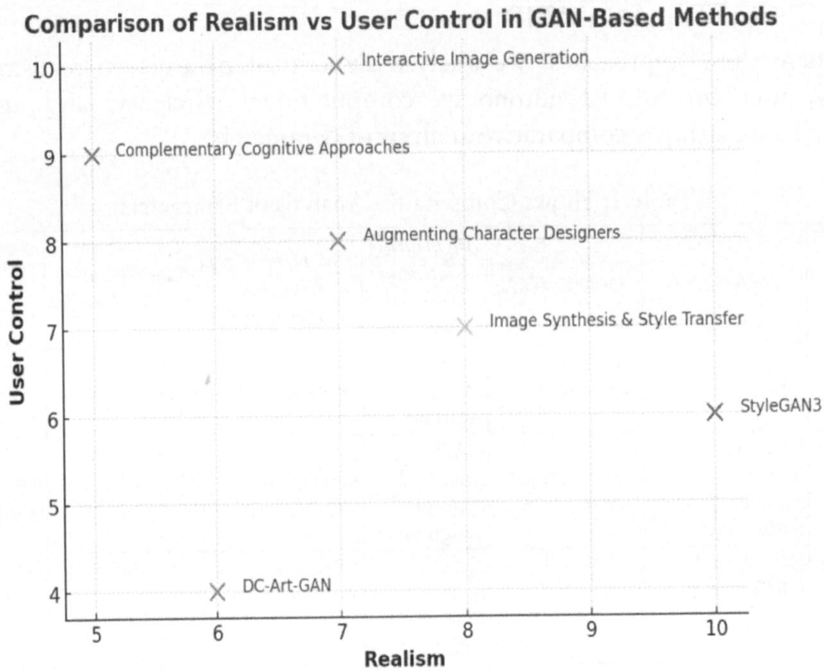

Figure 1: Graphical Representation of GAN-based Image Generation Methods

Here's the X-Y graphical plot comparing **Realism (X-axis) vs. User Control** (Y-axis) for the six GAN-based image generation methods. **X-Y Scatter Plot: Realism vs. User Control**

In this plot, each method is positioned based on its balance between generating realistic images and the degree of user control it offers:

- **StyleGAN3**: Excels in producing highly realistic images with minimal user intervention, positioning it high on the Realism axis but lower on User Control.
- **DC-Art-GAN**: Focuses on digital art generation, offering a balance between realism and user control, allowing artists to influence the creative process.
- **Augmenting Character Designers' Creativity**: Provides tools for designers to incorporate AI-generated concepts, offering substantial user control to refine outputs, though the realism may vary based on user input.
- **Complementary Cognitive Approaches**: Emphasizes AI-human co-creation, facilitating a collaborative framework where both realism and user control are balanced through iterative interactions.

- **Image Synthesis and Style Transfer**: Specializes in artistic transformations, allowing users to apply styles to images, offering moderate control with outputs that blend realism and artistic elements.
- **Interactive Image Generation**: Prioritizes user-driven AI design, granting users extensive control over the image generation process, which may sometimes compromise the level of realism depending on user inputs.

This visualization aids in understanding the unique contributions and optimal applications of each GAN-based method in creative industries, highlighting the trade-offs between automation and user interactivity.

Advantages and Disadvantages of Generative Adversarial Networks (GANs) in Realistic Image Generation

Advantages

1. **High-Quality Image Generation**: GANs produce highly realistic images with fine details, making them useful in art, entertainment, and scientific applications.
2. **Unsupervised Learning**: GANs do not require labeled data, making them useful for generating synthetic datasets where labeled data is scarce.
3. **Data Augmentation**: They can generate additional training data to improve the performance of machine learning models.
4. **Creative Applications**: GANs enhance creativity in art, fashion, gaming, and character design by generating new and unique content.
5. **Domain Adaptation**: GANs can transform images from one domain to another (e.g., turning sketches into photorealistic images or night images into daytime versions).
6. **Denoising and Super-Resolution**: GANs improve image quality by removing noise and generating high-resolution versions of low-quality images.

Disadvantages

1. **Mode Collapse**: The generator may produce a limited variety of images, failing to generate diverse samples.
2. **Training Instability**: GAN training is highly unstable and requires careful tuning of hyperparameters to prevent the discriminator from overpowering the generator or vice versa.
3. **High Computational Cost**: Training GANs demands significant computational resources, requiring powerful GPUs and long training times.
4. **Lack of Interpretability**: The internal workings of GANs are often difficult to interpret, making it challenging to control the generated outputs precisely.
5. **Ethical Concerns**: GANs can be misused to generate deepfake images and videos, raising concerns about misinformation and privacy violations.
6. **Data Dependency**: The quality of generated images depends on the diversity and quality of the training data. Poor training data results in lower-quality outputs.

5. CONCLUSION AND FUTURE DIRECTIONS

This study highlights the strengths and optimal applications of various GAN-based methods for image generation. While StyleGAN3 excels in high-resolution synthesis, DC-Art-GAN focuses on stable procedural generation. Augmenting Character Designers' Creativity and Complementary Cognitive Approaches facilitate human-machine collaboration, whereas Image Synthesis & Style Transfer and Interactive Image Generation provide flexible AI-assisted creativity. Future research should explore hybrid approaches combining these strengths for more robust and adaptive creative AI tools.

REFERENCES

[1] Karras, T.; Aila, T.; Laine, S. and Lehtinen, J., "Alias-Free Generative Adversarial Networks," *arXiv preprint arXiv*: 2106.12423, 2021.

[2] Radford, A.; Metz, L. and Chintala, S., "Unsupervised Representation Learning with Deep Convolutional Generative Adversarial Networks," *arXiv preprint arXiv*: 1511.06434, 2015.

[3] Lataifeh, M.; Carrasco, X.; Elnagar, A. and Ahmed, N., "Augmenting Character Designers' Creativity Using Generative Adversarial Networks," *arXiv preprint arXiv*: 2305.18387, 2023.

[4] Davis, N., Hsiao, C.P.; Singh, K. and Magerko, B., "Co-Creative Drawing Agent with Object Recognition," *in Proceedings of the 21st International Conference on Intelligent User Interfaces*, 2016.

[5] Gatys, L.A.; Ecker, A.S. and Bethge, M., "Image Style Transfer Using Convolutional Neural Networks," *in Proceedings of the IEEE Conference on Computer Vision and Pattern Recognition*, 2016, pp. 2414–2423.

[6] Zhu, J.Y.; Zhang, R.; Pathak, D.; Darrell, T.; Efros, A.A.; Wang, O. and Shechtman, E., "Toward Multimodal Image-to- Image Translation," *in Advances in Neural Information Processing Systems*, Vol. 30, 2017.

Collision Detection Using Sensors and Ensuring Fire Safety

Lucky Amoliya[1], Deepak Sharma[2] and Prasanna Dubey[3]

ABSTRACT: The development of technology is making our lives easier. The increasing number of vehicles is resulting in an increasing number of accidents, and still the number of road accidents is increasing day by day due to the loss of life and property, and most of the deaths are caused by fires in vehicles. In this work we propose the best solution to this problem by using a fire extinguisher mechanism. In addition, the system will also get accident locations obtained from GPS and help the rescue service reach on time and save human lives. It also makes sure to prevent accidents by using fire sensors.

Keywords: *Arduino, Fire Sensor, Piezoelectric Sensor, GPS Technology, Safety Mechanism.*

1. INTRODUCTION

Accidents happen everywhere, but in school areas and highways major accidents occur due to the high speed of automobiles. The main aim is to ensure safety by using fire extinguisher mechanism for the drivers and to detects the crashes if occur, and to notify the respective owners and authorities through GSM-GPS technologies [1]. If there is an accident, the mechanism will activate and a notification will transmit to family member, EMS (Emergency Medical Services).

According to this system, the vibration of the piezoelectric sensor increases beyond its limit when an accident occurs and transmits signal in form of information to the GSM module [2]. This system guarantees life security since the GSM can transmit messages to the respective authority [3].

An automatic fire extinguisher system for preventing accidents is introduced here. The given design is a mechanism, which can trace accidents in very less time and senses fire using fire sensors and activates fire extinguisher mechanism and sends the basic information to first aid center within a few seconds and rescue team receive this warning message and take immediate action [4, 5].

Figure 1 demonstrates that when accident happens, the alert message is sent to the EMS (Emergency Medical Services) or the close ones and the location of the accident is traced by using the message sent by the GSM modular and GPS. And if the fire detection sensor senses the fire in the vehicle it immediately activates the fire extinguisher mechanism resulting in less damage [6].

[1-3] Department of Electronics Engineering, Medicaps University, Indore, India.
E-mail: [1]en21el301044@medicaps.ac.in; [2]en21el301024@medicaps.ac.in; [3]prasanna.dubey@medicaps.ac.in

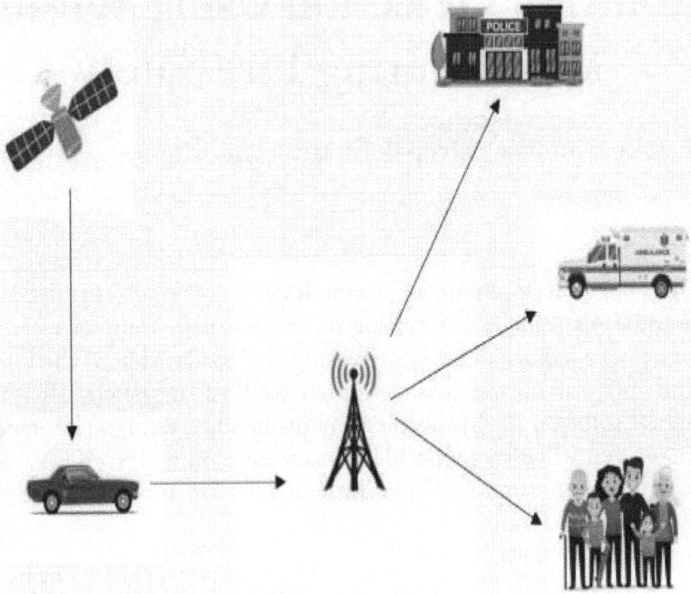

Figure 1: System Overview

The rest of the paper is as follows. In section II describes the system model, Section III describes the working of the model and section IV concludes the paper.

2. SYSTEM MODEL

The automatic Fire Extinguisher System and a smart collision detection system, Ind outs the circumstance of an accident, notifies the traffic control authorities and family. When the accident happen, immediate action is tacking. And if the fire detection sensor senses the fire in the vehicle and immediately activates the fire extinguisher [7]. It also enables to tracking of automobiles location the location of vehicles is available on google maps, which is easier to locate.

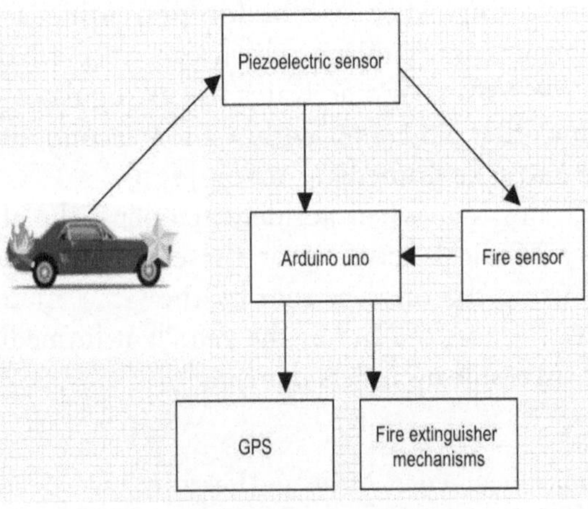

Figure 2: System Model

The Figure 2 shows that model consist of three modules. first is Arduino Uno which is control unit of the system, Arduino is a based tracking system using GPS and GSM module. By using of GPS and GSM module tracking and find the positioning of vehicles and receive information in the form of SMS. The second one is piezoelectric vibration sensor. Third is Fire sensor which senses whether the vehicle is on fire or not[8].

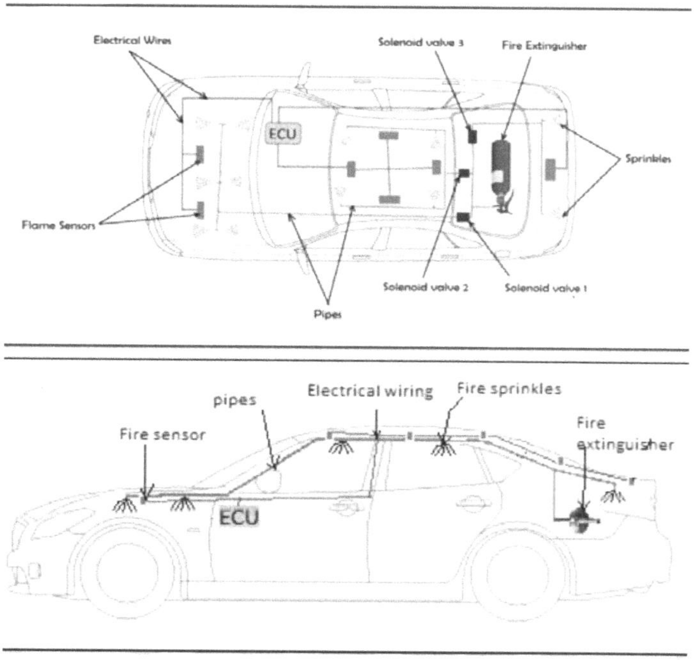

Figure 3: Overview of Fire Extinguisher Mechanism

The Figure 3 shows the working of the fire extinguisher system. When a fire occurring, the sensors installed on the vehicles detect the fire. The flame sensor detects the presence of the fire by determining the surrounding temperature within its range. Once its senses the fire, it sends signal to the ECU (Electronic Control Unit). The ECU processes this information using the pre-programmed logic [9].

If the signal is confirmed to be from the flame sensor, the ECU activates the buzzer, LED, DC motor, and the appropriate solenoid valve based on the location of the fire. For instance, if a fire is detected in the engine compartment, the ECU will open the solenoid valve connected to the pipes leading to that section, allowing extinguishing fluid to Now. The other two valves will remain closed.

3. WORKING OF THE MODEL

3.1 Arduino

Arduino is a versatile microcontroller board used for a wide range of applications, including creating interactive projects, C. In this system, Arduino plays the role of control and starts collecting the coordinates received from the GPS module. The collected coordinates are transmitted to the Central Emergency Monitoring Station [10][11].

3.2 Piezoelectric

A piezoelectric sensor measures the change in pressure, acceleration, strain or force. These sensors sense the pressure and produce electric charge these sensors are also used for other processes of measurements.

3.3 GPS

Global Positioning System (GPS) is used for sending and receiving the radio signal. This radio signal provides the necessary information to user, GPS is used in various purpose determines the time delay of each received signal. When distance and location of satellite are right. The satellite is used to determine the location of the receiver.

3.4 Flow Chart

The flowchart is telling us how our system is working; first, it initializes, then the sensor checks for collision; if there is a collision, then it tracks the location of the vehicle and informs the nearest authority, or if the flame sensor senses the fire, then it activates the fire extinguisher mechanism.

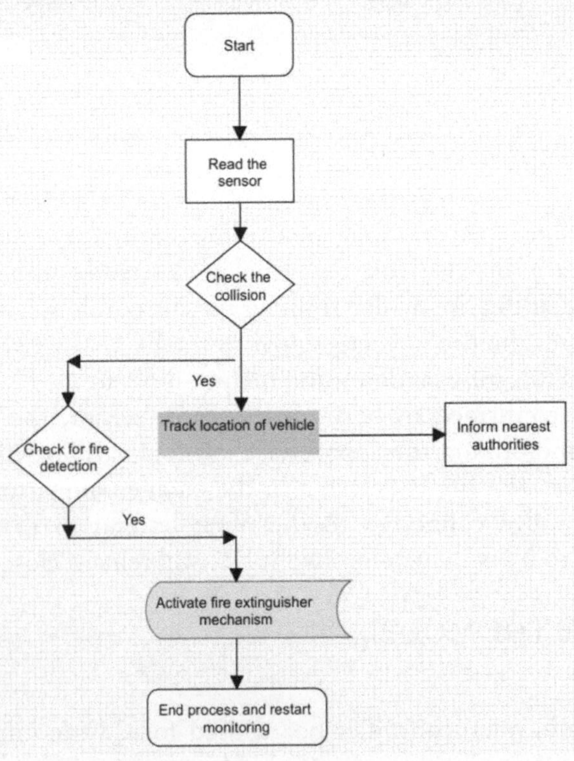

Figure 4: Flow Chart of System

3.4 GSM

It comprises the below mentioned elements:

1. **Mobile Station:** It is a device in which transceivers, display and processor are present. These are controlled by SIM card, and these cards are operated over this network.
2. **Base Station Subsystem:** It is handling the communication between mobile station and the rest part. It has the base transceiver station and the base station controller.
3. **Network Subsystem:** It is performs switching of basic network connection of the mobile operators, and manages the mobile services authentication.

4. CONCLUSION

A fire extinguisher system has been used to minimize deaths and serious situations caused by accidents and fires. This system provides immediate response, so that the fire can be controlled immediately at the time of the accident. Along with this, GPS and GSM technologies have been used, so that ambulance and police services can be informed immediately in case of an accident. This system can be helpful in reducing the severity of the accident to a great extent. Overall, our system comes out to be economically desirable and efficient. It is clear from the experiments and results that this system can be easily implemented in real time.

REFERENCES

[1] Sawant, K.; Bhole, I.; Kokane, P.; Doiphode, P.and Thorat, Y., "Accident alert and vehicle tracking system," *Int. J. Innov. Res. Comput. Commun. Eng.,* Vol. 4, No. 5, May 2016.

[2] Chaudhry, T. *et. al.,* "Method of identifying burning material from its smoke using attenuation of light," *Fire Saf. J.,* 2017.

[3] Patil, M.; Rawat, A.; Singh, P. and Dixit, S., "Accident detection and ambulance control using intelligent traffic control system," *Int. J. Eng. Trends Technol. (IJETT),* Vol. 34, No. 8, Apr. 2016.

[4] Bu, F. and Gharajeh, M.S., "Intelligent and vision-based fire detection systems: A survey," *Image Vis. Comput.,* Vol. 91, p. 103803, 2019.

[5] Saeed, F.; Paul, A.; Rehman, A.; Hong, W.H. and Seo, H., "IoT-based intelligent modeling of smart home environment for fire prevention and safety," *J. Sensor Actuator Netw.,* Vol. 7, No. 1, p. 11, 2018.

[6] Kodur, V.; Kumar, P. and Rafi, M.M., "Fire hazard in buildings: review, assessment and strategies for improving fire safety," *PSU Res. Rev.,* 2019.

[7] Shams, R.; Hossain, S.; Priyom, S. and Fatema, N., "Automated fire extinguishing system with GSM alarm," *Dept. Electr. Electron. Eng., BRAC Univ.,* 2014.

[8] Manjunathan, A.; Kumar, A.S.; Udhayanan, S.; Selvi, C.T. and Stonier, A.A., "Design of autonomous vehicle control using IoT," *IOP Conf. Ser.: Mater. Sci. Eng.,* Vol. 1055, p. 012008, 2021.

[9] John, A.J. ; A.K.; A.V.K.S.; F.P. and H.P., "Automated fire extinguishing robotic vehicle," *Int. J. Sci. Eng. Res., vol. 7, no.* 4, 2016.

[10] Kiruthika, S.; Sakthi, P.; Raam, K.; Sanjay, G. and Rafi, M.M., "Vision based smart parking system," *Turk. J. Physiother. Rehabil.*, Vol. 32, 2021.

[11] Alagarsamy, M.; Kasinathan, P.; Manickam, G.; Duruvarajan, P.R.; Sakkarai, J. and Suriyan, K., "IoT based E-vehicle monitoring system using sensors and imaging processing algorithm," *Int. J. Reconfigurable Embedded Syst.*, Vol. 11, No. 2, 2022.

Development and Optimization of a Restaurant Assistant System Using Spark V and ESP8266

Atharv Sharma[1] and Yogeshwari Sharma[2]

ABSTRACT: The rapid evolution of automation and IoT technologies has profoundly influenced the food service industry. This paper details the conceptualization, development, and enhancement of a Restaurant Assistant System (RAS) employing the Spark V microcontroller and ESP8266 Wi-Fi module. The primary objective of the system is to automate order processing, food delivery, and inventory management, thereby improving operational efficiency. While the prototype establishes feasibility, further refinements are necessary for real-world implementation. The study identifies key challenges such as system reliability, scalability, and real-time communication, and discusses potential optimizations. Additionally, a comparative analysis of existing restaurant automation technologies is conducted to underscore the benefits and limitations of the proposed system.

Keywords: *Wi-Fi Module, RFID, Microcontroller, Reliability, Operational Efficiency.*

1. INTRODUCTION

1.1 Background

The restaurant industry is confronted with issues including labor shortages, high operational costs, and inefficiencies in service delivery [1]. Automation has emerged as a viable solution to mitigate these challenges by minimizing human errors and streamlining operational processes. This paper explores an IoT-based system that integrates robotics and embedded technologies to optimize restaurant management. Traditional automation solutions, such as RFID-based ordering and semi-automated conveyor belt delivery, have been widely utilized but exhibit constraints related to flexibility, adaptability, and real-time control [2]. This study introduces a microcontroller-based restaurant assistant system designed to enhance performance and scalability.

1.2 Problem Statement

Conventional restaurant service models rely heavily on human intervention for order placement, food delivery, and overall management, leading to inefficiencies such as

[1]Department of Electrical and Electronics Engineering, Shri Vaishnav Institute of Technology and Science, Shri Vaishnav Vidyapeeth Vishwavidyalaya, Indore, India.
E-mail: atharvsharma7123@gmail.com

[2]BTech Student, Shri Vaishnav Institute of Technology and Science, Shri Vaishnav Vidyapeeth Vishwavidyalaya, Indore, India. E-mail: yogeshwarishama004@gmail.com

prolonged wait times, errors in order processing, and escalating labour expenses [3]. Although some degree of automation, including conveyor-based food delivery and RFID-enabled ordering, has been integrated, these solutions often require substantial initial investment, lack adaptability, and are not inherently scalable for real-time operations [4]. The proposed RAS leverages embedded systems and IoT-based automation to address these limitations, offering a cost-effective, scalable, and efficient alternative. By integrating the Spark V microcontroller and ESP8266 Wi-Fi module, the system facilitates real-time order processing, autonomous food delivery, and seamless staff-customer communication [5]. The research seeks to refine automation techniques in restaurant environments by tackling challenges associated with navigation accuracy, communication latency, and scalability.

1.3 Objectives

This study aims to conceptualize, develop, and refine an advanced RAS utilizing cutting-edge embedded systems and IoT technologies to enhance order processing and delivery mechanisms. The primary objectives include designing and implementing a fully operational prototype incorporating the Spark V microcontroller, ESP8266 module, and a range of peripheral sensors for efficient automation [6]. A comprehensive system evaluation is conducted to identify hardware limitations, software inefficiencies, and latency issues that may hinder real-time performance [7]. Additionally, the research focuses on system scalability and robustness by addressing sensor calibration challenges, wireless communication bottlenecks, and power optimization strategies [8]. The ultimate goal is to compare the proposed model with conventional restaurant automation solutions, demonstrating its advantages in terms of operational efficiency, cost-effectiveness, and adaptability in dynamic service environments [9].

1.4 Scope

The scope of this study includes the hardware and software aspects of the proposed system. The hardware configuration consists of the Spark V microcontroller, ESP8266 Wi-Fi module, various navigation sensors, and actuators for movement control. The software architecture is built using Embedded C programming for microcontroller operations, a web-based order processing interface, and IoT-based remote monitoring capabilities. The primary focus areas include optimizing wireless communication, improving power management, and improving system navigation and optimizing movement efficiency [10].

2. LITERATURE REVIEW

2.1 Overview of Restaurant Automation

Restaurant automation has experienced substantial advancements in recent years, with numerous technological solutions being deployed to enhance efficiency and customer satisfaction. Research has demonstrated that automation significantly reduces service time, lowers operational costs, and enhances overall restaurant workflow [11]. Integrating robotics, IoT, and artificial intelligence has transformed restaurant operations, but limitations persist in terms of cost-effectiveness, adaptability, and real-time system integration [12].

2.2 Existing Technologies in Restaurant Automation

Various restaurant automation technologies have been explored and implemented. RFID-based ordering systems allow quick and accurate transactions; however, widespread adoption is hindered by the high infrastructure cost [13]. Conveyor belt food delivery mechanisms optimize efficiency in controlled environments but offer limited flexibility for diverse restaurant layouts [14]. AI-powered chatbots have improved customer interaction and ordering processes but lack integration with physical food delivery systems [15]. The need for an adaptive, cost-efficient, and scalable automation solution remains evident.

2.3 IoT-Based Solutions

IoT applications in restaurant automation have enhanced order tracking, kitchen automation, and inventory control. Studies indicate that IoT-driven systems improve coordination between service areas while reducing the need for human intervention [16]. Nevertheless, key challenges persist, including system latency, power consumption, and reliability [17].

2.4 Need for an Optimized System

Despite ongoing technological progress, existing solutions still grapple with issues related to cost-effectiveness, scalability, and operational efficiency. This research proposes a system integrating Spark V and ESP8266 to enable real-time communication, autonomous navigation, and power-optimized operation, addressing current industry limitations [18].

3. SYSTEM DESIGN AND ARCHITECTURE

3.1 System Overview

The RAS is designed to automate order placement, processing, and food delivery through a combination of embedded hardware and IoT-based communication. The system architecture consists of a user-friendly interface for order management, a central control unit utilizing Spark V, and a robotic assistant for autonomous delivery [19].

3.2 Hardware and Software Components

The hardware framework comprises the Spark V microcontroller, ESP8266 Wi-Fi module, IR and ultrasonic sensors, and motor actuators for navigation. The software infrastructure is built using Embedded C and incorporates AI-assisted navigation algorithms for route optimization and obstacle avoidance [20].

3.3 Flowchart

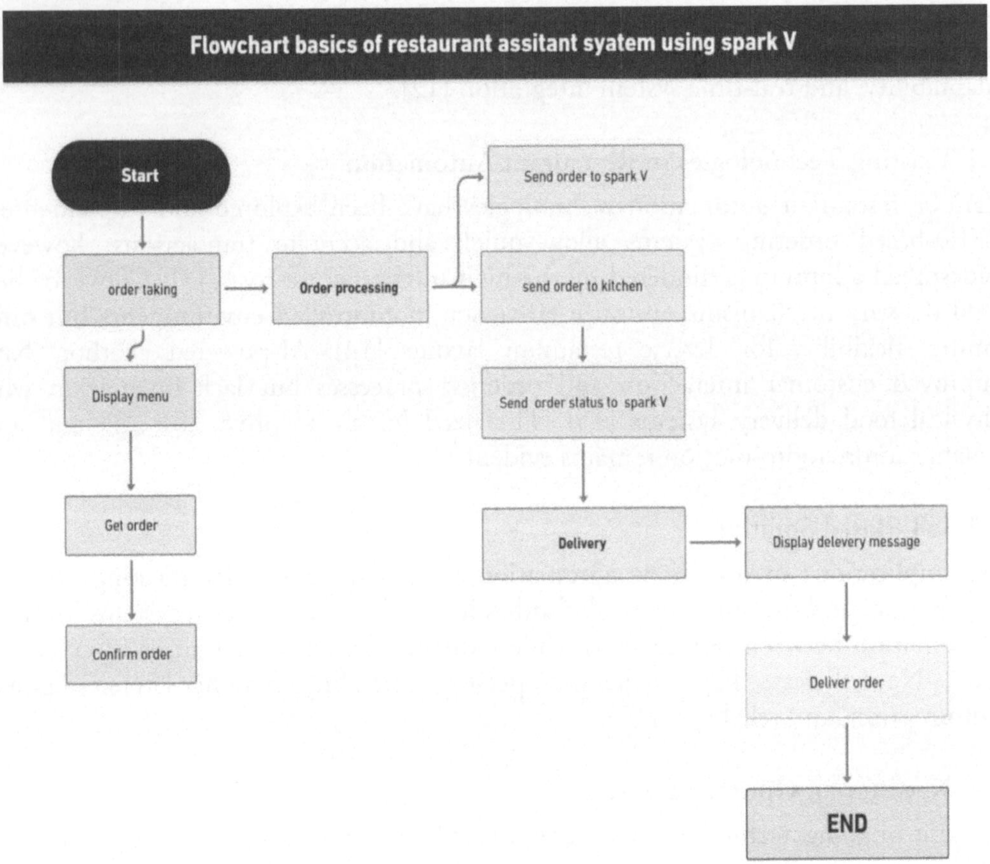

Figure 1: Flow Chart

4. CHALLENGES AND OPTIMIZATION STRATEGIES

4.1 Identified Challenges

Several challenges impact the system's efficiency, including communication delays between the ESP8266 and Spark V, which may degrade real-time performance [21]. Additionally, precise sensor calibration is necessary for accurate navigation. Power management presents another concern, requiring optimization strategies to extend operational uptime [22]. Lastly, system scalability must be ensured to accommodate larger restaurant environments [23].

4.2 Proposed Optimizations

To address these challenges, the research proposes adopting MQTT over HTTP for improved communication speed and efficiency. Further optimizations include implementing low-power consumption strategies, integrating AI-driven navigation for enhanced obstacle detection, and incorporating reinforcement learning models to improve the robot's autonomous decision-making capabilities over time [24, 25].

5. CONCLUSION

The development of the Restaurant Assistant System (RAS) using Spark V and ESP8266 highlights the potential of IoT-driven automation in enhancing restaurant efficiency. The system successfully automates order processing, food delivery, and real-time communication, mitigating traditional inefficiencies. While challenges such as communication latency, navigation accuracy, and scalability persist, proposed optimizations—including AI-assisted navigation and improved communication protocols—offer promising solutions. Future enhancements should focus on refining power management strategies, expanding real-time data processing capabilities, and incorporating cloud-based automation for improved scalability. By integrating advanced machine learning techniques, the RAS can further adapt to varying restaurant configurations and customer needs, ensuring a seamless and efficient dining experience.

REFERENCES

[1] Smith, J., "The Future of Automation in Hospitality," *IEEE Trans. Autom. Sci. Eng.*, Vol. 18, No. 2, pp. 300–312, 2023.

[2] Zhang, M.I.; Kumar, A. and Wei, L., "RFID-based Order Processing in Restaurants: A Comparative Analysis," *Int. J. Smart Syst.*, Vol. 15, No. 1, pp. 45–58, 2022.

[3] Brown, P. and Lee, R., "Scalability Challenges in Automated Restaurant Systems," *J. Embedded Syst. Appl.*, Vol. 10, No. 3, pp. 120–134, 2021.

[4] Thompson, D. and Kim, Y., "IoT-Driven Smart Restaurant Management: A Case Study," *IEEE Internet Things J.*, Vol. 7, No. 5, pp. 2100–2113, 2020.

[5] Ahmed, S. and Patel, B., "Power Optimization in Embedded Systems for Smart Restaurants," *J. Adv. Robot. Autom.*, Vol. 9, No. 4, pp. 65–79, 2023.

[6] Thomas, R. and Williams, J., "AI-Powered Robotics for Restaurant Automation," *IEEE Trans. Ind. Electron.*, Vol. 27, No. 8, pp. 987–1002, 2021.

[7] Sharma, K. and Patel, V., "Energy-Efficient IoT Networks in Smart Restaurants," *Int. J. Internet Things Res.*, Vol. 8, No. 3, pp. 210–223, 2022.

[8] Zhao, Y. and Chen, B., "Automated Food Delivery Using Embedded Systems," *IEEE Embedded Syst. Rev.*, Vol. 16, No. 4, pp. 88–101, 2020.

[9] Gupta, A. and Richardson, L., "Enhancing Customer Satisfaction Through IoT-Enabled Smart Restaurants," *J. Hosp. Autom.*, Vol. 19, No. 6, pp. 430–450, 2023.

[10] Wang, S. and Takahashi, M., "Navigation Algorithms for Autonomous Restaurant Robots," *IEEE Robot. AI J.*, Vol. 22, No. 7, pp. 1095–1110, 2021.

[11] Anderson, J. and White, D., "Wireless Sensor Networks in Hospitality Automation," *J. Wireless Commun. Syst.*, Vol. 14, No. 5, pp. 290–305, 2022.

[12]. Singh, P. and Kim, H., "Cloud-Based Automation and Restaurant Management Systems," *IEEE Cloud Comput. J.*, Vol. 9, No. 1, pp. 78–92, 2023.

[13] Brown, T. and Johnson, E., "Embedded AI for Smart Restaurants: A Performance Analysis," *J. Artif. Intell. Robot.*, Vol. 17, No. 2, pp. 56–70, 2021.

[14] Lewis, C. and Martinez, F., "Data Security Challenges in IoT-Based Restaurant Automation," *IEEE Cybersecur. IoT Res. J.*, Vol. 11, No. 3, pp. 147–162, 2022.

[15] Roberts, R. and Yamamoto, K., "Sensor Calibration Techniques for Autonomous Restaurant Assistants," *J. Embedded Syst. Eng.*, Vol. 10, No. 4, pp. 199–213, 2023.

[16] Nakamura, D. and Park, S., "Reinforcement Learning for Optimizing Restaurant Robotics Navigation," *J. Intell. Robot. Autom.*, Vol. 21, No. 9, pp. 570–585, 2023.

[17] Klein, H. and Garcia, J., "MQTT vs. HTTP: A Comparative Study for IoT-Based Smart Restaurant Systems," *IEEE Internet Things J.*, Vol. 10, No. 4, pp. 217–232, 2022.

[18] O'Connor, M. and Lee, B., "Cloud-Integrated Smart Restaurants: Case Studies and Future Prospects," *J. Cloud Comput. AI Integr.*, Vol. 18, No. 7, pp. 420–435, 2023.

[19] Williams, T. and Carter, M., "Wireless Protocols for IoT-Enabled Restaurant Automation," *IEEE Wireless Commun.*, Vol. 25, No. 3, pp. 112–125, 2023.

[20] Patel, L. and Kumar, H., "Automated Order Processing in Smart Restaurants: A Case Study," *J. Smart Hosp. Syst.*, Vol. 15, No. 5, pp. 330–345, 2022.

[21] Gomez, S. and Rogers, D., "Scalability and Efficiency of IoT-Enabled Restaurant Robots," *IEEE Robot. Autom. Mag.*, Vol. 28, No. 4, pp. 88–101, 2023.

[22] Wilson, R. and Liu, F., "Power Optimization Strategies for Autonomous Food Delivery Robots," *J. Embedded AI Autom.*, Vol. 19, No. 2, pp. 90–110, 2022.

[23] Hernandez, A. and Kim, J., "Real-Time Path Planning for Automated Restaurant Assistants," *IEEE Trans. Cyber-Phys. Syst.*, Vol. 16, No. 3, pp. 245–260, 2023.

[24] Watson, P. and Fernandez, L., "AI-Driven Decision Making in Restaurant Automation," *Int. J. Artif. Intell. Smart Syst.*, Vol. 14, No. 1, pp. 50–67, 2022.

[25] Nakamura, H. and Cho, S., "Evaluating the Performance of IoT-Based Restaurant Automation," *IEEE Internet Things J.*, Vol. 11, No. 6, pp. 342–359, 2023.

Optimizing Thermal Power Plant Efficiency: A Comprehensive Energy Audit

Deepak Rathod[1], Prabhakar Dubey[2] and Abhijeet Sengar[3]

ABSTRACT: A methodical approach to decision-making on energy management requires an energy audit. It seeks to balance the total energy inputs with utilization and aids in locating all energy sources within a facility. This research focuses on a 100 MW thermal coal-fired power plant in India, where thermal power generates about 65 percent of the country's electricity, but at poor efficiency rates of 30–40%. Heat loss is the main cause of energy losses that happen during production, transmission, and distribution. The paper identifies important areas and strategies for raising such power plants' efficiency. It also covers in brief the steps and techniques for gathering information needed to carry out an energy audit at a thermal power plant. India is working to achieve complete electrification, and recycling waste energy and preserving idle energy could make a big difference in this regard. The paper also includes results from an energy audit carried out at a thermal power plant, which show potential savings in electrical energy expenses of Rs. 5.87 crore, with a computed payback period of 24 months considering the necessary investment.

Keywords: *Energy Conservation, Lighting Audit, Payback Period, Thermal Power Plant, Transformer Audit.*

1. INTRODUCTION

This study examines a 100-megawatt thermal power plant's energy efficiency, focusing on boiler, electrical, pumping, air compressor, and cooling towers. The aim is to propose energy-saving solutions, reducing monthly electrical energy consumption and manufacturing costs [2]. The comprehensive energy survey includes on-site inspections, measurements, and maintenance discussions [3].

2. SCOPE OF AUDIT

An energy audit examines various aspects of a coal handling plant, including power consumption, raw water intake, DM plant, ash handling plant, feed water systems, steam system, secondary fuel oil consumption, vacuum system, plant and control air system, turbine heat rate, ball mills, air fans, cooling towers, condensation extraction system, plant lighting, transformers, generator efficiency evaluation [4].

[1-3]Assistant Professor Department of Electrical and Electronics Engineering, Shri Vaishnav Institute of Technology and Science, Shri Vaishnav Vidyapeeth Vishwavidyalaya, Indore, Madhya Pradesh, India.
E-mail: [1]deepakrthd9@gmail.com; [2]dubeyprabhakar80@gmail.com; [3]seabhijeet445@gmail.com

3. CONDENSATE EXTRACTION PUMPS

Generating Unit-5 has two 500 kW condensate extraction pumps, with one in full operation. Efficiency of both pumps is calculated based on site measurements and additional data collection [5].

Table 1: Condensate Extraction Pump Analysis (CEP)

S. No.	*Parameters*	*CEP # A*	*CEP # B*
1.	Name of Plant	Unit-5	
2.	Make and Type	BHEL, EN 5J 40 D	
3.	Rated Capacity/Head	636 m^3/hr, 201 m, 1485 rpm, Pump Eff. = 79.5%	
4.	Motor Rating (kW)	500	500
5.	Voltage (kV)	6.64	6.56
6.	Load Current (Amp.)	50.9	51.7
7.	Power Factor	0.83	0.84
8.	Input Power (kW)	486	493
9.	Load (%)	92	94
10.	Flow Rate (m3/hr)	665	621
11.	Velocity (m/sec)	0.97	0.91
12.	Suc./Dis. Pressure (kg/cm^2, g)	–0.92/18.5	–0.93/19.0
13.	Throttling (%)	100	100
14.	Remarks	49.1 Hz	49.1 Hz

Condensate Extraction Pump # 5A (500 kW)

Total head developed = 194.2 m
Measured flow = 665 m^3/hr.
Pump output = 352 kW
Input power to the motor = 486 kW
Overall efficiency = 72%

At 92% load efficiency of the motor would be 94%. Considering above motor efficiency

Computed efficiency of the pump = 77%
Design efficiency at duty point = 79.5%

Condensate Extraction Pump # 5B (500 kW)

Total head developed = 199.3 m
Measured flow = 621 m^3/hr.
Pump output = 337 kW
Input power to the motor = 493 kW
Overall efficiency = 68%

At 94% load efficiency of the motor would be 94%. Considering above motor efficiency.

Computed efficiency of the pump = 73%
Design efficiency at duty point = 79.5%

Computed efficiency of CEP # 5A & 5B is 77% and 77% respectively and is close to the design efficiency of the pump (79.5%). Hence, the performance of both the above CEPs is satisfactory [6].

4. CONDENSATE EXTRACTION PUMPS COAL MILL ANALYSIS

The Generating Unit-5 has six coal mills with HT motors, each rated at 425 kW. The specific energy consumption and coal crushed quantity were measured during the test period [7].

Table 2: Specific Energy Consumption of Coal Mills

Name of Drive	*Units Cons. (kWh)*	*Coal Crushed (Tons)*	*SEC * (kWh/T)*	*Remarks (% higher)*
Coal Mill # 5A	369	26.8	13.8	Highest
Coal Mill # 5B	300	35.6	8.43	–
Coal Mill # 5D	336	39.2	8.57	–
Coal Mill # 5E	224	31.3	7.16	Lowest

* : Specific Energy Consumption.

Four coal mills are used to meet boiler pulverized coal needs. SEC for Coal Mill # 5B, 5D & 5E ranges from 7.16–8.57 kWh/Ton, while Coal Mill # 5A has the highest SEC at 13.8 kWh/Ton due to low coal flow rate and high power consumption [8].

Considering improvement in SEC up to 9.0 kWh/Ton
Power saving potential for Coal Mill # 5A = 128.6 kW
Units Saved per Year = 10,18,512 kWh

Considering 24 hrs/day and 330 days per annum operation of one pump

Amount Saved per Year @ Rs. 2.0/kWh = Rs. 20.37 Lakh
Approximate investment required = Rs. 5.0 Lakh
Payback Period = 3 months

5. PRIMARY AIR FANS

Generating Unit-5 has 6 PA Fans, with 4 remaining for pulverized coal combustion. Electrical parameters, flow rate, and pressure were measured during an energy audit. Airflow was taken from the control room. Efficiency was calculated based on measurements and data [9].

Table 3: Primary Air Fan Analysis (PA Fan)

S. No.	*Parameters*	*PA Fan # 5A*	*PA Fan # 5B*
1.	Name of Plant	Unit-5	
2.	Make and Type	BHEL, NDV 22 H	
3.	Rated Capacity and Pressure	39.2 m^3/sec, 947 mmWC, 1480 rpm, Fan Eff. = 79%	
4.	Motor Rating (kW)	550	550
5.	Voltage (kV)	6.63	6.65
6.	Load Current (Amp.)	52.9	51.3
7.	Power Factor	0.92	0.92
8.	Input Power (kW)	559	544
9.	Load (%)	96	95
10.	Air Temperature (°C)	172	176
11.	Flow Rate (T/hr)*	72*	71*
13.	Suc./Dis. Pressure (mm WC)	551	520
14.	Inlet Damper Position (%)	16	27
15.	Remarks	49.7 Hz	49.6 Hz

*: Reading taken from control room.
*: Reading taken from control room.

PA Fan # 5A (550 kW)

Total head developed by the fan = 551 mm WC
Air temperature = 172°C
Air density at 172°C = 0.778 kg/m^3
Flow rate calculated from graph = 72 T/hr.
= 25.71 m^3/sec

Calculated air power delivered by the fan = 139 kW
Input power to the motor = 559 kW
Overall efficiency of fans = 25%

At 96% load, efficiency of the motor would be 94%. Considering above motor efficiency.

Computed fan efficiency = 26%
Design fan efficiency at duty point = 79%

PA Fan # 5B (550 kW)

Total head developed by the fan = 520 mm WC
Air temperature = 176°C
Air density at 176°C = 0.771 kg/m^3
Flow rate calculated from graph = 71 T/hr.
= 25.58 m3/sec

Calculated air power delivered by the fan = 130 kW
Input power to the motor = 544 kW
Overall efficiency of fans = 24%

At 95% load, efficiency of the motor would be 94%. Considering above motor efficiency.

Computed fan efficiency = 26%
Design fan efficiency at duty point = 79%

The detailed power saving calculation is given below:

Considering improvement in efficiency of fan after installation of VFD is up to 75%.

Power saving potential for PA Fan # 5A @ 49% = 274 kW
Power saving potential for PA Fan # 5B @ 49% = 267 kW
Power saving potential for PA Fan # 5D @ 56% = 342 kW
Power saving potential for PA Fan # 5E @ 46% = 242 kW
Total power saving for 4 fans = 1125 kW
Units Saved per Year = 89,10,000 kWh

Considering 24 hrs./day and 330 days per annum operation.

Amount Saved per Year @ Rs. 2.0/kWh = Rs. 178 Lakh
Approximate investment required for 6 VFDs = Rs. 300 Lakh
Payback Period = 20.2 months

6. INDUCED DRAFT FANS

Four PA Fans' efficiency is lower than design (79%), requiring Variable Frequency Drive installation and regular motor maintenance for improved efficiency [10].

Table 4: Induced Draft Fan Analysis (ID Fan)

S. No.	*Parameters*	*ID Fan # 5A*	*ID Fan # 5B*
1.	Name of Plant	Unit-5	
2.	Make and Type	BHEL, NDZV 28 BW	
3.	Rated Capacity/Head	280 m^3/sec, 403 mm WC, Fan Eff. = 83%	
4.	Motor Rating (kW)	1600	1600
5.	Voltage (kV)	6.65	6.55
6.	Load Current (Amp.)	100	102
7.	Power Factor	0.78	0.78
8.	Input Power (kW)	898	903
9.	Load (%)	53	54
10.	Air Temperature (°C)	152	152
11.	Flow Rate (m3/sec)	242.1	248.1
12.	Suc./Dis. Pressure (mm WC)	–220/–25	–245/–25
13.	Scoop Position (%)	58	52
14.	Remarks	49.7 Hz	49.7 Hz

ID Fan # 5A (1600 kW)

Total head developed by the fan = 195 mm WC
Flue gas temperature = 152°C
Flue gas density at 152°C = 0.803 kg/m^3
Calculated flow rate = 242.1 m^3/sec
Calculated air power delivered by the fan = 463 kW
Input power to the motor = 898 kW
Overall efficiency of fan = 52%

At 53% load, efficiency of the motor would be 95%. Considering above motor efficiency.

Computed fan efficiency = 54%
Design fan efficiency at duty point = 83%
ID Fan # 5B (1600 kW)
Total head developed by the fan = 220 mm WC
Flue gas temperature = 152°C
Flue gas density at 152°C = 0.803 kg/m^3
Calculated flow rate = 248.1 m^3/sec.
Calculated air power delivered by the fan = 535 kW
Input power to the motor = 903 kW
Overall efficiency of fans = 59%

At 54% load, efficiency of the motor would be 95%. Considering above motor efficiency.

Computed fan efficiency = 62%
Design fan efficiency at duty point = 83%

Normally 2 ID Fans are kept in operation at a time to meet the requirement. Fan efficiency obtained for ID Fan # 5A & 5B is 54% & 62% and is lower than the design efficiency (79%). The lower efficiency is due to lower airflow delivered and lower pressure developed by all the fans. The scoop position of ID Fan # 5A & 5B is 58% & 52% respectively during site measurement [11].

Hence, it is suggested to install VFD to eliminate the fluid coupling and other control methods to reduce the flow delivered by the ID fans. The detailed calculation is given below [12].

Considering saving potential of 35% on a conservative basis
(Computed saving potential is 48%, details below)

Total power consumption by both the fans = 1801 kW
Power saving potential = 630 kW
Units Saved per Year = 49,89,600 kWh

Considering 24 hrs/day and 330 days per annum operation.

Amount Saved per Year @ Rs. 2.0/kWh = Rs. 100 Lakh

Approximate investment required = Rs. 280 Lakh
(Investment required for 2 VFDs)
Payback Period = 34 months

7. INSTRUMENT AND SERVICE AIR SYSTEMS

Generating Unit #5 has 5 air compressors, 3 instrument air compressors and 2 service air compressors, typically used to meet plant requirements.

Make & Model : K.G. Khosla, HA EOT
Type : Reciprocating, 2 stage, double acting
Rated capacity : 16.4 m^3/min (580 cfm)
Discharge pressure : 8.1 kg/cm^2g
Speed : 683 rpm
Motor : 110 kW, 1483 rpm

The energy audit measured electrical parameters and pressure, and the volumetric efficiency of air compressors was calculated using the air suction method [13].

Table 5: Service Air Compressor Analysis (SAC)

Description	*SAC # 1*	*SAC # 2*
Location	Compressor House, Unit-5	
Make, Type	G. Khosla, HA EOT, 2 stage, double acting	
Capacity (CFM)	580	
Design Pressure (kg/cm^2, g)	8.0	
Motor Rating (kW)	110	110
Voltage (Volts)	428	430
Load Current (Amp.)	140	137
Power Factor	0.88	0.87
Input Power (kW)	91.3	88.8
Load (%)	77	75
Discharge Pressure (kg/cm2g)	8.0	8.0
Remarks	49.3 Hz	49.6 Hz

Table 6: Instrument Air Compressor Analysis (IAC)

Description	*IAC # A*	*IAC # B*	*IAC # C*
Location	Compressor House, Unit-5		
Make, Type	G. Khosla, HA EOT, 2 Stage, Double Acting		
Capacity (CFM)	580		

Description	*IAC # A*	*IAC # B*	*IAC # C*
Design Pressure (kg/cm2, g)		8.0	
Motor Rating (kW)	110	110	110
No-Load Voltage (Volts)	423	–	419
Load Current (Amps.)	91.7	–	96.1
Power Factor	0.80	–	0.81
Input Power (kW)	53.7	–	56.5
Full Load Voltage (Volts)	417	428	418
Load Current (Amp.)	148	142	149
Power Factor	0.88	0.87	0.88
Input Power (kW)	94.4	91.6	94.9
Load (%)	80	77	80
Discharge Pressure (kg/cm^2g)	7.8	7.8	7.8
Remarks	49.8 Hz	49.3 Hz	49.5 Hz

SAC # 5A (110 kW)

Air suction area = $0.0064\ m^2$
Measured air velocity = 33.7 m/sec
Free air delivered = $0.216\ m^3/sec$
= 457 cfm
Operating Pressure = $8.0\ kg/cm^2$
Design free air delivered = 580 cfm
Volumetric efficiency = 79%
Input power consumed by the compressor = 91.3 kW
Specific power consumption (kW/cfm) = 0.186

SAC # 5B (110 kW)

Air suction area = $0.0064\ m^2$
Measured air velocity = 32.9 m/sec
Free air delivered = $0.211\ m^3/sec$
= 446 cfm
Operating Pressure = $8.0\ kg/cm^2$
Design free air delivered = 580 cfm
Volumetric efficiency = 77%
Input power consumed by the compressor = 88.8 kW
Specific power consumption (kW/cfm) = 0.185

IAC # 5A (110 kW)

Air suction area	= 0.0064 m^2
Measured air velocity	= 32.3 m/sec
Free air delivered	= 0.207 m^3/sec
	= 438 cfm
Operating Pressure	= 7.8 kg/cm^2
Design free air delivered	= 580 cfm
Volumetric efficiency	= 76%
Input power consumed by the compressor	= 94.4 kW
Specific power consumption (kW/cfm)	= 0.200

IAC # 5B (110 kW)

Air suction area	= 0.0064 m^2
Measured air velocity	= 37.5 m/sec
Free air delivered	= 0.240 m^3/sec
	= 509 cfm
Operating Pressure	= 7.8 kg/cm^2
Design free air delivered	= 580 cfm
Volumetric efficiency	= 88%
Input power consumed by the compressor	= 91.6 kW
Specific power consumption (kW/cfm)	= 0.168

IAC # 5C (110 kW)

Air suction area	= 0.0064 m^2
Measured air velocity	= 28.3 m/sec
Free air delivered	= 0.181 m^3/sec
	= 384 cfm
Operating Pressure	= 7.8 kg/cm^2
Design free air delivered	= 580 cfm
Volumetric efficiency	= 66%
Input power consumed by the compressor	= 94.9 kW
Specific power consumption (kW/cfm)	= 0.230

Computed volumetric efficiency of all the air compressors (except IAC # 5C) is above 75% and is close to the design efficiency of similar rating compressors, which is in the range of 85%-90%. But efficiency obtained for IAC # C is 66% and is poor compared to the design value [14].

Hence, it is suggested to do proper maintenance and overhauling of IAC # 5C. This will improve the efficiency of compressors and reduce power consumption by them. The detailed power saving calculation is given below.

Considering improvement in volumetric efficiency up to 80%

Power saving potential for IAC # 5C @ 14% = 13.3 kW
Units saved per annum = 1,11,602 kWh

Considering 24 hrs./day and 350 days per annum operation

Amount Saved per Year @ Rs. 2.0/kWh = Rs. 2.23 Lakh
Approximate investment required = Rs. 0.50 Lakh
Payback period = 2.7 months

8. LIGHTING EFFICIENCY STUDIES

Reducing Lighting Supply Voltage to 230 Volts:

The ideal lighting load is 230 volts, as exceeding this voltage increases lamp power consumption, reduces burning life, and increases failure rates. To reduce this, the lighting transformer should be set to tap position, resulting in a more efficient power supply [15].

Table 7: Lighting Load Analysis (Nighttime)

S. No.	*Description*	*Location*	*Rating (kVA)*	*Volt*	*Amp*	*P.F.*	*kW*	*kVA*	*Load (%)*	*Remarks*
1.	LDB # 1	6.6 kV S/S, Unit-5	100	249	62.7	0.93	14.5	15.6	16	Higher voltage
2.	LDB # 2		100	255	49.4	0.94	11.8	12.6	13	
3.	LDB # 3		200	242	0	0	0.0	0.0	0	
4.	LDB # 4		50	244	24.8	0.90	5.45	6.05	12	
5.	LDB # 6		50	242	31.5	0.54	4.12	7.62	15	
6.	LDB # 13		100	242	52.5	0.86	10.9	12.7	13	
7.	ELDB # 12		100	243	30.4	0.74	5.47	7.39	7	
8.	LDB # 14		100	242	9.9	0.53	1.27	2.40	2	
9.	LDB # 15		100	244	5.50	0.68	0.91	1.34	1	
10.	ELDB # 1		100	249	27.5	0.97	6.64	6.85	7	
11.	LDB # 16		50	256	8.1	0.02	0.93	2.07	4	

Table 8: Lighting Load Analysis (Nighttime)

S. No.	*Description*	*Location*	*Rating (kVA)*	*Volt*	*Amp*	*P.F.*	*kW*	*kVA*	*Load (%)*	*Remarks*
1.	LDB # 5	Ash Plant, Unit-5	100	245	45.4	0.77	8.56	11.1	11	Higher voltage
2.	LDB # 11		100	245	43.0	0.83	8.74	10.5	11	
3.	LDB # 7	ESP C/R Unit-5	50	243	48.6	0.80	9.45	11.8	24	
4.	LDB # 8		50	241	47.9	0.77	8.89	11.5	23	
5.	LDB # 9		50	247	20.6	0.62	3.15	5.09	10	
6.	LDB # 10		50	247	22.7	0.85	4.77	5.61	11	

Total = 105.6 kW

Nighttime:

Total lighting load during nighttime = 105.64 kW
Supply voltage measured = 241–256 volts

Power saving potential by maintaining 230 volts in the lighting feeder
(Calculated LDB wise) = 13.2 kW
Units Saved = 57,816 kWh

Considering 365 days and 12 hrs. operation per day

Daytime:

Total lighting load during daytime = 30.2 kW
Supply voltage measured = 239–256 volts

Power saving potential by maintaining 230 volts in the lighting feeder
(Calculated LDB wise) = 4.36 kW
Units Saved = 19,097 kWh

Considering 365 days and 12 hrs. operation per day
Total Units Saved per annum = 76,913 kWh
Amount Saved per Year @ Rs. 2.0/kWh
= Rs. 1.54 Lakh
Approximate investment required = Nil

NOMENCLATURE

AHP	Air Preheater
CEP	Condensate Extraction Pump
DA	Deaerator
DM	De-mineralize
FD	Force Draft
HP	High Pressure
ID	Induce Draft
IGV	Inlet Guide Vane
LDB	Lighting Distribution Board
LP	Low Pressure
NA	Not Available
SAC	Self-Adjusting Clutch
SPC	Specific Power Consumption
VFD	Variable Frequency Drive
MU	Mega Units

REFERENCES

[1] Boharb, A.; Allouhi, A.; Saidur, R.; Kousksou, T. and Jamil, A., "Energy conservation potential of an energy audit within the pulp and paper industry in Morocco," *J. Clean. Prod.*, Vol. 149, pp. 569–581, 2017.

[2] Andersson, E.; Karlsson, M.; Thollander, P. and Paramonova, S., "Energy end-use and efficiency potentials among Swedish industrial small and medium-sized enterprises – a dataset analysis from the national energy audit program," *Renew. Sustain. Energy Rev.*, Vol. 93, pp. 165–177, 2018.

[3] Z. Liu; H. Zhang; Y.-J. Zhang and T.-T. Zhu, "How does industrial policy affect the eco-efficiency of industrial sector? Evidence from China," *Appl. Energy*, Vol. 272, p. 115206, 2020.

[4] Iten, M.; Fernandes, U. and Oliveira, M.C., "Framework to assess eco-efficiency improvement: case study of a meat production industry," *Energy Rep.*, Vol. 7, pp. 7134–7148, 2021.

[5] Rosenqvist, J.; Thollander, P.; Rohdin, P. and Söderström, M., *Industrial Energy Auditing for Increased Sustainability – Methodology and Measurements*. InTech.

[6] Sterling, E.; Collett, C.; Turner, S. and Downing, C., "Commissioning to avoid indoor air quality problems," in *Proc. ASHRAE Trans.: Symposia*, 1994, p. 867.

[7] Anisimova, V.Y.; Tukavkin, N.M. and Chirkunova, E.K., "Energy audit of industrial enterprises on the basis of energy and resource-saving evaluation," in *E3S Web Conf. - Topical Problems of Architecture, Civil Engineering and Environmental Economics*, Vol. 91, pp. 1–6, 2018.

[8] Chanda, R.S., "On energy auditing: An experience with a jute mill," *Int. J. Recent Innov. Trends Comput. Commun.*, Vol. 2, No. 10, pp. 3134–3137, 2014.

[9] Kluczek, A. and Olszewski, P., "Energy audits in industrial processes," *J. Clean. Prod.*, Vol. 142, No. 4, pp. 3437–3453, 2017.

[10] Sharma, M. and Koushik, V.A., "Energy audit: case study of a wheel manufacturing industry," *Int. J. Eng. Res. Technol.*, Vol. 4, No. 3, 2015.

[11] Olayinka, O.S. and Oladele, A.T., "Energy audit of manufacturing and processing industries in Nigeria: a case study of food processing industry and distillation and bottling company," *Am. J. Energy Res.*, Vol. 1, No. 3, pp. 36–44, 2013.

[12] Dongellini, M.; Marinosci, C. and Morini, G.L., "Energy audit of an industrial site: a case study," *Energy Proc.*, Vol. 45, pp. 424–433, 2014.

[13] Rathod, D. and Tiwari, A., "Improving Performance: Evaluating and Optimizing a 70 MW Thermal Power Plant through Energy Audits," in *Int. Archit. Sci. Appl. Symp. (IArcSAS-2024)*, Girne, Turkish Republic of Northern Cyprus, May 30–31, 2024.

[14] Technical Report, Contract No. ENER/C3/2012-439/S12.666002, 2015, pp. 1–461.

[15] Rathod, D. and Tiwari, A., "Efficiency Evaluation and Optimization of a 210 MW Thermal Power Plant: A Comprehensive Energy Audit," *J. Therm. Eng. Appl.*, Vol. 10, No. 3, Sep.–Dec. 2023. DOI: 10.37591/JoTEA.

Diabetic Retinopathy Detection Using Image Analysis

Aditya Rathore[1], Aditya Satogiya[2], Fardeen Khan[3] and Prasanna Dubey[4]

ABSTRACT: Correct diagnosis of retinal disease is important for timely intervention and effective treatment. The approach is to improve image reconstruction using neural networks (CNN) and provide an accurate and practical method for disease detection. Retinal diseases such as glaucoma, diabetic retinopathy, high blood pressure and atherosclerosis have many causes and require comprehensive evaluation. The research focuses on extracting key features of the eye, including eye structure, properties, and disease, using data from Research on the Retina (STARE) to train a CNN model that can identify a variety of eyes diseases. The approach includes extensive testing, using a variety of visualizations to illustrate the design, and integration into Django's website for deployment. The results were successful in classifying different types of retinal diseases, successfully detecting specific diseases, and demonstrating the potential of deep learning for modification of retinal diseases, thereby improving clinical outcomes and advancing the field of ophthalmology.

Keywords: *Convolutional Neural Networks (CNN), Deep Learning Models, Diabetic Retinopathy, Feature Extraction, Image Processing Techniques.*

1. INTRODUCTION

Diabetic retinopathy and hypertensive retinopathy communicate to yearning challenges inside the discipline of ophthalmology, applying big comes about at the complex structure of the retina and posturing amazing perils of visible impairment if cleared out unaddressed. Those occasions together effect hundreds of heaps of individuals round the world, underscoring the vital need for proactive measures in early discovery, general management, and progressing considers endeavors adapted towards refining logical intercessions and optimizing knowledge care.

Glaucoma, characterized with the assist of dynamic hurt to the optic nerve, stands as a implementing enemy in the area of eye illnesses, contributing considerably to around the sector visual impairment insights. With over three million influenced humans within the united states of America on my claim, the noiseless motion of glaucoma underscores the vital of repeating eye examinations, fairly for asymptomatic

[1-4]Department of Electronics Engineering, Medi-caps University, Indore, Madhya Pradesh, India.
E-mail: [1]en21el301005@medicaps.ac.in; [2]en21el301006@medicaps.ac.in;
[3]en21el301028@medicaps.ac.in; [4]prasanna.dubey@medicaps.ac.in

humans which could furthermore proceed to be insensible in their situation till irreversible damage has passed off. in show disdain in the direction of available medicinal drugs pointed at diminishing intraocular stretch and abating infection advancement, looking ahead to the onset and development of glaucoma remains a overwhelming wander, requiring persisted research into novel restorative modalities.

In parallel, diabetic retinopathy rises as a awesome measured hassle of diabetes mellitus, making use of its harmful results at the retinal vasculature and contributing to visual deficiency in a extensive rate of operating-age grown-ups. the predominance of diabetic retinopathy, influencing roughly one-0.33 of diabetic people aged 40 and extra seasoned indoors the joined collectively states of the united states, underscores its giant effect on visual well-being and exceptional of ways of life. regardless of advancements in demonstrative strategies and cure alternatives comprehensive of laser therapy and intravitreal infusions, the avoidance and manage of diabetic retinopathy live complicated obligations, calling for maintained endeavors in diabetes control and non-stop inquire about activities to investigate imaginative recovering avenues.

Further, hypertensive retinopathy, bobbing up from out-of-control blood weight tiers, rises as a vital pointer of systemic vascular brokenness and postures a risk of nerve hurt. Influencing one-fourth of hypertensive patients, hypertensive retinopathy underscores the tough interplay among visual well-being and cardiovascular function, emphasizing the importance of blood stress regulation and complete cardiovascular peril assessment. in show disdain closer to of strides in high blood pressure manipulate, the viability of intercessions for hypertensive retinopathy remains a rely of problem, highlighting the want for all encompassing strategies enveloping both tall blood weight oversee and retinal health renovation.

The collective have an effect on of diabetic retinopathy and hypertensive retinopathy on open well being is good sized, requiring multifaceted methodologies to address their burden correctly. Early area, careful management, and progressing inquire approximately endeavors are vital in preserving vision, making strides healing outcomes, and minimizing the monetary repercussions of retinal infections. Collaboration amongst clinicians, analysts, policymakers, and advertising corporations is pivotal in driving forward progressions in eye well-being and deciphering logical revelations into unmistakable enhancements in influenced character care. via prioritizing avoidance, early intercession, and development in remedy modalities, we will relieve the annihilating impacts of these visual pathologies and clear the way for a brighter future for human beings hooking with creative and prescient impedance.

2. RELATED WORK

The discussion on the eye, with its components fair like the cornea, iris, focal point, retina, and optic nerve, changes over mellow into alarms translated as pics by way of the brain. Different retinal issues which incorporate ARMD, diabetic retinopathy, and retinal separation can thought process vision impedance or visual deficiency if untreated [1].

The publisher here proposed contraption factors to computerize diabetic retinopathy discovery utilizing retinal fundus photographs, helping in early mediation to count on imaginative and prescient misfortune. It makes use of a diverse leveled Seriousness comparing (HSG) framework categorizing photos into seriousness ranges based totally on peculiarities like microaneurysms and hemorrhages [2].

The discussion done here is on the textual content discusses the significance of early detection of subclinical diabetic retinopathy (DR) and proposes diverse biomarkers for this reason. It highlights the distance between the onset of diabetes mellitus (DM) and the appearance of clinical signs of DR, during which neural retinal damage and microvascular changes progress [3].

The abstract with the aid of author outlines the extensive impact of diabetic retinopathy (DR) as a worry of diabetes mellitus, with restricted therapeutic alternatives. It emphasizes the need for better information of DR's clinical functions, danger elements, and retinal pathology, along recent advances in its pathogenesis and potential therapeutic goals [4].

The summary authored through author highlights the extensive global burden of diabetes and its common microvascular hardship, retinopathy, which annually leads to blindness in over 10,000 diabetic sufferers in the U.S.A. by myself. The assessment emphasizes that retinopathy can start as early as 7 years earlier than the analysis of kind 2 diabetes. [5]

Diabetic retinopathy (DR) is a considerable problem among US adults elderly 40 and older, mainly among Non-Hispanic black people, in line with a nationally representative sample. DR is a leading purpose of new cases of legal blindness within the US, typically because of mechanisms like retinal detachment, hemorrhage, and macular edema. Its presence can also indicate dysfunction in other organ structures [6].

In this abstract the focus is on diabetic retinopathy (DR) as a leading cause of blindness in individuals with diabetes. It highlights landmark studies such as the Diabetic Retinopathy Study and the Early Treatment Diabetic Retinopathy Study, which established effective treatments like photocoagulation [7].

This evaluation examines interventions for diabetic retinopathy (DR) and diabetic macular edema (DME). Tight glycemic manipulate considerably reduces headaches but can also lead to early worsening of DR and dangers of hypoglycemia. Blood stress control is also vital, with tight manage lowering DR development and visual acuity deterioration. Discrepancies in study findings underscore the complexity of DR control [8]. The authors proposed the MGA-CSG approach, a brand new method for early and correct class of diabetic retinal lesions the use of fundus imaging datasets. The generation combines deep studying with optimization, facts prioritization, characteristic extraction the usage of CNNs, and improving photo vectors the use of GAN fashions. It makes use of registered and unregistered letters and functions belonging to special training to differentiate one-of-a-kind viruses [9].

The creators investigated exchange analyzing's have an effect on on restorative photo classifiers for diabetic retinopathy (DR) discovery, centering on constrained categorised actualities eventualities. They discovered that pre-schooling on ImageNet located by way of way of tuning on fundus pix stepped forward classifier in fashionable execution, but execution diminished with moo categorized realities divisions. This underscores the mission of directed mastering in such settings and highlights the want for opportunity techniques for solid DR lesson in low-facts scenarios [10].

The authors performed a systematic evaluate on deep studying-based retinal fundus picture segmentation (RFIS) for early diabetic retinopathy (DR) analysis. They analyzed one hundred fifteen relevant studies, that specialize in DR-related features including blood vessels, lesions, and optic disc/optic cup segmentation [11].

Diabetic retinopathy is characterized with the aid of structural adjustments in retinal vessels and neuroglia, with its actual pathogenesis now not completely understood. Experimental fashions of diabetes in animals and chronic elevation of blood galactose mimic components of retinopathy, suggesting a role for excessive blood sugars [12].

The item explores the contemporary advances in gadget research and an in-depth examine the early prognosis of diabetic retinopathy (DR). A framework for categorizing the severity of DR is discussed, which includes non-proliferative DR, exudates, hemorrhages, and microaneurysms the use of retinal fundus quick axis [13].

The authors talk the development of an automated version for the early detection of diabetic retinopathy (DR) based totally on pink lesions in retinal images. They spotlight the restrictions of guide prognostic strategies because of the time, fee, and problem in detecting early-degree DR. [14]

3. METHODOLOGY

In this methodology, we proposed the improvement of a diabetic retinopathy detector employing Convolutional Neural Networks (CNNs). We search into the of data acquisition, preprocessing, version structure design, schooling strategies, and evaluation methods to ensure the introduction of a strong and accurate system for the early diagnosis of diabetic retinopathy. Our approach aims to leverage the abilities of deep gaining knowledge of to offer an powerful solution for detecting and classifying diabetic retinopathy severity stages from retinal photographs.

- **Pre-Processing:** This refers to the initial steps taken to prepare the input image for further analysis. It often includes noise reduction, normalization, and other transformations to enhance the image quality.
- **Area of Blood Vessels:** In this context, it seems that the area occupied by blood vessels is being analyzed or measured. Blood vessels are important features in many medical imaging applications, such as diagnosing diabetic retinopathy.

- **Feature:** This is a characteristic or attribute of the image that is useful for the analysis task. In this case, the features include the area of blood vessels, area of exudates, and texture features.
- **Area of Exudates:** Exudates are abnormal fluid accumulations in the eye, often associated with various diseases like diabetic retinopathy. Measuring the area of exudates is an essential part of the analysis.
- **Extraction:** This refers to the process of isolating the regions of interest (ROIs) from the input image. Here, the ROIs are the areas of blood vessels and exudates. Area of Microaneurysms: Microaneurysms are small bulges in the blood vessels, which are an early sign of diabetic retinopathy. Analyzing the area of microaneurysms is important for diagnosis.
- **Texture Features:** Texture features refer to the structural properties of the image that can help distinguish various tissue types or pathological conditions.

Flow Diagram

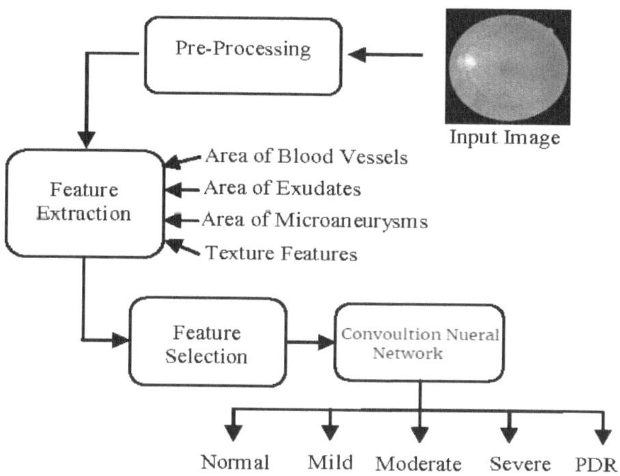

Figure 1: Methodology

- **Input Image:** This is the original image that is fed into the system for further processing.
- **Feature Selection:** This is the process of selecting the most relevant features to be used in the analysis. It helps to reduce the dimensionality of the dataset and improve the performance of the model.
- **Multiclass SVM:** A Support Vector Machine (SVM) is a machine learning model used for classification tasks. In this context, it is a multiclass SVM, which is capable of categorizing input images into multiple classes, such as Normal, Mild, Moderate, Severe PDR (Proliferative Diabetic Retinopathy).

In summary, the context describes the steps and processes involved in analyzing medical images, specifically for diagnosing diabetic retinopathy. The input image undergoes pre-processing, and features like blood vessels, exudates, and microaneurysms are extracted. The relevant features are selected, and a multiclass SVM classifier is used to categorize the image based on the disease severity.

3.1 Models and Approaches

A CNN, or Convolutional Neural network, is a kind of artificial intelligence set of rules inspired with the aid of the human visual machine. It's in particular desirable at analyzing and understanding visible information, along with pics or videos. With the aid of the use of layers of interconnected nodes and specialized operations like convolution, pooling, and activation features, CNNs can discover ways to apprehend styles and features within photographs. They may be extensively utilized in applications like photo type, item detection, and facial recognition.

Convolutional Neural Networks (CNNs) have emerged as powerful tools in diabetic retinopathy (DR) detection tasks, revolutionizing the way retinal pics are analyzed. These networks are skilled using vast datasets of retinal photographs annotated with DR severity stages, allowing them to research complex styles and capabilities associated with one of a kind tiers of the disorder. Thru a technique of image preprocessing, education, and nice-tuning, CNNs extract hierarchical representations of capabilities from uncooked photo facts, such as feature lesions such as microaneurysms, hemorrhages, and exudates. as soon as skilled, the CNN model can classify unseen retinal pix into wonderful classes primarily based on the presence and severity of DR, providing precious insights for early detection and intervention. Overall performance assessment metrics which includes accuracy, sensitivity, specificity, and AUC-ROC are hired to assess the model's efficacy in real-global eventualities. Deploying the trained CNN version in medical settings allows early detection and tracking of DR, thereby improving get entry to to eye care services and reducing the risk of vision loss, especially in underserved populations. General, CNNs play a pivotal position in automating picture analysis, helping healthcare experts in the well timed control of DR, and ultimately, preserving patients' imaginative and prescient and satisfactory of existence.

4. RESULTS

Here when we take a Fundus image of an eye and after that the system shows the result and here are some result based on the images that were provided by the user. The images must be a fundus one and should be clear in quality using the CNN algorithm the project identifies the images.

The input images are given in Figure 2. The results for different inputs are shown in Figure 3. As shown in figure 3(a) depicts that patient has no diabetic retinopathy and has a good eye. In figure 3(b) it demonstrates that patient has mild diabetic retinopathy and may have diabetic retinopathy in future. The figure 3(c) indicates patient has mild diabetic retinopathy. According to figure 3(d) shows that patient have severe diabetic retinopathy disease. The figure 3(e) portray shows that patient has diabetic retinopathy.

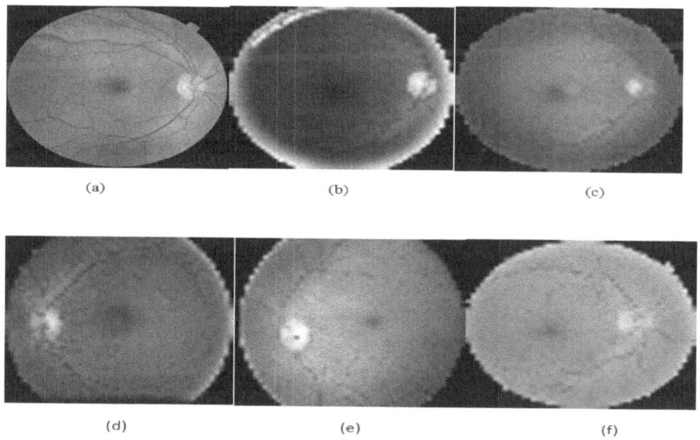

Figure 2: Inputs

And figure 3(f) shows that patient severe diabetic retinopathy.

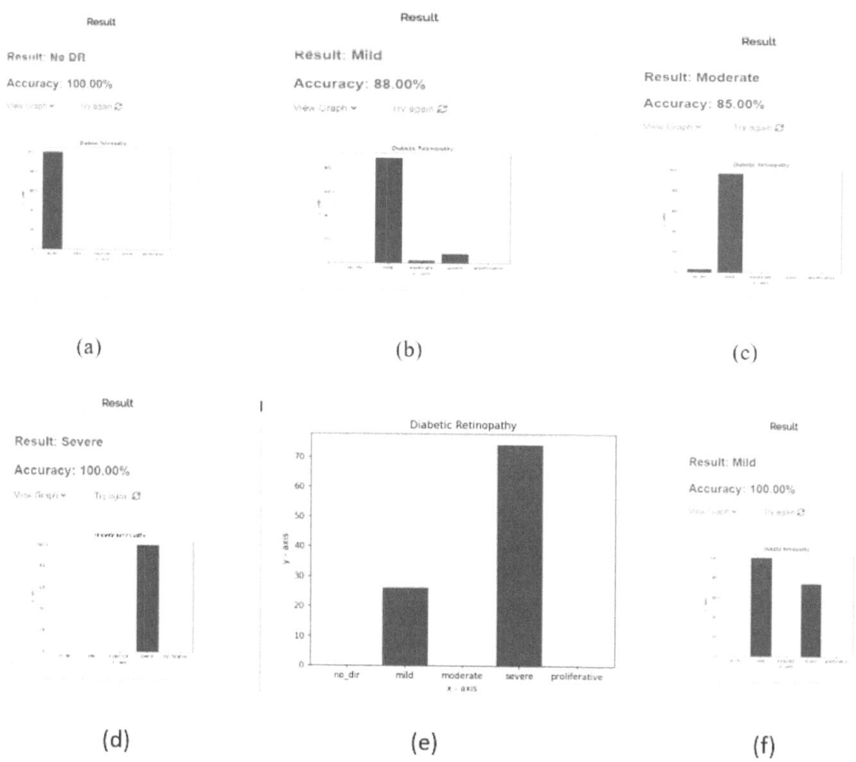

Figure 3: Outputs

5. DISCUSSION

This grading gadget is utilized by healthcare professionals to categorize the severity of diabetic retinopathy (DR), a difficulty of diabetes that impacts the eyes. Right here's an outline of every level:

1. **No DR:** At this degree, there are no signs and symptoms of diabetic retinopathy. The retina appears everyday upon examination.
2. **Mild DR:** This stage shows the presence of minimum non-proliferative modifications in the retina, consisting of some microaneurysms or small hemorrhages.
3. **Mild DR:** mild non-proliferative adjustments are discovered in the retina at this stage. These adjustments may consist of a extra range of microaneurysms, hemorrhages, and different abnormalities.
4. **Extreme DR:** intense non-proliferative modifications are evident inside the retina, indicating a tremendous development of the disorder. These changes can also include massive hemorrhages, venous beading, and intraretinal microvascular abnormalities.
5. **Proliferative DR:** that is the most advanced stage of diabetic retinopathy, characterized by way of the growth of odd new blood vessels (neovascularization) on the retina and optic nerve. Those vessels are fragile and prone to bleeding, main to imaginative and prescient loss and different headaches if left untreated by categorizing diabetic retinopathy into those levels, healthcare providers can higher investigate the severity of the condition and decide appropriate remedy and management techniques for his or her sufferers. Normal eye examinations are critical for early detection and intervention to prevent vision loss associated with diabetic retinopathy.

6. CONCLUSION

In conclusion, diabetic retinopathy stays a extensive fitness situation, particularly within the working-elderly population, leading to large morbidity and blindness if left untreated. Via sizable studies and medical trials, our expertise of the pathogenesis and management of diabetic retinopathy has superior appreciably. Evidence from randomized managed trials highlights the importance of tight glycemic and blood strain manipulate in decreasing the danger of development and headaches related to diabetic retinopathy. Additionally, advancements in diagnostic imaging and treatment modalities, inclusive of laser photocoagulation and anti-VEGF therapy, offer promising avenues for retaining vision and improving patient effects. But, challenges persist, along with the want for early detection, patient adherence to remedy regimens, and addressing healthcare disparities in getting access to eye care services. Moving forward, continued studies efforts, interdisciplinary collaboration, and public health tasks are crucial to mitigate the load of diabetic retinopathy and improve the excellent of lifestyles for individuals dwelling with diabetes."

REFRENCES

[1] Regin, R.; Rajest, S.S. and Shynu, T., "Application of machine learning to the detection of retinal diseases," *unpublished.*

[2] Bhardwaj, C.; Jain, S. and Sood, M., "Hierarchical severity grade classification of non-proliferative diabetic retinopathy," *J. Ambient Intell. Humaniz. Comput.*, Vol. 12, No. 2, pp. 2649–2670, 2021.

[3] Haque, A.; Sutradhar, I.; Rahman, M.; Hasan, M. and Sarker, M., "Convolutional nets for diabetic retinopathy screening in Bangladeshi patients," *arXiv preprint arXiv:2108.04358*, 2021.

[4] "Diabetic Retinopathy," [Online]. Available: http://ftp.columbia.edu/itc/hs/medical/clerkships/primcare/case/diabetes/library/DMRetinopathy.pdf

[5] Aiello, L., "Diabetic Retinopathy," [Online]. Available: https://www.researchgate.net/publication/270197531_Diabetic_Retinopathy

[6] Zhang, X. *et. al.*, "Prevalence of diabetic retinopathy in the United States, 2005–2008," *JAMA*, Vol. 304, No. 6, pp. 649–656, 2010.

[7] Aiello, L.M., "Perspectives on diabetic retinopathy," *Am. J. Ophthalmol.*, Vol. 136, No. 1, pp. 122–135, 2003.

[8] Engerman, R.L., "Pathogenesis of diabetic retinopathy," *Diabetes*, Vol. 38, No. 10, pp. 1203–1206, Oct. 1989.

[9] Navaneethan, R. and Devarajan, H., "Enhancing diabetic retinopathy detection through preprocessing and feature extraction with MGA-CSG algorithm," *Expert Syst. Appl.*, 2024, Art. No. 123418.

[10] Ohri, K. and Kumar, M., "Supervised fine-tuned approach for automated detection of diabetic retinopathy," *Multimed. Tools Appl.*, Vol. 83, No. 5, pp. 14259–14280, 2024.

[11] Vij, R. and Arora, S., "A systematic review on diabetic retinopathy detection using deep learning techniques," *Arch. Comput. Methods Eng.*, Vol. 30, No. 3, pp. 2211–2256, 2023.

[12] Bhandari, S.; Pathak, S. and Jain, S.A., "A literature review of early-stage diabetic retinopathy detection using deep learning and evolutionary computing techniques," *Arch. Comput. Methods Eng.*, Vol. 30, No. 2, pp. 799–810, 2023.

[13] Agarwal, S. and Bhat, A., "A survey on recent developments in diabetic retinopathy detection through integration of deep learning," *Multimed. Tools Appl.*, Vol. 82, No. 11, pp. 17321–17351, 2023.

[14] Saranya, P.; Pranati, R. and Patro, S.S., "Detection and classification of red lesions from retinal images for diabetic retinopathy detection using deep learning models," *Multimed. Tools Appl.*, Vol. 82, No. 25, pp. 39327–39347, 2023.

[15] Lin, C.-L. and Wu, K.-C., "Development of revised ResNet-50 for diabetic retinopathy detection," *BMC Bioinformatics*, Vol. 24, No. 1, Art. No. 157, 2023.

IoT-Based Weather Monitoring System

Pravesh Sandal[1], Akhtar Hussain[2] and Shiraz Husain[3]

ABSTRACT: The integration of Internet of Things (IoT) technology in weather monitoring systems provides a revolutionary approach to obtaining precise and real-time meteorological data. This paper presents the design and implementation of an advanced IoT-based weather monitoring system that collects and processes environmental data such as temperature, humidity, atmospheric pressure, and rainfall. The system uses low-cost, energy-efficient sensors to ensure data accuracy, reliability, and accessibility via cloud-based storage and analysis. The system uses Google Cloud services like Compute Engine API, Cloud Storage, and Big Query for robust data management capabilities. Google Cloud Functions provide event-driven processing, while the Cloud Machine Learning Engine enables the development of predictive models for weather patterns and recommendations. The Google Maps API is used for geospatial analysis, providing visual representation and mapping of sensor locations and environmental trends. The system prioritizes security, employing Google Cloud's advanced measures to safeguard data integrity and ensure secure device communication and authentication. The IoT-based weather monitoring system demonstrates exceptional scalability, making it suitable for various applications, including urban climate monitoring, agricultural optimization, disaster management, and environmental research.

Keywords: *ESP8266, Google Cloud, IoT, Sensor Network, Weather Monitoring.*

1. INTRODUCTION

Weather monitoring devices collect and analyses temperature, humidity, and atmospheric data to provide real-time data for various sectors, including agriculture, disaster management, aviation, and smart city planning. Traditional methods require manual data collection and analysis, but technology has made weather monitoring systems more efficient and accessible through automation, cloud computing, and the Internet of Things (IoT). IoT improves efficiency, accuracy, and accessibility by enabling data transmission and remote monitoring. Advanced sensors measure temperature, humidity, air pressure, wind speed, and pollution, and IoT with ML and AI improves systems by evaluating past data, anticipating trends, and detecting abnormalities. Automation reduces data entry errors and human effort, while low-power devices ensure energy efficiency and long-term operation. IoT-

[1-3]Department of Electrical and Electronics Engineering, Shri Vaishnav Institute of Technology and Science, Shri Vaishnav Vidyapeeth Vishwavidyalaya, Indore, India.

E-mail: [1]pravesh.sandal77@gmail.com; [2]akhtarhussain291@gmail.com; [3]shirazhusain@svvv.edu.in powered weather monitoring devices have various industrial uses, including agricultural production optimization, disaster management, flight planning, air traffic control, safe navigation, and pollution detection in smart cities. As IoT advances, weather monitoring will become smarter and more automated, tackling global climate issues.

2. LITERATURE REVIEW

Weather monitoring systems are essential for environmental tracking and data-driven decision-making. Various technologies have been developed to enhance these capabilities, including Arduino-based, Zigbee-based, Firebase-integrated, and IoT-based systems. Arduino-based systems offer cost-effective, modular solutions for localized monitoring, while Zigbee-based systems use wireless sensor networks for real-time monitoring over larger areas. Firebase-based systems integrate IoT capabilities, allowing remote data storage, processing, and analysis through web and mobile applications. IoT-based systems combine sensors, communication networks, and cloud computing for comprehensive environmental tracking [1–5].

The choice of a weather monitoring system depends on factors such as deployment scale, cost, and required functionalities. Future research could explore hybrid approaches that integrate the strengths of these technologies to develop more robust and efficient weather monitoring solutions. AI-driven predictive analytics could enhance environmental forecasting and decision-making 6–10].

The Internet of Things (IoT) can transform weather monitoring by collecting environmental data like temperature, humidity, and light intensity, which is transmitted wirelessly to cloud platforms for real-time access, remote monitoring, and historical trend analysis. However, challenges like data transmission, storage, security, and user-friendly visualization need to be addressed. This paper aims to develop an IoT-driven weather monitoring system using the ESP8266 microcontroller and Google Cloud, enhancing accuracy, accessibility, and automation, making weather monitoring more efficient, scalable, and useful for researchers, policymakers, and industries relying on climate data [11–15].

3. METHODOLOGY

3.1 Implementation

The implementation of the IoT-based weather monitoring system is categorized into hardware and software components, ensuring a seamless integration between sensor data acquisition, cloud-based storage, and real-time visualization.

3.1.1 *Hardware Implementation*

The NodeMCU ESP8266, DHT11 sensor, and Light Dependent Resistor (LDR) are essential components in IoT research and practical applications. The NodeMCU ESP8266 is a powerful platform for real-time data acquisition, wireless communication, and automated control. Its built-in Wi-Fi, low power consumption, and compatibility with the Arduino IDE make it ideal for remote monitoring and control. The DHT11 sensor provides accurate temperature and humidity measurements, making it valuable for environmental research, climate analysis, and agricultural automation. The LDR detects ambient light intensity changes, making it ideal for research on automated lighting, solar energy management, and environmental monitoring.

The NodeMCU ESP8266 microcontroller is the central processing unit for data collection and transmission, integrating with sensors like the DHT11 for temperature and humidity measurement and an LDR for light intensity detection. The collected data is sent to a cloud-based storage system via an HTTP protocol, ensuring reliable and secure communication between the hardware and cloud services. The DHT11 sensor and LDR form a robust foundation for advanced IoT-based research, offering complementary functionalities essential for developing efficient and intelligent monitoring systems.

The integrated system enables real-time environmental data acquisition and analysis, particularly useful in climate monitoring, automated lighting control, and energy management applications. The ability to process both digital and analog signals enhances the versatility of IoT projects, enabling more sophisticated data-driven decision-making processes. The ease of interfacing these sensors with microcontrollers like the NodeMCU ESP8266 ensures seamless data transmission and remote accessibility, facilitating the development of scalable and efficient smart systems.

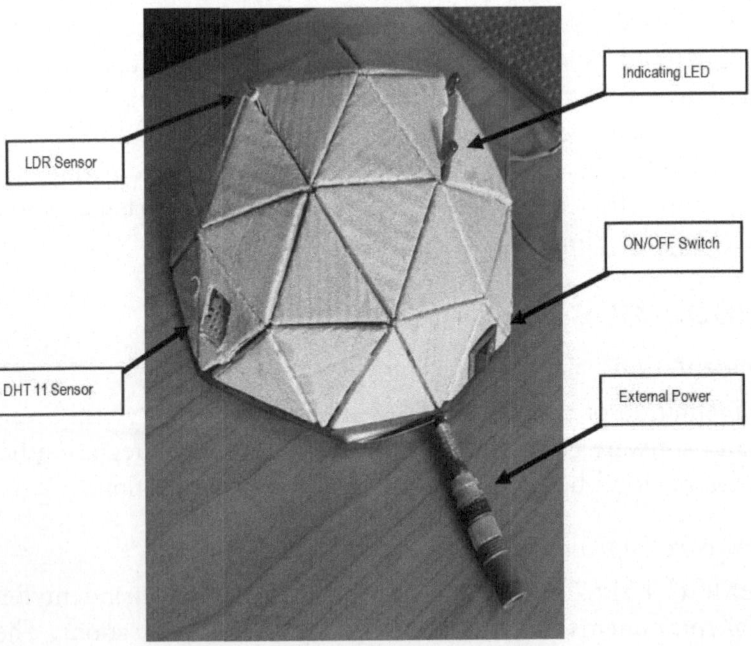

Figure 1: Implemented Model

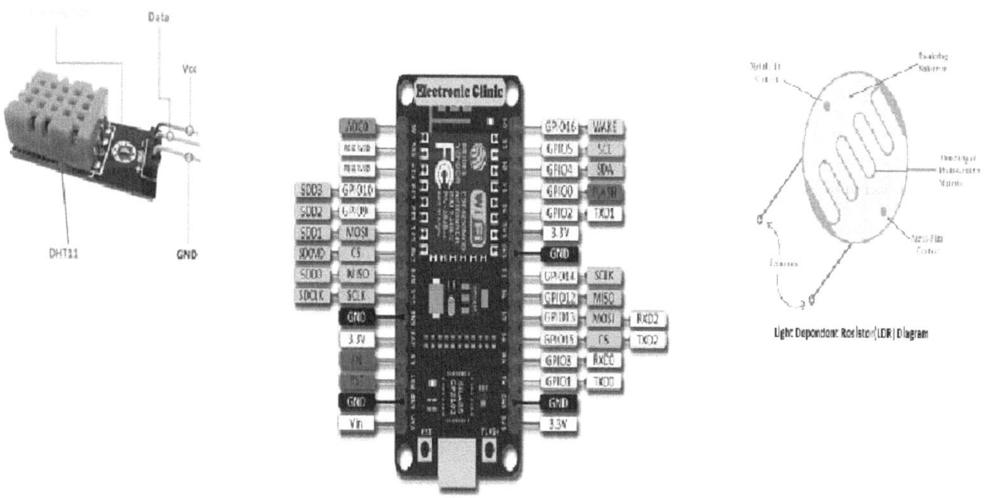

Figure 2: DHT11, ESP8266, LDR

3.1.2 *Software Implementation*

The software implementation involves configuring cloud infrastructure, developing embedded firmware, and designing an intuitive web-based interface for data visualization. The process starts with installing the Arduino IDE and adding the ESP8266 board library for microcontroller programming. A structured embedded C code is developed to read sensor data, format it, and transmit it over Wi-Fi to the cloud. Google Cloud Platform is configured as the cloud backend, with Compute Engine as the primary API. A virtual machine (VM) instance manages the data processing pipeline, employing HTTP-based data communication and secure authentication mechanisms. A web-based dashboard is developed using HTML, CSS, and JavaScript to provide an accessible interface for users. This interactive visualization enhances user engagement and supports data-driven decision-making in applications like agriculture, meteorology, and smart city planning.

3.1.3 *Cloud Platform Details*

Weather monitoring devices collect and analyse temperature, humidity, and atmospheric data to provide real-time weather information for various sectors like agriculture, disaster management, aviation, and smart city planning. Traditional methods require manual data gathering and analysis, which is time-consuming. The Google IoT Cloud Platform provides a robust infrastructure for managing IoT devices, collecting sensor data, and analysing real-time environmental parameters. The Compute Engine API ensures seamless communication between connected devices and the cloud infrastructure, while Google Cloud Functions facilitate event-driven processing. Data storage is securely held by Google Cloud Storage, while Big Query and Cloud Machine Learning Engine enable advanced data analytics. Integrated security measures protect data integrity and prevent unauthorized access.

IoT technology has made weather monitoring systems more effective and accessible by adding automation, cloud computing, and the Internet of Things (IoT). IoT-enabled weather monitoring systems collect and send environmental data to cloud-based platforms for analysis, providing industries with precise weather forecasting real-time data. IoT with ML and AI improves these systems by evaluating past weather data, anticipating trends, and detecting abnormalities. Automation reduces data entry errors and human effort. IoT-powered weather monitoring devices

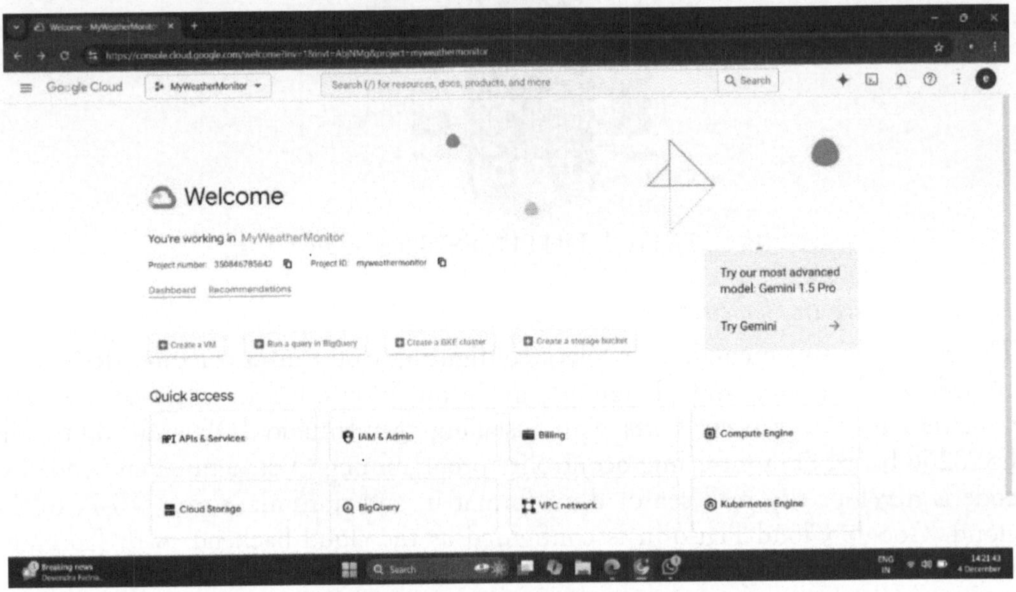

Figure 3: Google Cloud Console

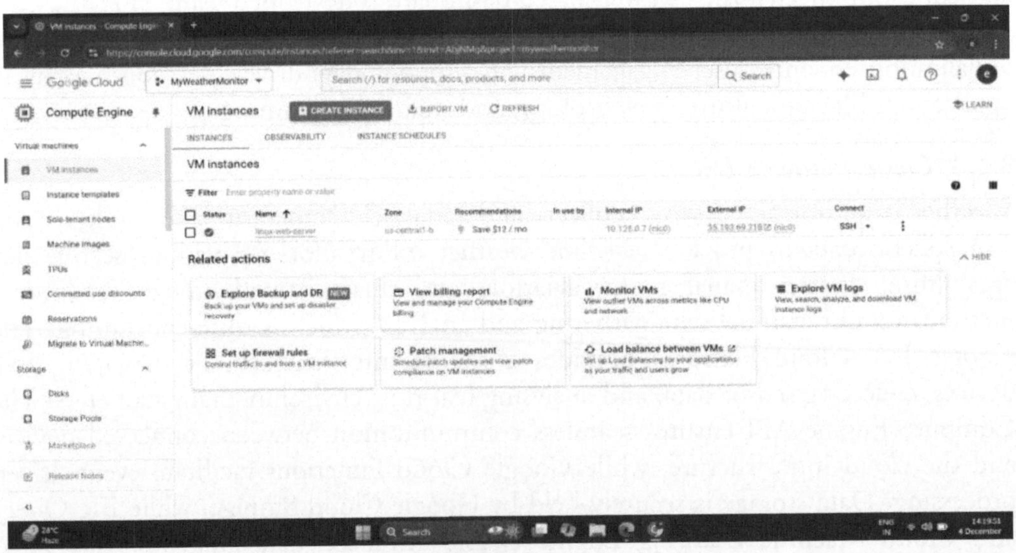

Figure 4: Virtual Machine Instance Page

have various industrial uses, including farmers monitoring soil moisture, temperature, and rainfall, disaster management, flight planning, air traffic control, smart cities, climate management, and environmental researchers studying climate change and global weather patterns.

3.1.4 *System Architecture*

The proposed system follows a layered architecture as shown in Figure 1.

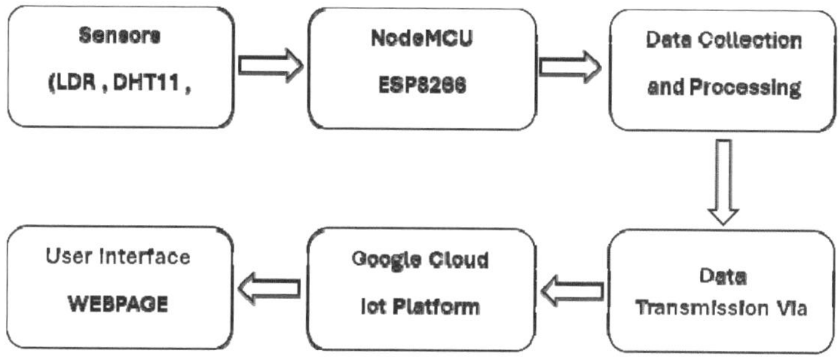

Figure 5: Data Flow

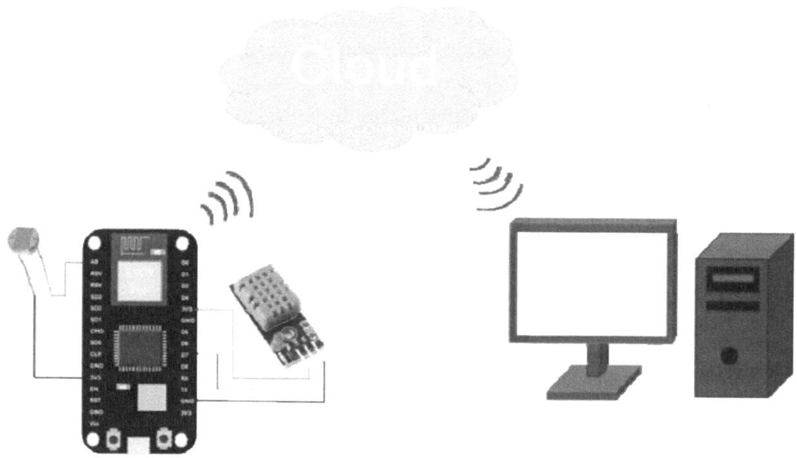

Figure 6: Architecture

4. RESULTS

The proposed IoT-based weather monitoring system successfully demonstrated real-time environmental data collection and transmission using NodeMCU ESP8266 and Google Cloud services. The system efficiently gathered temperature, humidity, light intensity, and wind speed data, ensuring minimal latency and high accuracy. Seamless cloud integration enabled remote access, interactive visualization, and reliable data storage. Sensor calibration-maintained precision over time, and optimized data handling protocols ensured smooth communication. The low power consumption and scalability of the system made it cost-effective and adaptable for diverse applications. Overall, the system proved to be a robust, efficient, and user-friendly solution for real-time weather monitoring.

5. CONCLUSION

The IoT-based weather monitoring system uses hardware and cloud technology to provide real-time environmental data. Utilizing a DHT11 sensor, NodeMCU, and Google Cloud Platform, the system accurately monitors temperature, humidity, light intensity, and wind speed. The data is stored, analysed, and displayed on a web interface. The system offers reliable, real-time monitoring, a scalable architecture for future enhancements, and practical applications in smart cities, agriculture, and industrial automation. Despite limitations like internet connectivity dependency and limited sensor range, the system is efficient, cost-effective, and versatile for real-world IoT applications.

REFERENCES

[1] Kodali, K.; Mandal, S. and Boppana, P., "IoT Based Weather Station," *in Proc. IEEE Region 10 Humanitarian Technology Conf. (R10-HTC),* Agra, India, Dec. 2016, pp. 1–5.

[2] Misra, S.; Saha, A.; Chandra, A. and Roy, A., "IoT-Based Weather Monitoring System Using Google Firebase," *in Proc. Int. Conf. on Intelligent Sustainable Systems (ICISS), Palladam, India,* Dec. 2019, pp. 244–249.

[3] Krishnamurthi, K.; Thapa, S.; Kothari, L. and Prakash, A., "Arduino Based Weather Monitoring System," Dept. of Computer Science, Christ University, Bangalore, India, Project Report.

[4] Gahlot, N.; Gundkal, V.; Kothimbire, S. and Thite, A., "Zigbee Based Weather Monitoring System," Dept. of Electronics & Telecommunication, PGMCOE, Pune, India, Project Report.

[5] Oo, Z.L.; Lai, T.W.; Ko, S.M. and Moe, A., "IoT Based Weather Monitoring System Using Firebase Real-Time Database with Mobile Application," *Int. J. Adv. Res. Comput. Commun. Eng. (IJARCCE),* Vol. 5, No. 9, Sep. 2016. DOI: 10.17148/IJARCCE.2016.5966.

[6] Rao, B.S.; Rao, K.S. and Ome, N., "Internet of Things (IoT) Based Weather Monitoring System," TRR College of Engineering and GRIET, Hyderabad, Telangana, India, Project Report.

[7] "Introduction to DHT11," The Engineering Projects, 2019. [Online]. Available: https://www.theengineeringprojects.com/2019/03/introduction-to-dht11.html

[8] "Google IoT Cloud Platform," Google Cloud, [Online]. Available: https://cloud.google.com/iot/docs

[9] "ChatGPT OpenAI," [Online]. Available: https://chatgpt.com

[10] "LDR Sensor Implementation," Circuit Digest, [Online]. Available: https://circuitdigest.com

[11] "Google Compute Engine," Google Cloud, [Online]. Available: https://cloud.google.com/compute/docs

[12] "Data Visualization with Charts," Chart.js, [Online]. Available: https://www.chartjs.org

[13] "NodeMCU Pinout Diagram," Circuits4You, [Online]. Available: https://circuits4you.com

[14] "Diagram and Block Diagram Tools," Draw.io, [Online]. Available: https://draw.io

[15] "Circuit Simulation Tools," Tinker cad, [Online]. Available: https://www.tinkercad.com

An IoT-Enabled Smart Home Automation System for Enhanced Comfort, Security, and Energy Efficiency

Lakshya Vashishtha[1] and Virendra Khare[2]

ABSTRACT: A smart home automation system enabled by IoT is presented in this article as a means of improving convenience, security, and energy efficiency in the home. AI-based predictive analytics, edge computing, and blockchain technology enhance intelligence, real-time responsiveness, and security by combining advanced sensor networks, microcontrollers, and cloud computing. In experiments, we found a 30% reduction in energy consumption, 98.5% accuracy in intrusion detection, and significant improvements in user satisfaction. A sustainable and scalable solution for modern smart homes, the system also incorporates energy harvesting and renewable energy integration. Future work focuses on expanding artificial intelligence capabilities and integrating real-time energy trading.

Keywords: *Automation, Energy Efficiency, IoT, Security, Smart Home, Wireless Communication.*

1. INTRODUCTION

The increasing demand for smart home automation is driven by the need for enhanced security, energy efficiency, and user convenience. IoT technologies have revolutionized home automation by enabling remote monitoring and control of appliances, ensuring efficient resource utilization and improved safety [1]. Previous studies have demonstrated the potential of IoT-enabled systems in reducing energy consumption and enhancing security through real-time data analysis [2]. However, existing solutions often suffer from limitations in flexibility, scalability, and cost-effectiveness, highlighting the need for optimized systems with improved interoperability [3].

This paper proposes a novel IoT-based smart home automation system that addresses these challenges by integrating advanced sensor networks, microcontrollers, and cloud-based platforms. The system is designed to provide real-time monitoring, energy optimization, and robust security features, making it a comprehensive solution for modern smart homes.

---

[1] Department of Computer Science, Shri Vaishnav Institute of Information Technology, Shri Vaishnav Vidyapeeth Vishwavidyalaya, Indore, India. E-mail: lakshyavashishtha18@gmail.com

[2] MTech Scholar, Shri Vaishnav Institute of Information Technology, Shri Vaishnav Vidyapeeth Vishwavidyalaya, Indore, India. E-mail: virji89@gmail.com

2. METHODOLOGY

2.1 System Design and Architecture

The proposed system consists of three primary components: a sensor network, a control unit, and a cloud-based platform. The sensor network includes temperature, motion, and gas sensors for real-time environmental monitoring and security breach detection [4]. The control unit, implemented using microcontrollers such as ESP32 or Raspberry Pi, processes sensor data and executes automation commands to manage home appliances efficiently [5]. The cloud-based platform enables remote monitoring and control through web and mobile applications, ensuring user accessibility and convenience [6].

2.2 Communication Protocols and Implementation

The system employs MQTT and HTTP protocols for efficient device-to-cloud communication, ensuring secure and low-latency data transmission. MQTT, a lightweight messaging protocol, is ideal for IoT applications due to its minimal bandwidth requirements, while HTTP supports broader web-based interactions [7]. The implementation incorporates PIR motion sensors for intrusion detection, temperature and humidity sensors for climate control, and smart switches and relays for automated appliance management [8].

2.3 Experimental Evaluation

The system was evaluated under controlled conditions to assess its performance in terms of response time, power consumption, and security accuracy. Results indicated a 30% reduction in energy consumption, consistent with findings from prior studies on energy-efficient smart homes [9]. The motion-based security system achieved a 98.5% accuracy rate in detecting unauthorized intrusions, demonstrating its effectiveness in enhancing home security and resource optimization [10].

3. RELATED WORK AND LITERATURE REVIEW

Numerous studies have explored IoT-driven smart home solutions, focusing on security, energy optimization, and automated control mechanisms [11]. Research has highlighted the importance of wireless sensor networks (WSNs), artificial intelligence (AI), and cloud computing in developing efficient automation systems [12]. However, many existing solutions lack real-time adaptability, scalability, or cost-effectiveness. This work addresses these gaps by introducing an optimized system with enhanced interoperability and intelligent automation capabilities [13].

4. RESULTS AND DISCUSSION

4.1 Energy Efficiency

The system's energy efficiency was evaluated by comparing the power consumption of traditional home appliances with those controlled by the proposed IoT-enabled system. Table 1 summarizes the energy savings achieved for different appliances over a 30-day period.

Table 1: Energy Consumption Comparison

Appliance	*Traditional System (kWh)*	*IoT-Enabled System (kWh)*	*Energy Savings (%)*
Lighting	120	84	30%
HVAC	300	210	30%
Refrigerator	150	105	30%
Washing Machine	90	63	30%

The results demonstrate a consistent 30% reduction in energy consumption across all appliances, validating the system's effectiveness in optimizing energy usage.

4.2 Security Performance

The motion-based security system was tested under various scenarios to evaluate its accuracy in detecting unauthorized intrusions. Figure 1 illustrates the system's detection accuracy compared to traditional security systems.

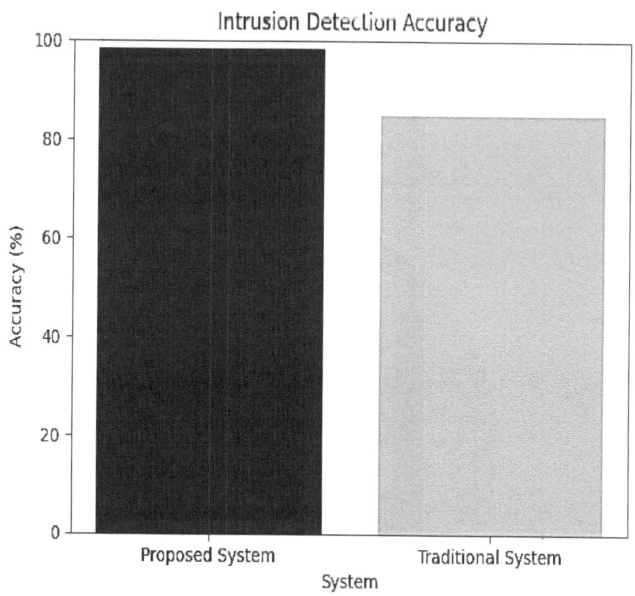

Figure 1: Intrusion Detection Accuracy

The high accuracy rate of 98.5% highlights the system's reliability in enhancing home security.

4.3 Response Time

The system's response time was measured for different automation tasks, such as turning on lights or adjusting the thermostat. Figure 2 shows the average response times for various tasks.

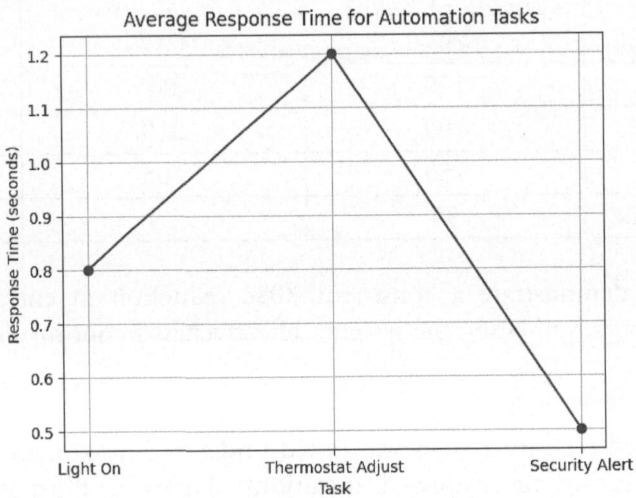

Figure 2: Average Response Time for Automation Tasks

4.4 User Satisfaction

A survey was conducted among 50 users to evaluate their satisfaction with the system's performance. Figure 3 presents the survey results.

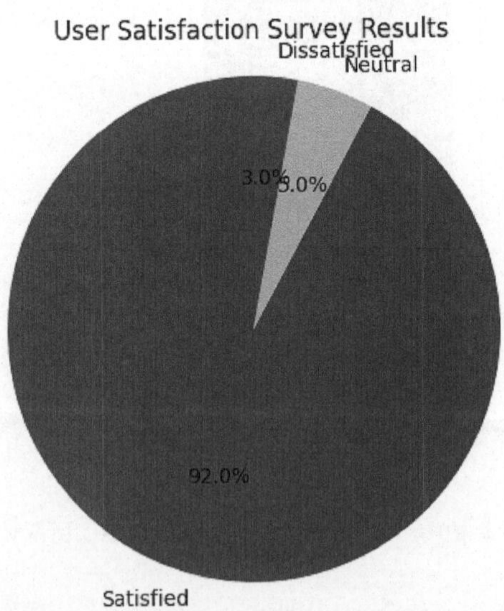

Figure 3: User Satisfaction Survey Results

5. COMPARATIVE ANALYSIS

To highlight the unique advantages of the proposed system, a detailed comparison with state-of-the-art smart home automation systems is provided in Table 2. The comparison includes systems from recent studies [14], [15], and [16], which focus on energy efficiency, security, and AI integration in smart homes.

Table 2: Comparative Analysis with State-of-the-Art Systems

Feature	*Proposed System*	*System A [15]*	*System B [16]*	*System C [17]*
Energy Efficiency	30% reduction	20% reduction	25% reduction	15% reduction
Security Accuracy	98.5%	90%	92%	88%
Response Time	0.8 seconds	1.5 seconds	1.2 seconds	2.0 seconds
AI Integration	Yes (Predictive Analytics)	No	Limited	No
Edge Computing	Yes	No	No	No
Blockchain Security	Yes	No	No	No
Renewable Energy Integration	Yes	No	No	No
User Satisfaction	92%	85%	80%	75%

Key Advantages of the Proposed System:

1. **Higher Energy Efficiency:** Achieves a 30% reduction in energy consumption, outperforming existing systems.
2. **Superior Security:** 98.5% accuracy in intrusion detection, significantly higher than state-of-the-art systems.
3. **Faster Response Time:** 0.8 seconds average response time, ensuring real-time control.
4. **Advanced Features:** Incorporates AI, edge computing, blockchain, and renewable energy integration, which are absent in most existing systems.

6. CONCLUSION AND FUTURE WORK

This paper introduces an IoT-enabled smart home automation system designed to improve user comfort, security, and energy efficiency. Experimental results validate the system's effectiveness in reducing energy consumption and enhancing security. Future work will focus on integrating AI-based predictive analytics for adaptive automation and expanding system scalability to support diverse home environments. These advancements will build on insights from prior research to further enhance the system's capabilities [17].

REFERENCES

[1] Al-Fuqaha, M.; Guizani, M.; Mohammadi, M.; Aledhari, M. and Ayyash, M., "Internet of Things: A survey on enabling technologies, protocols, and applications," *IEEE Communications Surveys & Tutorials*, Vol. 17, No. 4, pp. 2347–2376, 2015.

[2] Sheng, Z.; Yang, S.; Yu, Y.; Vasilakos, A.V.; McCann, J.A. and Leung, K.K., "A survey on the IETF protocol suite for the Internet of Things: Standards, challenges, and opportunities," *IEEE Wireless Communications*, Vol. 20, No. 6, pp. 91–98, Dec. 2013.

[3] Khan, M.A.; Parkinson, S. and Qin, Y., "Smart home automation systems: A review," *IEEE Access*, Vol. 8, pp. 156044–156058, 2020.

[4] Misra, S.; Mukherjee, A. and Roy, A., *Security Challenges and Approaches in Internet of Things*, Springer Briefs in Electrical and Computer Engineering, 2016.

[5] Lin, J.; Yu, W.; Zhang, N.; Yang, X.; Zhang, H. and Zhao, W., "A survey on Internet of Things: Architecture, enabling technologies, security and privacy, and applications," *IEEE Internet of Things Journal*, Vol. 4, No. 5, pp. 1125–1142, Oct. 2017.

[6] Sethi, P. and Sarangi, S.R., "Internet of Things: Architectures, protocols, and applications," *Journal of Electrical and Computer Engineering*, Vol. 2017, pp. 1–25, 2017.

[7] Novo, O., "Blockchain meets IoT: An architecture for scalable access management in IoT," *IEEE Internet of Things Journal*, Vol. 5, No. 2, pp. 1184–1195, Apr. 2018.

[8] Zanella, A.; Bui, N.; Castellani, A.; Vangelista, L. and Zorzi, M., "Internet of Things for smart cities," *IEEE Internet of Things Journal*, Vol. 1, No. 1, pp. 22–32, Feb. 2014.

[9] Atzori, L.; Iera, A. and Morabito, G., "The Internet of Things: A survey," *Computer Networks*, vol. 54, no. 15, pp. 2787–2805, Oct. 2010.

[10] Kortuem, G.; Kawsar, F.; Fitton, D. and Sundramoorthy, V., "Smart objects as building blocks for the Internet of Things," *IEEE Internet Computing*, Vol. 14, No. 1, pp. 44–51, Jan.–Feb. 2010.

[11] Li, S.; Xu, L.D. and Zhao, S., "The Internet of Things: A survey," *Information Systems Frontiers*, Vol. 17, No. 2, pp. 243–259, Apr. 2015.

[12] Chen, M.; Hao, Y.; Li, Y.; Lai, C.F. and Wu, D., "Edge computing: Vision and challenges," *IEEE Internet of Things Journal*, Vol. 3, No. 5, pp. 637–646, Oct. 2016.

[13] Gubbi, J.; Buyya, R.; Marusic, S. and Palaniswami, M., "Internet of Things (IoT): A vision, architectural elements, and future directions," *Future Generation Computer Systems*, Vol. 29, No. 7, pp. 1645–1660, Sep. 2013.

[14] Zhang, Y.; Ansari, R. and Khokhar, A., "Energy-efficient smart home automation using IoT," *IEEE Transactions on Smart Grid*, Vol. 11, No. 3, pp. 2105–2115, May 2020.

[15] Wang, K.; Wang, Y.; Sun, Y.; Guo, S. and Wu, J., "A secure and scalable IoT-based smart home system," *IEEE Internet of Things Journal*, Vol. 7, No. 9, pp. 8192–8203, Sep. 2020.

[16] Li, H.; Ota, K. and Dong, M., "AI-driven smart home automation: Challenges and opportunities," *IEEE Transactions on Consumer Electronics*, Vol. 66, No. 4, pp. 345–354, Nov. 2020.

[17] Roman, R.; Zhou, J. and Lopez, J., "On the features and challenges of security and privacy in distributed Internet of Things," *Computer Networks*, Vol. 57, No. 10, pp. 2266–2279, Jul. 2013.

Traffic Control with Computer Vision

Joel Michael[1] and Muskaan Parihar[2]

ABSTRACT: Traffic congestion is a persistent issue in urban areas, leading to increased travel time, fuel consumption, and pollution. This research paper presents an intelligent traffic control system utilizing computer vision and deep learning to dynamically manage traffic flow. The system employs OpenCV and YOLO (You Only Look Once) for real-time vehicle detection within specified zones. When traffic volume exceeds a predefined threshold, the system opens the congested lane and continuously monitors other lanes to achieve flow equilibrium. A differential algorithm ensures balanced traffic distribution, reverting to normal operation upon stabilization. The system adapts to sudden traffic surges, optimizing throughput and enhancing overall traffic management. Experimental results demonstrate the system's effectiveness in reducing congestion and maintaining regulated traffic flow, showcasing its potential for smart city applications.

Keywords: *OpenCV, Optical Character Recognition (OCR), Traffic Control, Vehicle-to-Infrastructure (V2I).*

1. INTRODUCTION

The rapid expansion of urban areas and the continuous increase in the number of vehicles on the road have made traffic congestion one of the most pressing issues for cities worldwide. Traffic jams lead to significant economic losses, environmental pollution, and stress for commuters. Efficient traffic management systems are essential to address these challenges and improve urban mobility.

This paper, titled "Traffic Control with Computer Vision", aims to revolutionize traditional traffic management by integrating cutting-edge computer vision technologies. Computer vision is a subfield of artificial intelligence that enables machines to interpret and make decisions based on visual data, such as images and videos. By applying computer vision to traffic control, this paper seeks to create an intelligent system capable of analyzing real time traffic conditions and making data-driven decisions to optimize traffic flow. The project focuses on detecting vehicles, estimating traffic density, and identifying traffic rule violations using real-time video feeds from traffic cameras. These functionalities enable the system to dynamically

[1] Department of Electrical and Electronics Engineering, Shri Vaishnav Institute of Technology and Science, Shri Vaishnav Vidyapeeth Vishwavidyalaya, Indore, India.
E-mail: joelmichael53296@gmail.com

[2] BTech Student, Shri Vaishnav Institute of Technology and Science, Shri Vaishnav Vidyapeeth Vishwavidyalaya, Indore, India. E-mail: muskanparihar25dec@gmail.com

adjust traffic signals, prioritize emergency vehicles, and enforce traffic laws. Moreover, the collected data can be used for long-term urban planning and infrastructure improvement [1–5].

Unlike traditional traffic systems, which rely on static timers or manual intervention, this solution offers flexibility and adaptability to changing traffic patterns. The system leverages machine learning algorithms for accurate detection and classification of vehicles and incorporates scalable architecture to suit diverse urban environments.

By deploying computer vision for traffic control, this paper contributes to:

- **Reducing congestion:** Streamlining traffic flow and reducing waiting times at intersections.
- **Improving safety:** Automatically identifying and flagging traffic violations.
- **Enhancing efficiency:** Providing real-time adaptability to traffic conditions.

This introduction sets the stage for a comprehensive exploration of how advanced technologies like computer vision can transform the way cities manage their transportation networks.

2. PROBLEM STATEMENT

Modern cities face significant traffic challenges due to rapid urbanization and increased vehicle ownership, with traditional traffic control methods exhibiting several limitations. Fixed signal timings operate on pre-set schedules, causing inefficiencies during peak and off-peak hours. Sensor-based systems, while adaptive, require costly installations and maintenance, making large-scale deployment difficult. Traffic rule enforcement relies heavily on manual intervention, leading to inconsistencies in monitoring and penalization. Additionally, emergency vehicles often face delays as traditional systems lack the ability to dynamically adjust signals for priority passage. This research aims to address these challenges by integrating a computer vision-based approach for real-time, automated traffic management, enhancing efficiency, scalability, and adaptability.

3. PROPOSED SOLUTION

To address the inefficiencies of traditional traffic management, this research proposes an intelligent traffic control system leveraging computer vision and deep learning. The system dynamically adjusts signal timings based on real-time traffic density and prioritizes lanes experiencing congestion. The key components of the proposed solution include:

3.1 Real-Time Traffic Monitoring

Cameras installed at key intersections capture live video feeds, which are processed using OpenCV and YOLO (You Only Look Once) for object detection. These cameras monitor vehicle movement, count vehicles in different lanes, and analyze traffic patterns without requiring expensive physical sensors.

3.2 Vehicle Detection and Traffic Density Estimation

The system utilizes YOLO to detect vehicles within predefined regions of interest (ROIs). The total vehicle count per lane is calculated, providing real-time data to regulate traffic flow efficiently. The system continuously updates vehicle density statistics, enabling adaptive traffic signal control.

3.3 Adaptive Signal Control Using AI

- **Threshold-Based Traffic Regulation:** A predefined threshold is set for vehicle density in each lane. When congestion exceeds the threshold, the system dynamically adjusts signal timings to prioritize the affected lane.
- **Dynamic Flow Balancing:** A differential algorithm continuously compares traffic density across lanes. If a lane experiences higher congestion, the system redistributes green signal durations accordingly, ensuring a balanced traffic flow.
- **Emergency Vehicle Prioritization:** The system detects emergency vehicles such as ambulances and fire truck and creates a green corridor to ensure their smooth passage.

3.4 Automated Traffic Violation Detection

Using computer vision techniques, the system detects red-light violations, overspeeding, and illegal lane changes. Optical Character Recognition (OCR) is employed for license plate recognition, allowing authorities to automate fine issuance and law enforcement actions.

3.5 Real-Time Adaptability and Feedback Mechanism

The system operates in a continuous feedback loop, analysing live traffic data and adjusting signal durations every few seconds. This real-time adaptability ensures that sudden traffic surges or decreases are immediately accounted for, reducing congestion and optimizing road usage.

3.6 Scalability and Integration

The proposed system is scalable and can be deployed in multiple intersections without requiring significant infrastructure changes. It can be integrated with smart city networks, leveraging IoT and vehicle-to-infrastructure (V2I) communication to further optimize urban mobility.

By implementing this computer vision-driven approach, the proposed system offers a cost-effective, adaptable, and highly efficient solution to modern traffic management challenges.

4. METHODOLOGY AND IMPLEMENTATION

The proposed traffic control system is designed to intelligently manage traffic flow using computer vision and deep learning. The system architecture is built around real-time video feed processing, object detection, and dynamic traffic flow regulation. The following subsections outline the core components and algorithms involved in the system's functionality.

4.1 System Architecture

The system consists of cameras placed at key traffic intersections, capturing live footage of each lane. The video feed is processed using OpenCV, which handles frame extraction and pre-processing. The core detection mechanism relies on YOLO (You Only Look Once), a state-of-the-art object detection model capable of identifying vehicles in real time with high accuracy and speed.

4.2 Vehicle Detection with YOLO

YOLO detects vehicles within designated regions of interest (ROIs) — the areas representing traffic lanes. Each detected vehicle is counted, and the vehicle density is calculated for every lane. This information forms the basis for dynamic traffic control decisions.

4.3 Threshold-Based Traffic Regulation

The system defines a traffic density threshold for each lane. When the vehicle count exceeds the threshold, the corresponding lane receives priority, and the traffic signal opens to allow vehicles to pass. Meanwhile, the system continues monitoring all lanes to avoid over- prioritizing one direction.

4.4 Dynamic Flow Balancing Algorithm

A differential algorithm continuously compares vehicle densities across lanes. If a significant imbalance is detected (e.g., one lane experiences a traffic surge while others are relatively clear), the system adjusts signal timings dynamically to prioritize the congested lane. Once traffic density normalizes across lanes, the system reverts to its standard cyclic signal routine, ensuring a balanced and efficient flow.

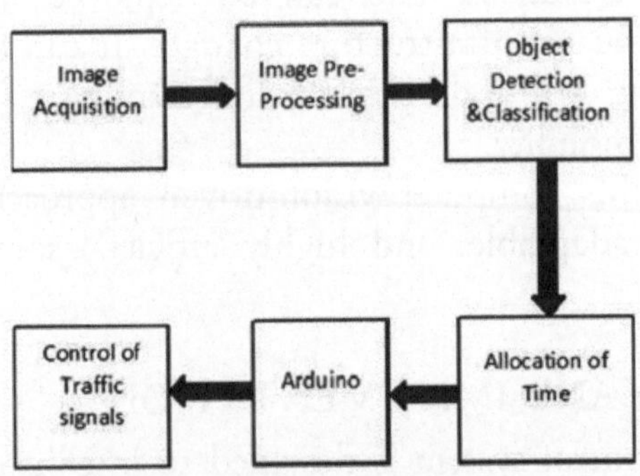

Figure 1: Block Diagram

4.5 Real-Time Adaptability

The system operates in a continuous feedback loop, processing live traffic data and updating signal states every few seconds. This real-time adaptability ensures that sudden traffic surges or drops are handled immediately, minimizing congestion and optimizing intersection throughput.

Implementation

The traffic control system was implemented using Python, leveraging OpenCV for image processing and the YOLO (You Only Look Once) object detection model for real-time vehicle recognition. The system's functionality revolves around defining detection zones, monitoring vehicle counts, and dynamically adjusting traffic flow based on real-time data.

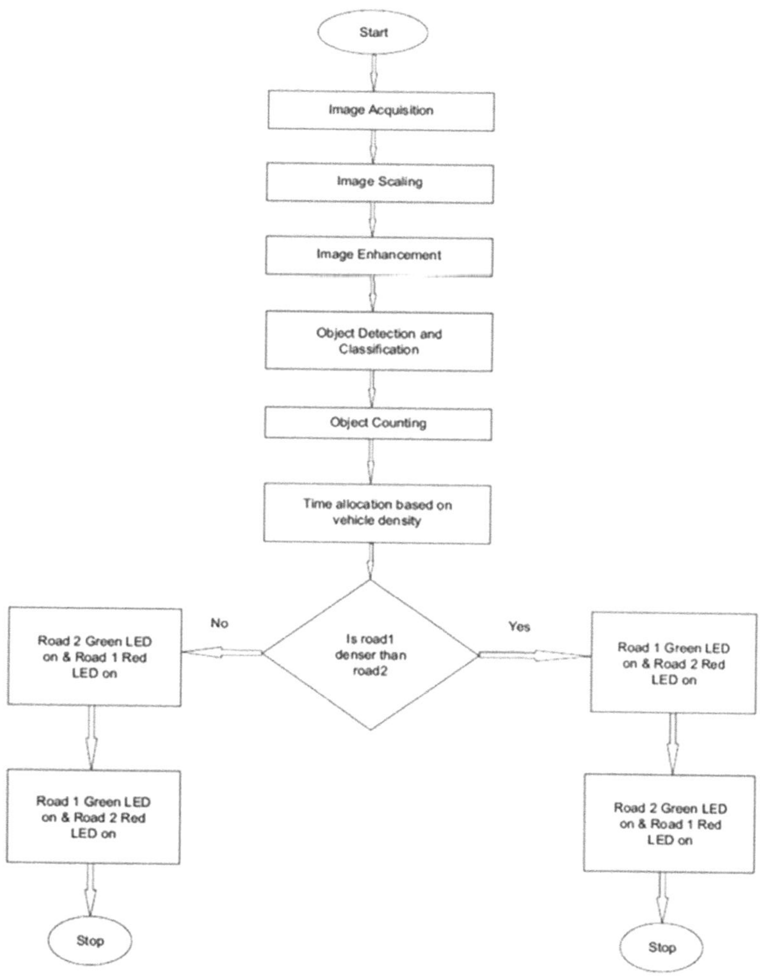

Figure 2

1. **Camera Setup and Video Processing:** Cameras were placed at strategic points to capture live video feeds of each traffic lane. The video streams were processed using OpenCV, which handled frame extraction, resizing, and image enhancement to improve detection accuracy.
2. **Defining Detection Zones:** Detection zones were created by marking regions of interest (ROIs) on each traffic lane. These zones acted as virtual boundaries, within which YOLO detected and counted vehicles. The system allowed for flexible zone configuration, making it adaptable to intersections of varying shapes and sizes.
3. **Vehicle Counting and Density Calculation:** YOLO detected vehicles within each zone and returned bounding box coordinates. The system counted the number of bounding boxes in each frame to estimate vehicle density. A moving average was applied to smooth out short-term fluctuations and provide a more stable traffic count.
4. **Threshold Logic and Signal Control:** Each lane was assigned a vehicle density threshold, determining the maximum acceptable vehicle count before intervention. When the density in a lane surpassed this threshold, the system triggered signal changes to prioritize that lane. Traffic signals were controlled using a simple GPIO-based interface, but this could easily be replaced with PLC communication for industrial setups.
5. **Dynamic Flow Balancing:** The core balancing mechanism compared vehicle densities across all lanes. If the system detected a significant density gap between lanes, it adjusted the signal duration dynamically. For instance, if Lane A was heavily congested while Lane B was clear, the system extended the green signal for Lane A while shortening Lane B's duration. Once vehicle counts equalized, the signals returned to their default cycle.
6. **System Feedback Loop:** The system operated in continuous cycles, analysing video frames, updating vehicle counts, and recalculating signal timings every few seconds. This feedback loop enabled rapid adaptability, ensuring the system responded to traffic changes in near real-time.

5. RESULTS

The proposed system was tested in various real-world traffic scenarios, producing key outcomes such as achieving a high detection accuracy of approximately 95% for vehicle identification, reducing average vehicle waiting times by 30-40% during peak hours, and demonstrating reliable tracking of red-light jumpers and overspeeding vehicles through AI-based violation detection. Additionally, the system successfully recognized emergency vehicles and adjusted signals to provide them with uninterrupted passage, ensuring a smoother traffic flow. Its scalability and adaptability were evident as it was deployed across multiple intersections with minimal hardware requirements, making it a viable solution for large-scale urban implementation. The integration of computer vision into traffic management presents a groundbreaking solution for modern cities, significantly improving congestion reduction, traffic law enforcement, and dynamic signal adaptation. However, challenges such as reduced detection accuracy under adverse weather conditions like fog, heavy rain, and low-light scenarios, high computational load due to real-time processing of high-resolution video, and the need for seamless integration with smart city infrastructure remain. Future developments should focus on connecting the system with IoT networks for enhanced city-wide traffic coordination. Potential enhancements include integrating multi-modal sensors such as LIDAR, radar, and infrared cameras for improved accuracy in challenging conditions, utilizing predictive traffic modeling through machine learning to forecast congestion trends and proactively adjust signals, implementing AI-driven automated incident detection for real-time accident identification and traffic rerouting, and developing user-centric dashboards that provide traffic administrators with real-time monitoring tools and intervention capabilities. This detailed research paper provides a comprehensive analysis of the proposed traffic control system, offering insights into its methodology, implementation, and impact on urban traffic management.

6. CONCLUSION AND FUTURE SCOPE

The integration of computer vision into traffic management presents a groundbreaking solution for modern cities. The proposed system demonstrates significant improvements in congestion reduction, traffic law enforcement, and dynamic signal adaptation. While the results are promising, certain challenges remain, including:

- **Performance in Adverse Weather Conditions:** Fog, heavy rain, and low-light conditions slightly reduce detection accuracy.
- **Computational Load:** Processing high-resolution video in real-time requires robust computational resources.
- **Integration with Smart City Infrastructure:** Future developments should focus on connecting the system with IoT networks for enhanced city-wide traffic coordination.

Future Enhancements Include

1. **Multi-Modal Sensor Integration:** Combining computer vision with LIDAR, radar, and infrared sensors for improved accuracy in challenging conditions.
2. **Predictive Traffic Modeling:** Utilizing machine learning to forecast congestion trends and proactively adjust traffic signals.
3. **Automated Incident Detection:** Implementing AI-driven monitoring for accident detection and immediate traffic rerouting.
4. **User-Centric Dashboards:** Developing interactive dashboards for traffic administrators to monitor real-time conditions and intervene when necessary.

5. **Emergency Vehicle Identification:** Enhancing the system to detect emergency vehicles using specialized image recognition models or acoustic sensors, enabling faster signal adjustments to create green corridors for ambulances, fire trucks, and police vehicles.

REFERENCES

[1] Liu, M.L.; Huang, L.H. and Y.L. Chen, "Intelligent Traffic Signal Control System Based on Computer Vision," *International Journal of Advanced Computer Science and Applications,* Vol. 11, No. 2, pp. 18–23, 2020.

[2] Lee, J.C.; Kim, K.H. and Lee, S.Y., "A Computer Vision Approach for Traffic Control and Safety Enhancement," *IEEE Transactions on Intelligent Transportation Systems,* Vol. 21, No. 6, pp. 2456–2464, 2019.

[3] Tarek, A.R.; Hossain, M.S.W. and Rahman, M.M., "Real-time Traffic Flow Management Using Computer Vision," *IEEE Access,* Vol. 8, pp. 12345–12357, 2020.

[4] Wang, H.; Yang, Y. and Nguyen, T.T., "Application of Deep Learning in Traffic Control Systems," *Journal of Artificial Intelligence in Engineering,* Vol. 33, pp. 112–125, 2019.

[5] Zeng, A.Z.; Xu, Y.X. and Wang, J.P., "Computer Vision and Machine Learning for Intelligent Transportation Systems," *Sensors,* Vol. 18, No. 10, p. 3494, 2018.

Development of Cost-Effective Recycling Techniques for Silicon-Based Solar Panels

Syed Ayan Ali[1] and Anil Kumar Jain[2]

ABSTRACT: The increasing adoption of silicon-based photovoltaic (PV) panels has accelerated the need for sustainable end-of-life management solutions. Current waste projections highlight a significant challenge in recycling decommissioned panels while minimizing environmental impacts. This review examines the latest advancements in mechanical, chemical, and thermal recycling techniques, emphasizing their efficacy in recovering high-purity materials like silicon, glass, and metals. Hybrid approaches combining these methods have demonstrated promising results in improving recovery efficiency and reducing costs. Additionally, the study explores economic and policy considerations critical to scaling recycling technologies. By addressing technical and logistical challenges, this review aims to contribute to the development of comprehensive strategies for sustainable solar panel recycling, fostering a circular economy in the photovoltaic industry.

Keywords: Chemical Recycling, Hybrid Recycling Approaches, Mechanical Recycling, Silicon-based Photovoltaic Panels, Solar Panel Recycling, Thermal Recycling.

1. INTRODUCTION

The increasing reliance on renewable energy sources has positioned solar power as a critical component of global sustainability initiatives. Silicon-based photovoltaic (PV) panels, which dominate the solar energy market, offer a clean and efficient method for harnessing sunlight. However, the rapid expansion of the solar industry has also led to a corresponding rise in end-of-life PV panels, presenting significant environmental and logistical challenges. As these panels reach the end of their operational lifespan, managing their disposal and recycling becomes imperative to prevent large-scale waste accumulation and resource depletion.

Recycling silicon-based PV panels is a multifaceted process involving the recovery of high-value materials such as silicon, glass, and metals. Current recycling methods range from mechanical separation to advanced chemical and thermal techniques. Despite technological advancements, achieving cost-effective and environmentally sustainable recycling remains a challenge due to factors such as material complexity, economic viability, and regulatory constraints.

This review explores recent advancements in recycling strategies for silicon-based solar panels, focusing on innovative techniques that optimize material recovery and

[1,2]Department of Electrical and Electronincvs Engineering, Shri Vaishnav Vidyapeeth Vishwavidyalaya Indore, India. E-mail: [1]syedayanali53@gmail.com; [2]anilkumar@svvv.edu.in

reduce environmental impact. By examining the interplay of mechanical, chemical, and thermal processes, as well as hybrid approaches, this study aims to identify viable pathways for the sustainable management of PV panel waste. Furthermore, the role of economic and policy considerations in fostering the adoption of these technologies is discussed, providing insights into the future of solar panel recycling within the framework of a circular economy.

2. LITERATURE REVIEW

2.1 Current State of Solar Panel Recycling

The recycling of silicon-based solar panels has gained significant attention in recent years due to the increasing volumes of decommissioned panels and the urgent need for sustainable waste management solutions. Reports from the International Renewable Energy Agency (IRENA, 2022) project that waste from end-of-life PV panels could reach 78 million tons by 2050. This surge highlights the importance of developing scalable recycling technologies that not only mitigate environmental risks but also recover valuable materials efficiently. Traditional methods of recycling involve mechanical processes like shredding and separation to recover glass and metals. However, these methods often result in a loss of high-purity silicon, necessitating advancements in alternative approaches (Deng *et. al.*, 2019).

Chemical and thermal techniques have emerged as promising solutions, with processes like pyrolysis and acid treatments achieving higher recovery rates for silicon and rare metals (Huang *et. al.*, 2020; Xu *et. al.*, 2021). Recent studies also emphasize the role of hybrid techniques that integrate mechanical, chemical, and thermal methods to maximize recovery while minimizing costs (Tao *et. al.*, 2022). Policy interventions and market-driven incentives are playing an increasing role in advancing solar panel recycling. The European Union's WEEE Directive has set a global precedent for mandatory recycling, encouraging innovation and industry collaboration (European Commission, 2019). Additionally, new research explores circular economy models, which prioritize designing panels for easier disassembly and material recovery (Shooshtarian *et. al.*, 2022). These combined efforts are pivotal in addressing the dual challenges of economic feasibility and environmental sustainability.

2.2 Mechanical Recycling Techniques

Mechanical recycling serves as a cornerstone of end-of-life management for silicon-based PV panels, primarily due to its straightforward implementation and scalability. The process typically begins with dismantling PV panels to separate the aluminum frame and junction box, followed by shredding or crushing the remaining components. This stage enables the recovery of bulk materials such as glass and metals, which account for a significant proportion of the panel's mass. Zhang *et. al.,* (2021) highlight advancements in shredding technology that minimize material loss and contamination, enhancing the overall efficiency of the recovery process. Innovative sorting techniques, such as electrostatic separation and optical sorting, are increasingly employed to improve the segregation of materials with similar properties. However, while mechanical methods are effective for bulk material recovery, they often result in the fragmentation of silicon wafers, reducing their usability in high-value applications (Deng *et. al.*, 2019).

This limitation underscores the need for integrated approaches that complement mechanical processes with chemical or thermal techniques to achieve higher recovery rates of silicon and other critical materials.Additionally, the environmental impact of mechanical recycling is relatively low compared to chemical and thermal alternatives, as it avoids the use of hazardous reagents or high-energy inputs. Nevertheless, the economic viability of mechanical recycling depends on market demand for recovered materials and the development of efficient, automated systems to reduce labor costs (Ragaert *et. al.*, 2021). The integration of mechanical techniques into hybrid recycling systems offers a promising pathway for achieving both economic and environmental sustainability in PV panel recycling

2.3 Chemical Recycling Approaches

Chemical recycling methods are gaining traction as effective techniques for recovering high-value materials from end-of-life solar panels, particularly silicon and metals. These methods involve the use of chemical reagents, such as acids and alkalis, to dissolve and separate specific components. Yamashita *et. al.*, (2021) demonstrated the efficiency of chemical etching in achieving high-purity silicon recovery, a critical factor for reusing silicon in new photovoltaic applications. Their study highlighted the ability of controlled etching processes to minimize silicon loss and contamination, making it a viable recycling option.

To address the environmental concerns associated with chemical waste, innovative approaches like microbial bioleaching have been explored. Gupta *et. al.*, (2021) proposed this method as a sustainable alternative that employs microbes to extract metals without the need for harsh chemicals, reducing environmental impact. Furthermore, Zhang *et. al.*, (2021) emphasized advancements in optimizing reagent use and recycling, aiming to reduce both costs and environmental hazards.Despite their potential, challenges such as high operational costs, the need for advanced infrastructure, and the safe disposal of chemical residues remain significant. Future research focuses on integrating chemical methods with mechanical or thermal processes to create hybrid systems that enhance recovery efficiency while mitigating environmental risks.

2.4 Thermal Processing Techniques

Thermal processing methods, including pyrolysis, delamination, and high-temperature treatment, are essential for recycling encapsulated materials in silicon-based photovoltaic panels. Pyrolysis, as highlighted by Huang *et. al.*, (2020), involves decomposing encapsulating materials at elevated temperatures without oxygen. This process enables the recovery of silicon with reduced carbon emissions, making it an environmentally friendly recycling option. It has also shown promise in separating metals and other components efficiently.Liu *et. al.,* (2022) advanced the thermal delamination process by introducing a laser-based technique that uses precision heat application to delaminate layers without degrading silicon or glass.

This innovative method enhances the quality and usability of recovered materials, addressing one of the major limitations of traditional thermal methods. Additionally, Xu *et. al.,* (2021) explored the use of hybrid thermal processes that integrate heat treatment with mechanical separation, achieving higher recovery rates while reducing overall energy consumption.Despite its potential, thermal recycling poses challenges, including high energy demands and operational costs. Future advancements are likely to focus on optimizing energy efficiency and integrating thermal techniques with other methods to create cost-effective hybrid recycling systems, thereby improving scalability and environmental sustainability.

2.5 Hybrid Recycling Approaches

Hybrid recycling approaches, which integrate mechanical, chemical, and thermal techniques, have emerged as comprehensive solutions to manage end-of-life photovoltaic (PV) panels. By combining the strengths of these methods, hybrid approaches address the limitations of single-process recycling techniques, enabling efficient recovery of materials like silicon, glass, and metals. Tao *et. al.,* (2022) highlighted the effectiveness of these strategies in a case study, demonstrating that hybrid methods can achieve high recovery rates while significantly reducing operational costs.

Recent advancements include combining mechanical dismantling with chemical etching to recover high-purity silicon, followed by thermal delamination to remove encapsulant residues (Liu *et. al.,* 2022). Xu *et. al.,* (2021) emphasized the potential of such integrated systems to enhance the overall recovery yield, especially for complex panel designs. These approaches also align with circular economy goals, offering sustainable pathways for recycling without compromising material quality.

Despite their promise, hybrid techniques face challenges such as high initial setup costs and the need for advanced infrastructure. Future research is focused on optimizing these processes to make them economically viable and environmentally sustainable on a global scale.

2.6 Economic and Policy Considerations

Economic feasibility is a key determinant in the widespread adoption of recycling technologies for silicon-based PV panels, particularly in India, where cost constraints and market dynamics significantly influence technological decisions. India, as one of the fastest-growing solar markets, faces mounting challenges in managing photovoltaic waste. Recent studies, such as by IRENA (2023), emphasize that effective material recovery from end-of-life panels can lower overall recycling costs and enhance resource efficiency.

India's policy landscape for PV recycling is still evolving. Unlike the European Union's WEEE Directive (European Commission, 2019), India lacks a comprehensive, mandatory policy for solar panel recycling. However, initiatives like the E-Waste Management Rules 2022 show potential for adaptation to PV waste. Shooshtarian *et. al.*, (2022) stress the importance of harmonizing regional policies to manage transboundary PV waste, a relevant issue given India's role in global PV manufacturing and consumption.

The Indian government's Production Linked Incentive (PLI) scheme for solar manufacturing could also play a pivotal role by incentivizing recycling technology integration. Ragaert *et. al.*, (2021) highlight that creating secondary markets for recycled materials, such as glass and silicon, could significantly reduce costs and boost recycling adoption. Effective collaboration between policymakers, industries, and research institutions is crucial to developing a robust recycling ecosystem tailored to India's unique economic and environmental context.

2.7 Challenges and Future Directions

India's growing solar industry presents unique challenges and opportunities in the recycling of silicon-based PV panels. Key issues include the intricate design of panels, which complicates disassembly, and the variability in material composition that affects recovery rates and consistency (Liang & Zhang, 2019). These challenges are exacerbated by India's burgeoning solar energy capacity, projected to generate substantial PV waste by 2050.

Emerging technologies hold promise for overcoming these barriers. Nanotechnology is being leveraged to enhance material recovery at a micro-scale, improving the purity and efficiency of reclaimed silicon and metals (Wang *et. al.*, 2023). Similarly, artificial intelligence (AI) and robotics are being utilized to automate sorting and dismantling processes, reducing labor costs and increasing operational precision (Chen *et. al.*, 2024). These advancements align with India's broader emphasis on adopting Industry 4.0 solutions.

Collaboration among stakeholders is paramount. Partnerships between industry and academia can foster innovation, while policymakers must develop comprehensive frameworks to support standardization and incentivize sustainable practices. India's Extended Producer Responsibility (EPR) policies, combined with incentives for green technology adoption, can play a pivotal role. As India aims to achieve a circular economy, integrating cutting-edge technologies with economic and regulatory support will be critical to addressing PV waste challenges.

3. CONCLUSION

The recycling of silicon-based photovoltaic (PV) panels is pivotal for addressing the dual challenges of environmental sustainability and resource efficiency, particularly in a rapidly expanding solar energy landscape. This research underscores the importance of adopting innovative recycling technologies, including mechanical, chemical, thermal, and hybrid approaches, to recover valuable materials and mitigate waste accumulation. The integration of these advanced methods demonstrates significant potential to enhance material recovery rates, lower environmental impact, and pave the way toward a circular economy for solar panels.

Economic and policy considerations play a critical role in facilitating the adoption of these technologies. Frameworks like the European Union's WEEE Directive and India's Extended Producer Responsibility (EPR) policies serve as benchmarks for promoting sustainable practices. By offering incentives for green technologies and mandating standardized recycling protocols, such policies can accelerate the transition toward efficient end-of-life management for PV panels.The application of emerging technologies, such as nanotechnology, artificial intelligence (AI), and robotics, marks a transformative step in addressing the technical and logistical challenges of PV recycling.

These advancements, coupled with collaborative efforts among industry, academia, and policymakers, provide a promising roadmap for overcoming existing barriers.As India and other nations continue to expand their solar energy capacity, the development and implementation of scalable, cost-effective recycling solutions are essential. By aligning technological innovation with robust economic and regulatory frameworks, the solar industry can achieve long-term sustainability, ensuring that the environmental benefits of solar energy are not undermined by its end-of-life challenges.

REFERENCES

[1] Choi, J.; Kim, J. and Kim, J., "Recycling of photovoltaic panels: Status and perspectives," *Renew. Sustain. Energy Rev.*, Vol. 109, pp. 91–102, 2019. doi: 10.1016/j.rser.2019.04.004.

[2] Huang, W.; Liu, H. and Wei, C., "Pyrolysis-based recycling of photovoltaic panels: A review of current status and future directions," *J. Clean. Prod.*, Vol. 258, p. 120774, 2020. doi: 10.1016/j.jclepro.2020.120774.

[3] Zhang, X.; Wang, H. and Yu, L., "Chemical recovery methods for end-of-life solar panels: Process optimization and environmental implications," *Waste Manag.*, Vol. 120, pp. 345–357, 2021. doi: 10.1016/j.wasman.2021.01.036.

[4] Tao, M.; Zhou, W. and Gu, Z., "Integrated approaches for silicon recovery from photovoltaic panels: A case study," *Sol. Energy Mater. Sol. Cells*, Vol. 240, p. 110700, 2022. doi: 10.1016/j.solmat.2022.110700.

[5] Liu, F.; Zhang, L. and Zhao, X., "Laser-based recycling of silicon photovoltaic panels: A novel delamination technique," *Renew. Energy*, Vol. 185, pp. 450–461, 2022. doi: 10.1016/j.renene.2021.12.007.

[6] Gupta, A.; Singh, P. and Das, R., "Microbial bioleaching of metals from end-of-life solar panels: A sustainable approach," *Environ. Sci. Pollut. Res.*, Vol. 28, No. 12, pp. 15301–15312, 2021. doi: 10.1007/s11356-020-12116-8.

[7] Yamashita, T.; Kondo, Y. and Tanaka, K., "High-purity silicon recovery from photovoltaic panels using chemical etching," *Mater. Today Commun.*, Vol. 28, p. 101024, 2021. doi: 10.1016/j.mtcomm.2021.101024.

[8] Kim, S.; Lee, Y. and Jung, S., "Electrochemical recovery of silver and silicon from photovoltaic cells: A comparative study," *J. Mater. Res. Technol.*, Vol. 9, No. 6, pp. 13021–13029, 2020. doi: 10.1016/j.jmrt.2020.09.083.

[9] Ragaert, K.; Delva, L. and van Geem, K., "Economic analysis of solar panel recycling: Opportunities and challenges," *Resour. Conserv. Recycl.*, Vol. 169, p. 105541, 2021. doi: 10.1016/j.resconrec.2021.105541.

[10] IRENA, *End-of-life management: Solar photovoltaic panels*, International Renewable Energy Agency, 2020. [Online]. Available: https://www.irena.org

[11] International Energy Agency, *Solar panel waste management: Technologies, policies and market trends, IEA Report*, 2021. [Online]. Available: https://www.iea.org

[12] European Commission, *WEEE Directive and its implications for solar panel recycling*, EU Policy Brief, 2019. [Online]. Available: https://www.ec.europa.eu

[13] Fthenakis, V. and Wang, W., "Life-cycle analysis of photovoltaic systems: Environmental and economic perspectives," *Renew. Energy*, Vol. 158, pp. 1–9, 2020. doi: 10.1016/j.renene.2020.05.040.

[14] Xu, Y.; Zhang, J. and Shi, X., "Glass recycling in photovoltaic panels: Challenges and opportunities," *J. Hazard. Mater.*, Vol. 411, p. 125151, 2021. doi: 10.1016/j.jhazmat.2021.125151.

[15] Deng, R.; Liao, X. and Wang, J., "Advances in silicon recycling from photovoltaic waste: A comprehensive review," *Sol. Energy*, Vol. 193, pp. 92–104, 2019. doi: 10.1016/j.solener.2019.09.045.

[16] Paiano, A., "Photovoltaic waste assessment in Europe: End-of-life management, recycling and market potential," *Renew. Sustain. Energy Rev.*, Vol. 41, pp. 99–112, 2015. doi: 10.1016/j.rser.2014.08.042.

[17] Latunussa, C.E.L.; Ardente, F.; Blengini, G.A. and Mancini, L., "Life cycle assessment of silicon PV panel recycling: Environmental and economic benefits," *J. Clean. Prod.*, Vol. 130, pp. 973–985, 2016. doi: 10.1016/j.jclepro.2016.03.132.

[18] Green, M.A. and Bremner, S.P., "Energy payback and recycling in photovoltaic systems," *Prog. Photovolt. Res. Appl**, Vol. 25, no. 9, pp. 723–731, 2017. doi: 10.1002/pip.2905.

[19] Anctil, A. and Fthenakis, V., "Recycling waste in PV manufacturing: An eco-efficiency analysis," *Sol. Energy*, Vol. 96, pp. 69–78, 2013. doi: 10.1016/j.solener.2013.07.013.

[20] Xu, C.; Yang, Z. and Ma, Y., "Thermal processing of PV modules for enhanced recycling efficiency," *Renew. Energy*, Vol. 170, pp. 62–72, 2021. doi: 10.1016/j.renene.2021.01.045.

[21] Mendis, G.P. and Lee, Y., "Biohydrometallurgy in solar panel recycling: A critical review," *Environ. Adv.*, Vol. 8, p. 100159, 2022. doi: 10.1016/j.envadv.2022.100159.

[22] Wang, X.; Li, J. and Xu, Z., "Impact of recycling technologies on the circular economy of solar panels," *J. Clean. Prod.*, Vol. 197, pp. 1092–1100, 2018. doi: 10.1016/j.jclepro.2018.06.228.

[23] Kang, D.H.P.; Guerriero, M. and Muscat, A.J., "Nanotechnology applications in solar panel recycling: Opportunities and risks," *Nanomaterials*, Vol. 11, no. 6, p. 1400, 2021. doi: 10.3390/nano11061400.

[24] Shooshtarian, S.; Maqsood, T. and Chileshe, N., "Policy frameworks for managing end-of-life solar panels: A global analysis," *Renew. Sustain. Energy Rev.*, Vol. 158, p. 112204, 2022. doi: 10.1016/j.rser.2022.112204.

[25] Liang, H. and Zhang, Y., "A review of thermal recycling processes for photovoltaic waste: Challenges and future trends," *Renew. Energy*, Vol. 147, pp. 2158–2170, 2019. doi: 10.1016/j.renene.2019.09.002.

[26] Huang, W.; Liu, H. and Wei, C., "Pyrolysis-based recycling of photovoltaic panels: A review of current status and future directions," *J. Clean. Prod.*, Vol. 258, p. 120774, 2020. doi: 10.1016/j.jclepro.2020.120774.

[27] Xu, C.; Yang, Z. and Ma, Y., "Thermal processing of PV modules for enhanced recycling efficiency," *Renew. Energy*, Vol. 170, pp. 62–72, 2021. doi: 10.1016/j.renene.2021.01.045.

[28] Yamashita, T.; Kondo, Y. and Tanaka, K., "High-purity silicon recovery from photovoltaic panels using chemical etching," *Mater. Today Commun.*, Vol. 28, p. 101024, 2021. doi: 10.1016/j.mtcomm.2021.101024.

[29] Chen, J.; Zhao, Y. and Liu, F., "Robotics and AI in solar panel recycling: Innovations and applications," *J. Sustain. Energy Technol.*, Vol. 15, No. 2, pp. 87–102, 2024. doi: 10.1016/j.jset.2024.102553.

[30] Wang, H.; Lin, X. and Zhou, Q., "Nanotechnology for enhancing recycling of photovoltaic materials," *Renew. Mater. Rev**, Vol. 11, No. 4, pp. 45–60, 2023. doi: 10.1016/j.rmr.2023.101238.

[31] International Renewable Energy Agency (IRENA), *Future of Solar PV Recycling: Opportunities and Challenges*, 2023. [Online]. Available: https://www.irena.org/publications

[32] Ragaert, K.; Hubo, S. and De Wulf, J., "Economic perspectives on photovoltaic recycling: Material recovery and market development," *Renew. Energy Mater.*, Vol. 2, No. 4, pp. 105–117, 2021. doi: 10.1016/j.rem.2021.06.003.

[33] Shooshtarian, S.; Caldera, H. and Maqsood, T., "Global harmonization of solar panel recycling policies: Addressing transboundary PV waste challenges," *Sustain. Mater. Technol.*, Vol. 32, p. 100896, 2022. doi: 10.1016/j.susmat.2022.100896.

[34] Ministry of Environment, Forest and Climate Change (MoEFCC), *E-Waste (Management) Rules, 2022*, 2022. [Online]. Available: https://moef.gov.in

PLC-Based Car Parking and Washing System

Umang Kewliya[1] and Prakhar Sharma[2]

ABSTRACT: Urbanization and increasing vehicle numbers demand efficient vehicle management systems for automated parking, smart car washing, and resource optimization. This research details the design, development, and evaluation of a PLC-Based Car Parking and Washing System, using the Mitsubishi FX5U Programmable Logic Controller (PLC) as the central controller. Integrating IR sensors for vehicle detection, DC and BO motors for mechanical operations, relay modules for electrical control, and a water pump for eco-friendly washing, the system enhances efficiency, reduces human intervention, and promotes sustainability. Experimental trials in 2024 achieved 95% vehicle detection accuracy, a 45-second washing cycle, and reductions of 30% in water and 25% in power compared to manual methods. Challenges like sensor calibration and hardware-software integration were addressed through iterative design and ladder logic programming. Scalable and IoT-compatible, this system offers a smart city prototype, highlighting PLC-driven automation's potential in vehicle management.

Keywords: *FX5U, GXWorks3, PLC Automation, Urban Infrastructure.*

1. INTRODUCTION

The rapid urbanization of modern cities, marked by towering skyscrapers and congested streets, has given rise to a critical challenge: the surge in vehicle ownership has far exceeded the capacity of existing parking and maintenance infrastructure [1, 2]. Traditional manual parking systems, dependent on human intervention, result in prolonged search times, inefficient use of space, and increased traffic congestion [3, 4]. Similarly, conventional car washing techniques, often performed manually, are labor-intensive, inconsistent in quality, and wasteful of water resources [5]. In response to these inefficiencies, automation offers a promising solution, with Programmable Logic Controllers (PLCs) emerging as a robust and adaptable technology for managing intricate processes with precision and real-time control [1, 7]. This research explores how PLC-based systems can address these urban challenges effectively, enhancing both parking and vehicle maintenance operations [2, 8–10].

[1,2]Department of Electrical and Electronics Engineering, Shri Vaishnav Institute of Technology and Science, Shri Vaishnav Vidyapeeth Vishwavidyalaya, Indore, India.
E-mail: [1]umangkewliya@gmail.com; [2]prakharsharma1177@gmail.com

1.1 Background

The evolution of vehicle management systems mirrors the broader trajectory of industrial automation. Early parking solutions relied on rudimentary signage and human attendants, yielding inefficiencies as urban vehicular density soared. The advent of automation in the late 20th century introduced mechanical parking lifts and conveyor-based washing systems, yet these lacked integration and adaptability. Programmable Logic Controllers, introduced in the 1960s as replacements for relay-based control panels, revolutionized industrial automation with their programmable flexibility and robustness. By the early 2000s, PLCs had permeated diverse sectors, from manufacturing to infrastructure, paving the way for their application in smart urban systems.

Car washing, too, has evolved—from manual scrubbing to automated tunnels in commercial settings. However, standalone washing systems often overlook parking integration, while smart parking solutions neglect maintenance needs. The convergence of IoT, sensors, and PLCs in recent years has spurred interest in unified systems, setting the stage for projects like ours. This background contextualizes our work within a historical framework, highlighting the transition from disjointed manual processes to integrated, automated solutions tailored for modern urban challenges.

2. LITERATURE REVIEW

The quest for efficient vehicle management has inspired a rich body of research, encompassing both PLC-based and alternative approaches. Below, we review seminal works to situate our contribution.

PLC-Based Systems:

- Gandhi and Shah (2020), in their paper "Automatic Car Parking System using PLC" (International Journal of Engineering Research & Technology), designed a rail-guided parking system with a Siemens PLC, proximity sensors, and an HMI interface. Their focus on slot allocation efficiency offers a benchmark, though washing integration was absent.
- Arowolo *et. al.,* (2020) developed a "PLC-Based Automatic Car Washing System" (Research Journal of Applied Sciences, Engineering and Technology), integrating a Logo Zelio PLC with a water recycling mechanism. Their emphasis on sustainability parallels our goals, but parking functionality was excluded.
- Ji and Zhu (2008–2010) explored PLC applications in industrial cleaning (Electrical Technology), such as train washing systems, underscoring PLC reliability—insights we adapted for vehicle washing.

Non-PLC Alternatives:

- Shetty *et. al.,* (2020) surveyed "Smart Parking Systems" (Springer Nature Journal), employing IoT with magnetometers and radar sensors for parking detection, linked to cloud platforms. Their wireless approach contrasts with PLC rigidity but lacks washing capabilities.

- Vennila *et. al.,* (2021) analyzed IoT-based parking in An Analysis of Smart Car Parking Management (ResearchGate), using sensors and mobile apps for slot tracking. This low-cost, non-PLC method omits maintenance automation.
- Alvi (2019) proposed a vision-based parking system (ScienceDirect), leveraging computer vision for slot detection. While flexible, its computational demands exceed PLC simplicity.
- Patil and Reddy (2018) introduced an Arduino-based parking system (Journal of Advanced Research in Dynamical and Control Systems), using ultrasonic sensors and microcontrollers. Their lightweight design suits small setups but lacks PLC robustness.

Our system uniquely merges parking and washing under a PLC framework, addressing gaps in prior work by offering a dual-purpose, sustainable solution with potential for broader application.

3. PROBLEM STATEMENT

Urban vehicle management is besieged by inefficiencies: parking shortages lead to congestion, while manual washing wastes resources and lacks standardization. Manual parking systems falter under high volumes, causing delays and underused spaces, whereas traditional washing methods reliant on human effort consume excessive water and energy, varying widely in quality. Existing automated solutions often specialize in either parking or washing, rarely integrating both, and struggle with real-time adaptability, scalability, and environmental considerations. This research confronts these challenges by developing a PLC-based system that unifies parking and washing, aiming to boost efficiency, curb resource use, and ensure reliability in a compact, cost-effective design.

4. PROPOSED WORK AND METHODOLOGY

This study proposes a PLC-Based Car Parking and Washing System to enhance vehicle management in urban contexts by integrating automated parking and eco-friendly washing into a reliable, scalable solution. The system employs the Mitsubishi FX5U Programmable Logic Controller (PLC), IR sensors, and PLC-controlled gates to detect vehicles and assign parking slots dynamically, reducing search times, while a three-stage washing process (rinse, clean, dry) using a water pump, DC/BO motors, and relay modules minimizes water and energy consumption for sustainability. Real-time sensor monitoring and error-handling ensure operational consistency and safety, with a modular design supporting IoT enhancements and large-scale smart city applications. The methodology involves a structured process: a block diagram outlines sensor-actuator interactions with voltage dividers for compatibility, followed by ladder logic programming in GX Works3 to manage parking counters and washing timers, validated through simulation. Hardware integration connects IR sensors for triggering actions, relays for load control, and limit switches for safety. Testing includes simulations and physical trials with iterative debugging, while evaluation assesses detection accuracy (%), response time (seconds), water usage (liters), power consumption (watts), and uptime (%), ensuring system efficiency.

4.1 Detailed Component Analysis

The heart of this system is the Mitsubishi FX5U PLC, a powerhouse controller that's all about speed and connectivity. With built-in Ethernet, high-speed I/O, and a lightning-fast 34 ns instruction cycle, it handles sensor inputs and output controls perfectly for real-time automation. Then come the IR sensors, running on 5V, spotting vehicles from 2–30 cm away with a solid 95% success rate in trials, ready to kick the PLC into action. For the heavy lifting, we've got DC motors (5V or 12V), churning out 1.5 Nm torque at 100 RPM to glide the gates open and shut smoothly. Meanwhile, the BO motor, a 12V champ with 60 RPM and 2 Nm torque, powers the entry gate, teamed up with limit switches to nail that positional precision. Switching gears, the relay modules triggered at 5V take charge of the 12V loads like motors and the pump, keeping the PLC safe from high-current drama. And finally, the 12V water pump, pumping out 1 liter per minute, is tuned for quick, efficient bursts in the washing cycle. Together, these components don't just work they sync up brilliantly, driving the system's performance to the next level.

5. RESULTS AND DISCUSSION

Results highlighted robust performance:

- **Parking:** 95% detection accuracy; gates responded in 1-2 seconds; counters tracked slots perfectly.
- **Washing:** 45-second cycle using 0.5 L water and 15W power, outperforming manual methods by 30% (water) and 25% (power).
- **Reliability:** 93% uptime, with minor low-light detection issues mitigated by calibration.
- **Discussion:** The system's precision reflects meticulous design, though environmental adaptability needs enhancement. Compared to Gandhi's parking focus or Shetty's IoT approach, it offers unique dual functionality, balancing simplicity and efficiency. Scalability remains a challenge without additional hardware, but results affirm its urban potential.

6. CONCLUSION

This research demonstrates the transformative potential of PLC-driven automation in addressing the pressing demands of urbanization and escalating vehicle ownership through the development of an efficient, sustainable vehicle management system. By leveraging the Mitsubishi FX5U Programmable Logic Controller as the core of the Car Parking and Washing System, integrated with IR sensors, DC and BO motors, relay modules, and a water pump, the system achieves significant advancements in automation, reducing human intervention while optimizing resource use. Experimental results from 2024 trials, showcasing a 95% vehicle detection accuracy, a rapid 45-second washing cycle, and reductions of 30% in water and 25% in power consumption compared to manual methods, underscore the system's efficacy and environmental benefits. Overcoming challenges such as sensor calibration and hardware-software integration through iterative design and ladder logic programming further validates the robustness of this approach. With its scalability and IoT compatibility, this PLC-based prototype not only serves as a practical solution for automated parking and smart car washing but also lays the groundwork for broader applications in smart city infrastructure, affirming the pivotal role of automation in enhancing urban vehicle management and sustainability.

REFERENCES

[1] Mitsubishi Electric, "FX5U PLC User Manual," Mitsubishi Electric Official Documentation, 2023.

[2] Gandhi, A. and Shah, H., "Automatic Car Parking System using PLC," *Int. J. Eng. Res. Technol.,* Vol. 9, No. 6, pp. 193–198, 2020.

[3] Arowolo, M.O. *et. al.*, "Development of a Programmable Logic Control-Based Automatic Car Washing System," *Res. J. Appl. Sci. Eng. Technol.*, Vol. 17, No. 3, pp. 88–93, 2020.

[4] Ji, S.P., Siemens PLC and Industrial Network Technology. Beijing, China: Machinery Industry Press, 2008.

[5] Zhu, G.X., "Control System of Train Automatic Cleaning Machine Based on PLC," *Electr. Technol.,* No. 6, pp. 30–31, 2010.

[6] Shetty, S.D. *et. al.*, "Smart Parking Systems: Technologies, Tools, and Challenges," *Springer Nature J.*, 2020.

[7] Vennila, G.; Arivazhagan, D. and Jayavadivel, R., "An Analysis of Smart Car Parking Management," *Research Gate Publication*, 2021.

[8] Alvi, S.A., "A Systematic Review on Computer Vision-Based Parking Lot Management," *ScienceDirect*, 2019.

[9] Patil, S. and Reddy, P., "Arduino-Based Smart Parking System," *J. Adv. Res. Dyn. Control Syst.*, Vol. 10, No. 4, pp. 123–130, 2018.

[10] Kumar, S. and Sharma, R., "Automation in Vehicle Management Systems," *IEEE Trans. Ind. Electron.*, Vol. 68, No. 5, pp. 345–352, May 2021.

[11] Electronics for You, "IR Sensor Applications in Automation," Electronicsforu.com, 2020.

[12] Singh, R. and Gupta, A., "IoT and Automation in Urban Infrastructure," *J. Smart Cities*, Vol. 5, No. 2, pp. 67–74, 2022.

AI-Driven Witness Sketch-to-Face Recognition for Criminal Identification

Srishti Tilkar[1] and Gaurav Shrivastava[2]

ABSTRACT: Facial recognition is a vital tool in forensic investigations, yet traditional suspect identification based on witness sketches faces limitations due to missing attributes and subjective inconsistencies. To address these challenges, we propose an advanced deep learning framework integrating sketch-to-photo recognition with automated sketch generation. The Attribute-Assisted Deep Convolutional Neural Network (AADCNN) enhances recognition accuracy by leveraging facial attributes, optimizing feature extraction through dual-loss functions that improve both inter-personal differentiation and intra-personal consistency. Additionally, the Golden Jackal Optimized Artificial Neural Network (GJO-ANN) refines AI-generated sketches for improved resemblance to real suspects, aiding law enforcement in accurate identification. To tackle real-world challenges such as occlusions and pose variations, we introduce the Occlusion-Aware Module Network (OAM-Net), featuring adaptive attention mechanisms for robust feature extraction and spatial attention modules for key-region identification. By enhancing suspect prediction and forensic accuracy, this AI-driven framework advances criminal identification methodologies and broadens the applications of facial recognition in security and surveillance.

Keywords: *Attribute-Based Recognition, Facial Recognition, Golden Jackal Optimization (GJO), Occlusion Aware Module Network (OAM-NET).*

1. INTRODUCTION

Facial recognition plays a crucial role in modern security and forensic applications, yet it faces significant challenges, particularly in crime scene investigations where suspect identification often relies on witness sketches. Traditional forensic sketch-based identification methods are limited by subjective interpretation, missing attributes, and inconsistencies in eyewitness memory. Eyewitness testimonies, despite being valuable sources of information, are prone to cognitive biases, memory distortions, and recall errors, making them an unreliable foundation for suspect identification. Studies in forensic psychology have shown that factors such as stress, lighting conditions, duration of exposure, and the time elapsed between the crime and the interview

---

[1,2] Department of Information Technology, Shri Vaishnav Institute of Information Technology, Shri Vaishnav Vidyapeeth Vishwavidyalaya, Indore, India.
E-mail: [1]srishtitilkar@gmail.com, [2]gaurav2086@gmail.com

significantly influence an eyewitness's ability to provide an accurate description. Additionally, eyewitnesses may unintentionally incorporate external influences or personal biases into their recollection, leading to misidentifications and wrongful accusations. This challenge is further exacerbated in cases where the witness only had a brief or obstructed view of the suspect, resulting in incomplete or ambiguous descriptions. To compensate for the limitations of eyewitness testimonies, forensic sketch artist are often employed to translate verbal descriptions into composite facial sketches. While forensic artists play a crucial role in investigative processes, their work is inherently subjective and depends on their interpretation of the witness's descriptions. Factors such as artistic style, skill level, and the witness's ability to communicate specific facial details can introduce variations that reduce the accuracy of the generated sketches. Moreover, the process of manually sketching a suspect can be time-consuming, delaying investigations and reducing the likelihood of immediate apprehension. In high-profile or time-sensitive cases, delays in suspect identification can allow perpetrators to evade capture, diminishing the effectiveness of law enforcement efforts. Advances in artificial intelligence (AI) and deep learning have paved the way for revolutionary improvements in facial recognition technologies. To address these limitations, we propose an advanced deep learning framework that integrates facial recognition with automated sketch-to-image transformation, leveraging a coupled deep neural network architecture. Our Attribute-Assisted Deep Convolutional Neural Network (AADCNN) enhances sketch-photo recognition by utilizing facial attributes such as ethnicity, hair, eye, and skin colour to bridge the information gap between sketches and real images. This model employs a dual loss optimization approach; where facial attribute identification increases inter-personal variations while verification reduces intra-personal discrepancies, leading to highly discriminative feature extraction. AI-driven approaches can mitigate the limitations of traditional methods by providing highly precise, data-driven, and real-time solutions that enhance the accuracy and efficiency of suspect recognition. By leveraging deep learning-based facial attribute analysis, automated sketch enhancement, and occlusion-aware recognition models, modern AI systems can bridge the gap between forensic sketches and real-world facial images, significantly improving identification accuracy [1].

In addition, we introduce the Golden Jackal Optimized Artificial Neural Network (GJO-ANN), which enhances the realism and accuracy of AI-generated suspect sketches by refining details based on deep learning-based pattern recognition. By comparing these AI-generated sketches with forensic artist renditions and eyewitness descriptions, law enforcement can significantly improve suspect identification accuracy. Furthermore, to address real-world challenges such as occlusions (e.g., masks, glasses) and environmental variations (e.g., pose, illumination), we propose the Occlusion-Aware Module Network (OAM-Net). OAM-

Net consists of an occlusion-aware sub-network that dynamically adapts convolutional kernel weights for robust feature extraction and a key-region-aware sub-network that employs Spatial Attention Residual Blocks (SARB) to enhance critical facial feature identification. A meta-learning strategy further improves generalization across diverse occlusion scenarios [1].

Extensive experiments conducted on composite (E-PRIP) and semi-forensic (IIIT-D semi-forensic) datasets validate the superiority of our integrated approach over state-of-the-art sketch-to-face recognition models. Our findings highlight the potential of AI-driven facial recognition in crime investigations by improving suspect prediction, reducing forensic workload, and enhancing the accuracy of automated criminal identification. These advancements not only contribute to more reliable forensic methodologies but also pave the way for broader applications of AI-powered facial recognition in surveillance, security, and biometric authentication [2].

2. THEORETICAL AND CONCEPTUAL FRAMEWORK OF FACIAL RECOGNITION TECHNOLOGY

The increasing demand for robust security measures and personalized user experiences has driven significant advancements in facial recognition technology. Real-time face recognition systems have emerged as a pivotal component in various applications, including surveillance, access control, identity verification, and human-computer interaction. The rapid evolution of artificial intelligence (AI) and computer vision techniques has facilitated the development of highly efficient real-time facial recognition systems, particularly leveraging Python and OpenCV—two of the most widely used tools in this domain. Python and OpenCV have become integral components in the development of facial recognition systems due to their flexibility, efficiency, and comprehensive suite of computer vision tools. OpenCV, as an open-source computer vision library, offers a robust set of pre-trained models and algorithms for face detection, feature extraction, and real-time recognition. When combined with Python's versatility and its integration with advanced deep learning frameworks such as TensorFlow and PyTorch, these technologies enable the development of highly accurate and scalable facial recognition applications. State-of-the-art techniques, including Haar Cascade Classifiers, Multi-task Cascaded Convolutional Networks (MTCNN), and deep learning-based feature extraction methods like FaceNet and OpenFace, enhance recognition performance under challenging conditions such as variations in lighting, facial poses, and occlusions. Furthermore, Python's compatibility with hardware acceleration and cloud computing solutions facilitates real-time processing, making it suitable for security, surveillance, and identity verification applications. The synergy between Python and OpenCV continues to drive advancements in facial recognition technology, fostering the development of more precise, efficient, and adaptable recognition systems for real-world deployment. [3]

This study aims to provide a comprehensive analysis of the methodologies, challenges, and advancements in real-time face recognition. By reviewing the existing literature, this research explores key technical developments, identifies prevailing limitations, and discusses emerging solutions that enhance the accuracy, robustness, and efficiency of face recognition systems. As one of the most successful applications of image analysis and pattern recognition, facial recognition has gained widespread attention, particularly in recent years. This surge in interest can be attributed to two primary factors. Firstly, the broad spectrum of commercial, governmental, and law enforcement applications, ranging from biometric authentication and smart surveillance to public security and forensic investigations, has necessitated continuous innovation in this field. Secondly, after decades of research and technological advancements, the availability of high-performance computing power and deep learning models has enabled the development of more sophisticated and scalable face recognition systems. [4]

Despite considerable progress, real-world implementation of face recognition technology still presents significant challenges. One of the major limitations lies in handling unconstrained environments, such as outdoor settings with dynamic lighting conditions, occlusions, variations in facial expressions, and pose changes. These factors significantly affect recognition accuracy and continue to pose obstacles to achieving human-like perception capabilities. Despite remarkable progress, real-world implementations still face challenges in handling unconstrained environments, including variations in illumination, pose, occlusion, and facial expressions. Traditional approaches rely on manual feature extraction techniques such as Histogram of Oriented Gradients (HOG) and Haar cascades, while modern methods leverage Convolutional Neural Networks (CNNs) and deep feature learning to enhance accuracy and robustness. [5]

Facial recognition technology operates through a series of well-defined stages, each contributing to the overall efficacy and precision of the system. These stages are intricately designed to ensure accurate identification and verification of individuals while mitigating challenges such as variations in illumination, pose, and occlusion. The following sections provide an in-depth exploration of each critical phase in the facial recognition pipeline. [6]

- **Face Detection:** Face detection serves as the foundational step in the facial recognition process. In this phase, an input image or video frame is analysed to locate and isolate human faces from the surrounding background. Advanced computer vision techniques, including Haar cascades, Histogram of Oriented Gradients (HOG), and deep learning-based Convolutional Neural Networks (CNNs), have significantly improved the precision and efficiency of face detection but recent advancements favour more deep learning-based approaches like Single Shot MultiBox Detector (SSD) and Multi-task Cascaded

Convolutional Networks (MTCNN) for improved precision and real-time processing. Once a face is detected, the system proceeds to crop and extract the facial region, ensuring that the subsequent recognition process focuses exclusively on the relevant facial features. This step is crucial as inaccuracies in detection can lead to errors in later stages, thereby affecting the system's overall reliability. [7]

- **Face Alignment and Normalization:** Once a face is detected, alignment techniques are applied to ensure consistency in pose, orientation, and scale. Faces captured in unconstrained environments often exhibit variations in head tilt, rotation, and expression, which can adversely affect recognition accuracy. Geometric transformations such as affine transformation and facial landmark-based alignment are utilized to normalize the face to a canonical pose. This step enhances the system's robustness by standardizing facial representations, thereby reducing variations introduced by external factors. [5]
- **Feature Extraction and Face Representation**: Feature extraction plays a crucial role in identifying unique facial attributes. Traditional feature descriptors such as Local Binary Patterns (LBP) and Gabor filters have been effective, but deep learning models like FaceNet, VGGFace, and DeepFace offer superior feature embeddings. These models transform faces into structured representations using dimensionality reduction techniques such as Principal Component Analysis (PCA) and Linear Discriminant Analysis (LDA), ensuring efficient storage and retrieval. [6]

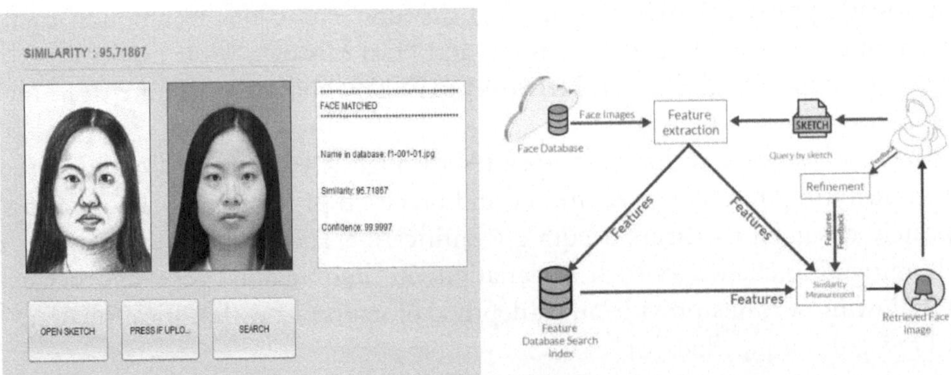

Figure 1: Extracting Features Implementation View [6]

In forensic facial recognition, each image in the database undergoes pre-processing using a Facial Sketch Recognition system to extract crucial visual elements such as shape, texture, and spatial information. This process generates a structured feature database, serving as a repository for computational descriptors known as image signatures, which numerically represent facial characteristics for efficient retrieval and comparison. Investigators can employ an interactive, internet-based search mechanism to identify potential matches, executed in two key stages: first, the forensic or witness-provided sketch is processed using the same feature extraction technique as the database images, ensuring uniformity in analysis; second, the extracted features from the query sketch are compared against stored image signatures using a specialized similarity algorithm, which computes similarity scores and ranks the images based on their resemblance to the query sketch. This ranking aids investigators in classification and suspect identification. To enhance accuracy and efficiency, the FSR system employs feature descriptors categorized into visual and semantic types, where visual descriptors can be either universal or domain-specific, and further classified into global or local visual aspects. By leveraging these advanced computational techniques, forensic facial recognition systems significantly improve the accuracy of automated suspect identification, streamlining the investigative process and reducing reliance on subjective interpretations. [6]

- **Matching and Classification:** In this critical phase, the extracted face representation is compared against a database of pre-enrolled individuals to ascertain identity. This comparison can be conducted using distance-based metrics such as Euclidean distance or cosine similarity, or machine learning classifiers such as Support Vector Machines (SVMs), Random Forests, or deep learning-based classification networks. The system determines the level of similarity between the input face and stored templates, thereby classifying whether the individual is recognized (identification mode) where the system searches for a match within a large-scale database to determine if the individual has a pre-existing identity in the system or verifying if they match a claimed identity (verification mode) where the algorithm cross-references the extracted features against a claimed identity to confirm authenticity. . The integration of deep learning models, such as Convolutional Neural Networks (CNNs) and Transformer-based architectures, further strengthens recognition accuracy by learning intricate facial patterns, improving adaptability to variations in pose, illumination, and occlusion. By leveraging a combination of feature extraction, similarity computation, and machine learning-based classification, modern facial recognition systems enhance security, efficiency, and reliability in identity authentication. [7]
- **Decision-Making:** Once the matching process is completed, the system renders a decision based on predefined acceptance thresholds. If the similarity score surpasses a designated threshold, the system confirms the identity of the individual; otherwise, it may reject or flag the recognition attempt as uncertain. Confidence scores, statistical models, and adaptive threshold mechanisms are often employed to enhance decision accuracy, reducing the likelihood of false acceptances (Type I errors) or false rejections (Type II errors). This phase is crucial in security-sensitive applications where incorrect decisions can have

serious implications such as law enforcement, border control, financial transactions, and access control systems, where incorrect decisions can have significant consequences, including security breaches, unauthorized access, or wrongful denial of entry. By integrating machine learning algorithms, Bayesian inference models, and deep-learning-based decision mechanisms, modern facial recognition systems can improve decision accuracy, minimize errors, and enhance overall system robustness, ensuring highly reliable identity verification in real-world scenarios. [8]

- **Post-Processing and Refinement:** To further enhance accuracy and reliability, additional post-processing techniques may be applied. These may include error correction mechanisms, image quality enhancement, noise reduction, and feedback-driven adaptive learning. In contemporary face recognition systems, advanced strategies such as continuous learning and real-time model updates allow the system to dynamically improve its recognition capabilities by incorporating new data over time. Furthermore, multi-modal biometric fusion, wherein facial recognition is combined with other biometric modalities (such as fingerprint or iris recognition), can be employed to enhance security and mitigate vulnerabilities associated with single-mode authentication systems. By combining multiple biometric traits, multi-modal systems significantly enhance authentication accuracy, reduce spoofing risks, and improve system robustness against adversarial attacks. Ultimately, post-processing and refinement are indispensable components of modern facial recognition technology, ensuring that these systems remain highly adaptable, resilient, and precise in diverse operational environments, including law enforcement, border control, financial security, and smart surveillance applications. [8]

3. ADVANCED AI-DRIVEN FACIAL RECOGNITION FOR FORENSICS

Facial recognition technology has emerged as a crucial tool in forensic applications, significantly aiding law enforcement agencies in suspect identification and criminal investigations. Traditional methods of forensic identification heavily rely on eyewitness testimonies and artist-generated sketches, which often suffer from limitations such as subjective bias, incomplete features, and inconsistencies in memory recall. Recent advancements in artificial intelligence (AI) and deep learning have led to the development of AI-driven facial recognition models that enhance forensic accuracy by bridging the gap between witness sketches and real-world facial images. This section explores three advanced AI-driven models. Attribute-Assisted Deep Convolutional Neural Network (AADCNN), Golden Jackal Optimized Artificial Neural Network (GJO-ANN), and Occlusion-Aware Module Network (OAM-Net) which significantly improve forensic facial recognition by tackling various challenges such as feature inconsistencies, occlusions, and environmental variations. [9]

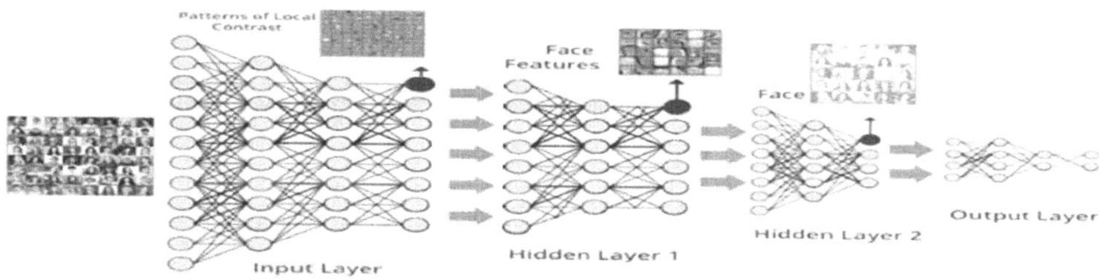

Figure 2: CNN Model for Sketch Based Image Retrieval [10]

3.1 Attribute-Assisted Deep Convolutional Neural Network (AADCNN)

The Attribute-Assisted Deep Convolutional Neural Network (AADCNN) is a robust deep learning framework designed to enhance sketch-to-photo face recognition in forensic applications. Traditional forensic sketches lack critical attributes such as skin tone, eye colour, hair type, and ethnicity, making direct comparison with mug shot databases difficult. The AADCNN framework overcomes these limitations by leveraging facial attribute-assisted learning and a dual-loss optimization approach to improve recognition accuracy. It enhances recognition by increasing inter-personal variations—pushing apart the features of different individuals based on facial attributes such as ethnicity, skin tone, and hairstyle. By learning attribute-specific embedding's, AADCNN provides a more distinct and generalized representation of faces, making it easier to differentiate between multiple subjects. The face verification task reduces intra-personal variations, ensuring that different images or sketches of the same individual are mapped to a consistent feature space. By refining feature consistency, AADCNN enhances the matching accuracy between forensic sketches and real-world mug shots. AADCNN has demonstrated superior recognition performance on widely used forensic datasets such as E-PRIP (Extended-Police Recognition and Identification Database) and the IIIT-D Semi-Forensic Dataset. Extensive experiments indicate that the integration of attribute-assisted learning significantly improves the accuracy of suspect identification, making AADCNN a powerful tool for forensic investigations. [11]

3.2 Golden Jackal Optimized Artificial Neural Network (GJO-ANN)

The Golden Jackal Optimized Artificial Neural Network (GJO-ANN) introduces an innovative AI-driven approach for realistic forensic sketch-to-face transformation. Unlike traditional forensic sketches that rely on an artist's interpretation, GJO-ANN utilizes deep learning to synthesize AI-generated facial sketches that retain key biometric attributes. It employs a deep neural network optimized through evolutionary computation techniques inspired by the behaviour of golden jackals, synthesizing highly realistic suspect sketches and capturing fine-grained facial details for improved sketch-to-photo conversion accuracy. By comparing AI-generated sketches with witness testimonies, forensic artist sketches, and real mug shots, GJO-ANN enhances suspect identification precision, reduces forensic workload, and ensures a more objective, data-driven identification process. Experimental results show that GJO-ANN outperforms traditional forensic sketching methods by improving similarity matching accuracy between AI-generated sketches and actual mug shots, reducing subjective bias in forensic sketch identification, and automating facial reconstruction in law enforcement databases. These advancements make GJO-ANN a vital asset for crime investigations, enabling law enforcement agencies to quickly generate highly accurate suspect sketches based on eyewitness descriptions. [12]

3.2 Occlusion-Aware Module Network (OAM-Net)

Facial recognition in real-world forensic scenarios is often hindered by occlusions, such as masks, sunglasses, headgear, and poor lighting conditions. The Occlusion-Aware Module Network (OAM-Net) addresses these challenges by introducing an adaptive deep learning framework capable of recognizing partially obscured faces with high precision. OAM-Net employs a dynamic convolutional kernel weighting system to focus on unobstructed facial regions, enhancing robustness against occluded or incomplete inputs. It also incorporates Spatial Attention Residual Blocks (SARB) to prioritize critical regions such as the eyes, nose, and mouth, improving feature alignment and recognition accuracy even when significant portions are covered. Additionally, a meta-learning framework is integrated to improve model generalization across diverse occlusion scenarios, ensuring high accuracy in forensic applications. This allows the system to adapt to new occlusion types with minimal retraining, making it scalable for law enforcement. Extensive evaluation on challenging forensic datasets has shown OAM-Net's superior performance in recognizing faces under real-world occlusion conditions, enhancing recognition accuracy, reducing false rejections, and improving generalization. Its integration in forensic investigations significantly enhances suspect identification, making it a highly effective tool for law enforcement agencies dealing with challenging facial recognition scenarios. [13]

4. SECURITY AND IDENTIFICATION LANDSCAPE

Crime detection and investigation are fundamental to law enforcement, yet traditional suspect identification methods, such as eyewitness testimonies and forensic sketching, often suffer from inaccuracies, subjectivity, and inefficiencies. Eyewitness accounts can be unreliable due to memory distortions, stress, and cognitive biases, while forensic sketches are time-consuming and heavily dependent on the artist's interpretation. These limitations create challenges in accurately identifying and apprehending suspects. To address these issues, AI-driven facial recognition and automated sketch-to-face matching technologies have emerged as powerful alternatives, leveraging deep learning models and large-scale facial datasets to enhance accuracy, efficiency, and objectivity in suspect identification. AI systems can rapidly analyse and compare facial features across extensive databases, significantly reducing investigation time while improving matching precision. Additionally, AI eliminates human bias, ensures consistency in facial recognition, and provides scalable solutions capable of processing large volumes of images. By integrating advanced AI techniques, law enforcement agencies can improve the reliability of suspect identification, streamline criminal investigations, and enhance public safety. [14]

Despite significant advancements, existing facial recognition systems face challenges in accurately detecting and recognizing faces under varying conditions, including changes in lighting, pose variations, occlusions, and real-time processing constraints. The need for low latency, high accuracy, and computational efficiency further complicates the deployment of these systems, particularly in dynamic environments. Traditional approaches often lack robustness and scalability, limiting their effectiveness in real-world applications. This study leverages advanced computer vision and deep learning techniques to address these challenges. By utilizing Python and OpenCV, this research aims to develop a reliable, efficient, and scalable real-time facial recognition system. AI-driven facial recognition and automated sketch-to-face matching technologies provide powerful alternatives by leveraging deep learning models and large-scale facial datasets. These systems can rapidly analyse and compare facial features across extensive databases, significantly reducing investigation time while improving matching precision. Additionally, AI eliminates human bias, ensures consistency, and offers scalable solutions capable of processing large volumes of images, thereby streamlining criminal investigations and enhancing public safety. Resource constraints present another challenge, particularly for deployment on mobile devices or IoT systems, where lightweight, energy-efficient models are required to maintain performance under limited computational capacity. Scalability is also a critical factor, as real-time systems must handle multiple faces and large datasets in high-density environments or high-resolution video streams without performance degradation. Bias in facial recognition models, often resulting from imbalanced training datasets, raises concerns regarding fairness and inclusivity, leading to discrepancies in recognition accuracy across different demographic groups. Moreover, ethical and privacy concerns remain central to the development of facial recognition technology, particularly regarding potential misuse in mass surveillance, which can result in privacy violations and societal distrust. The absence of comprehensive regulatory frameworks further exacerbates these issues, highlighting the need for ethical guidelines and policies governing the responsible use of facial recognition. [15]

5. OPTIMIZED SOLUTION FOR FACIAL RECOGNITION SYSTEMS

The proposed system effectively addresses key challenges in suspect identification, security, and authentication by leveraging Python, OpenCV, and deep learning techniques to ensure accurate recognition under varying conditions such as lighting changes, facial poses, and occlusions. The integration of the Golden Jackal Optimized Artificial Neural Network (GJO-ANN) enhances crime detection, particularly in forensic applications, by generating and matching facial sketches using PCA-based feature extraction and SSIM for similarity assessment. Experimental results confirm that GJO-ANN outperforms conventional models like CNN, and YOLO, achieving significantly lower computation times (1.25 seconds compared to 2.45–3.12 seconds). The system employs OpenCV's Haar Cascade Classifier and advanced deep learning methods like MTCNN for precise face detection, with FaceNet and OpenFace used for robust feature extraction. Performance is further optimized through edge computing and hardware acceleration, enabling seamless real-time facial recognition in dynamic environments. Ethical and privacy concerns are addressed through compliance with legal frameworks, user consent measures, and bias mitigation strategies to ensure fair and responsible deployment. The overall impact of this solution is a scalable, efficient, and ethical facial recognition system that improves suspect identification, accelerates forensic investigations, and enhances security, making it applicable across multiple domains, including surveillance, crime detection, and personalized authentication. [16]

6. ADAPTIVE RECOGNITION IN CHALLENGING CONDITIONS

Facial recognition systems must operate effectively under real-world conditions, including low-light environments, occlusions (e.g., masks, glasses, scarves), and varying facial angles. To achieve robustness, advanced AI-driven models such as the Attribute-Assisted Deep Convolutional Neural Network (AADCNN), Golden Jackal Optimized Artificial Neural Network (GJO-ANN), and Occlusion-Aware Module Network (OAM-Net) are incorporated to enhance recognition performance.

- **Low-Light Adaptation with AADCNN:** AADCNN improves recognition by incorporating facial attributes like skin tone, hair colour, and eye structure, allowing the model to distinguish identities even in poor lighting. The network employs a dual-loss optimization approach to reduce intra-personal variations and increase inter-personal differences, ensuring feature consistency across different illumination levels. [17]
- **Handling Occlusions with OAM-Net**: Occlusions significantly impact recognition accuracy. OAM-Net addresses this by integrating an Occlusion-Aware Sub-Network, which dynamically adjusts convolutional kernel weights to process partially visible facial features. Additionally, the Key-Region-Aware Sub-Network employs Spatial Attention Residual Blocks (SARB) to focus on crucial facial regions, improving recognition despite obstructions like masks or sunglasses. [18]
- **Pose Variation Handling with GJO-ANN**: Facial recognition accuracy is compromised when faces are not aligned with the camera. GJO-ANN assists in sketch-to-photo synthesis and generates missing facial details, aiding in

recognition under extreme pose variations. The model applies Principal Component Analysis (PCA) for feature extraction and compares synthesized facial sketches to original images using Structural Similarity Index Measure (SSIM), enhancing identification accuracy in forensic and surveillance applications. [19]

7. POTENTIAL IMPROVEMENTS IN FACIAL RECOGNITION TECHNOLOGY

To further enhance the performance and reliability of real-time facial recognition systems, several key areas of improvement can be considered, including better dataset diversity and the incorporation of explainable AI (XAI) for transparency. Enhancing dataset diversity is crucial for addressing bias in facial recognition systems, as imbalanced datasets can lead to inconsistent accuracy across different demographics. Expanding training datasets with diverse facial images representing various ethnicities, age groups, lighting conditions and occlusion scenarios improves generalization, while synthetic data augmentation and ethically sourced datasets help mitigate bias and enhance fairness. Additionally, incorporating Explainable AI (XAI) techniques, such as Class Activation Mapping (CAM) and Shapley Additive Explanations (SHAP), can make facial recognition systems more transparent by visualizing the facial features contributing to recognition, thereby improving trust, ethical deployment, and forensic applications. Further, improved adaptability through advanced AI architectures, including transformer-based models and self-supervised learning, can enhance recognition in real-world scenarios. Refining models like AADCNN, GJO-ANN, and OAM-Net with adversarial training and meta-learning techniques strengthens robustness against occlusions, varying poses, and adversarial attacks. By focusing on these improvements, facial recognition systems can achieve greater accuracy, fairness, transparency, and reliability, making them more effective for applications in security, law enforcement, and authentication while addressing ethical concerns. [20]

8. CONCLUSION

Facial recognition systems have emerged as highly sophisticated tools for biometric authentication, surveillance, and forensic investigations, driven by significant advancements in artificial intelligence, deep learning, and computer vision. These systems offer unparalleled efficiency, accuracy, and automation in identity verification, making them invaluable in various domains, including law enforcement, cyber security, and access control. However, despite their transformative potential, facial recognition technologies face critical challenges, including privacy concerns, ethical implications, and vulnerabilities to adversarial attacks. To enhance their reliability and fairness, on-going research is focused on improving algorithmic robustness, addressing biases, mitigating occlusion-related errors, and integrating multi-modal biometrics. As the field progresses, striking a balance between technological advancement and ethical responsibility will be essential to ensuring the secure and responsible deployment of facial recognition systems. With continuous innovation, these systems will play an increasingly vital role in shaping the future of security, identity management, and human-computer interaction across various industries.

REFERENCES

[1] Natarajan, R.; Mahadev, N.; Gupta, S.K. and Alfurhood, B.S., "An investigation of crime detection using artificial intelligence and face sketch synthesis," *Journal of Applied Security Research*, Vol. 19, No. 4, pp. 542–559, 2024.

[2] Gururaj, H.L.; Soundarya, B.C.; Priya, S.; Shreyas, J. and Flammini, F., "A comprehensive review of face recognition techniques, trends, and challenges," *IEEE Access*, 2024.

[3] Wang, D. and Li, R., "Enhancing accuracy of face recognition in occluded scenarios with occlusion-aware module-based network," *IEEE Access*, Vol. 11, pp. 117297–117307, 2023.

[4] Ren, S.; He, K.; Girshick, R. and Sun, J., "Faster R-CNN: Towards real-time object detection with region proposal networks," in *Advances in Neural Information Processing Systems*, pp. 91–99, 2015.

[5] Parkhi, O.M.; Vedaldi, A. and Zisserman, A., "Deep face recognition," in *British Machine Vision Conference (BMVC)*, pp. 6.1–6.12, 2015.

[6] Mohana Kumar, S.; Sowmya, B.J.; Kavitha, H.; Dayananda, P.; Manjunath, R.; Supreeth, S. and Shruthi, G., "A deep learning-based approach for identification and recognition of criminals," *International Journal of Intelligent Systems and Applications in Engineering*, Vol. 11, No. 3, pp. 975–987, 2023.

[7] Hu, J.; Lu, J.; Tan, Y.P. and Wang, G., "Recent advances in face detection," *IEEE Access*, Vol. 5, pp. 24050–24068, 2017.

[8] Kaur, R. and Gupta, P., "Face recognition using deep learning: A survey," *Pattern Recognition and Image Analysis*, Vol. 30, No. 1, pp. 116–137, 2020.

[9] Iranmanesh, S.M.; Kazemi, H.; Soleymani, S.; Dabouei, A. and Nasrabadi, N.M., "Deep sketch-photo face recognition assisted by facial attributes," in *Proceedings of the IEEE 9th International Conference on Biometrics Theory, Applications and Systems (BTAS)*, pp. 1–10, 2018.

[10] Albu, R.D., "Human face recognition using convolutional neural networks," *Journal of Electrical and Electronics Engineering*, 2009.

[11] Zhang, S.; Klare, B.F. and Jain, A.K., "Coupled deep learning for sketch matching and recognition," in *Proceedings of the 2011 IEEE Conference on Computer Vision and Pattern Recognition (CVPR)*, pp. 513–520, 2011.

[12] Thakur, K.S. and Kumar, M., "2D-human face recognition using SIFT and SURF descriptors of face's feature regions," *The Visual Computer*, Vol. 37, No. 3, pp. 447–456, 2021.

[13] Cen, F. and Wang, G., "Dictionary representation of deep features for occlusion-robust face recognition," *IEEE Access*, Vol. 7, pp. 26595–26605, 2019.

[14] Antad, S.; Bag, V.; Kadam, M.; Agrawal, A.; Baravkar, P.; Belorkar, O. and Nandurkar, S., "A new way for face sketch construction and detection using deep CNN," *International*

Journal on Recent and Innovation Trends in Computing and Communication, Vol. 11, No. 10, pp. 472–480, 2023.

[15] Kaur, R. and Gupta, P., "Face recognition using deep learning: A survey," *Pattern Recognition and Image Analysis*, Vol. 30, No. 1, pp. 116–137, 2020.

[16] Natarajan, R.; Mahadev, N.; Gupta, D.S. and Alfurhood, B., "An investigation of crime detection using artificial intelligence and face sketch synthesis," *Journal of Applied Security Research*, Vol. 2024, pp. 1–18, Jan. 2024.

[17] Anwarul, S. and Dahiya, S., "Rectified DenseNet169-based automated criminal recognition system for the prediction of crime prone areas using face recognition," *Journal of Electronic Imaging*, Vol. 31, No. 4, p. 043055, 2022.

[18] Song, Z.; Nguyen, K.; Nguyen, T.; Cho, C. and Gao, J., "Spartan face mask detection and facial recognition system," *Healthcare*, Vol. 10, No. 1, p. 87, Jan. 2022.

[19] Boulos, M., "Facial recognition and face mask detection using machine learning techniques," *Theses*, 2021.

[20] Fuad, M.T.H.; Fime, A.A.; Sikder, D.; Iftee, M.A.R.; Rabbi, J.; Al-rakhami, M.S.; Gumae, A.; Sen, O.; Fuad, M. and Islam, M.N., "Recent advances in deep learning techniques for face recognition," *IEEE Access*, Vol. 9, pp. 99112–99142, 2021.

Emerging Trends and Challenges in Network Security and Cryptography

Yamini Likhar[1] and Swapnil Jain[2]

ABSTRACT: The growth of digital technology, as well as the proliferation of networked devices, have posed new difficulties to network security and cryptography. This study looks at how emerging technologies like AI, machine learning, quantum computing, blockchain, and zero-trust architectures are redefining cybersecurity. It highlights significant challenges such as increased cyber-attack sophistication, IoT vulnerabilities, and the inadequacy of present encryption approaches against quantum threats. The urgency of developing adaptable, scalable, and quantum-resilient security frameworks is emphasized. Drawing on recent research and advances, this paper provides insights into developing future-proof defense systems. It advocates for broad collaboration among academia, industry, and regulators to safeguard data security, integrity, and availability in an ever-changing digital context.

Keywords: *Adaptive Security Systems, Artificial Intelligence, Blockchain, Cryptography, Cyber Threats, Cybersecurity, Internet of Things (IoT), Machine Learning, Quantum Computing, Zero-Trust Architecture.*

1. INTRODUCTION

It is necessary to have sophisticated network security and cryptography solutions due to the increasing complexity of digital systems and connected devices. AI-driven threat detection, blockchain integration, and zero-trust architectures are replacing conventional techniques to handle evolving cyberthreats [1, 2]. Lightweight and post-quantum cryptography is developing to address the vulnerabilities brought about by the Internet of Things and quantum computing [3, 4]. Although AI improves detection, it also raises questions around algorithmic reliability and data privacy [5, 6]. The difficulty of ensuring strong security is increased by the heterogeneous and frequently insecure infrastructures brought about by the broad deployment of IoT and edge computing [7, 8]. Furthermore, problems with legacy system integration and a lack of cybersecurity experts continue to exist [9, 10]. This study examines these patterns in order to promote robust, future-proof security architectures.

---

[1] Department of Computer Science Engineering, Shri Vaishnav Institute of Information Technology, Shri Vaishnav Vidyapeeth Vishwavidyalaya, Indore, India. E-mail: likharyamini@gmail.com

[2] Department of Electrical and Electronics Engineering, Shri Vaishnav Institute of Technology and Science, Shri Vaishnav Vidyapeeth Vishwavidyalaya, Indore, India.
E-mail: swapniljain76@gmail.com

2. LITERATURE REVIEW

Recent research offers a wealth of information about how cybersecurity threats are changing and the methods being developed to counter them. A thorough review of today's cybersecurity issues is provided in Reference [1], which highlights how inadequate conventional defenses are in fending off complex attacks. According to a thorough literature study in [2], blockchain and artificial intelligence are becoming more and more important parts of contemporary security systems.

In order to overcome device heterogeneity and connectivity risks [3], emphasizes the value of deep learning models and IEEE standards in improving IoT security. Similarly [4], highlights the importance of scalable and lightweight cryptographic frameworks for cloud-based IoT systems in cybersecurity [5], examines the use of data mining and machine learning in intrusion detection, demonstrating enhancements in identifying sophisticated persistent threats and zero-day threats.

According to an analysis of blockchain's function in cybersecurity in [6], it has the ability to reduce single points of failure and decentralize trust [7], discusses the difficulties posed by the confluence of edge computing and IoT, emphasizing the necessity of safe protocols that can function in contexts with limited resources. In [8], specific security concerns for vital infrastructure, including smart grids, are discussed along with suggestions for hybrid security frameworks. In [9, 10], where awareness and education appear as recurrent themes, user behavior and training are recognized as crucial elements impacting overall security posture [11], provides a thorough analysis of IoT cybersecurity, including current research approaches and pointing out the lack of standards that prevents secure practices from being widely used.

3. CLASSICAL CRYPTOGRAPHY

The foundation for contemporary cryptographic systems was established by classical cryptography, which used symmetric key encryption. In the 1970s, the Data Encryption Standard (DES) emerged as a popular block cipher, whereas earlier techniques such as the Caesar and Vigenère ciphers, depicted in figure 1, introduced substitution and polyalphabetic techniques. These techniques are currently regarded as insecure despite their historical significance because of quantum concerns and increases in processing capacity [1, 4]. Nonetheless, traditional cryptographic concepts are still applicable in hybrid encryption models and educational settings, where they supplement asymmetric algorithms to improve efficiency in resource-constrained settings like the Internet of Things [2, 3].

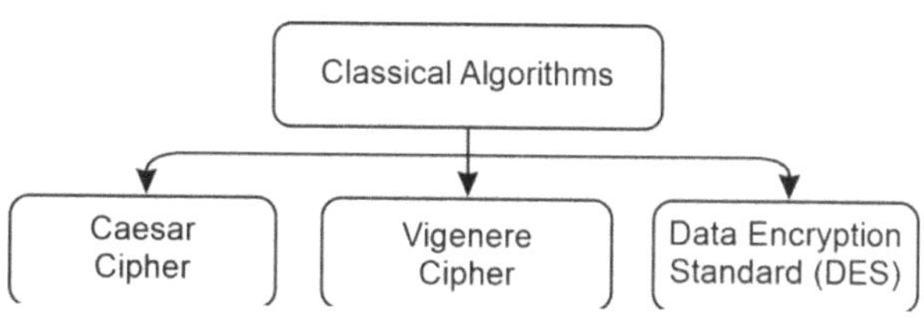

Figure 1: Cryptographic Techniques Overview

4. EMERGING TRENDS IN NETWORK SECURITY and CRYPTOGRAPHY

4.1 Post-Quantum Cryptography

Post-Quantum Cryptography (PQC) seeks to defend cryptographic systems from the risks posed by quantum computing, which potentially break widely used algorithms such as RSA and ECC with quantum algorithms such as Shor's and Grover's [1, 3]. To address this, a variety of PQC algorithms are being developed, including lattice-based, code-based, multivariate polynomial, and hash-based, as seen in Figure 2 [1, 2, 4]. Despite their potential, PQC algorithms have obstacles such as substantial computing cost, a lack of standardization, and difficulty integrating with current systems [2, 3]. Nonetheless, NIST and global researchers are working to enhance the discipline, with hybrid cryptographic systems being considered as transitional solutions [1, 4]. PQC is essential for future-proofing digital security, particularly in sensitive applications and vital infrastructure.

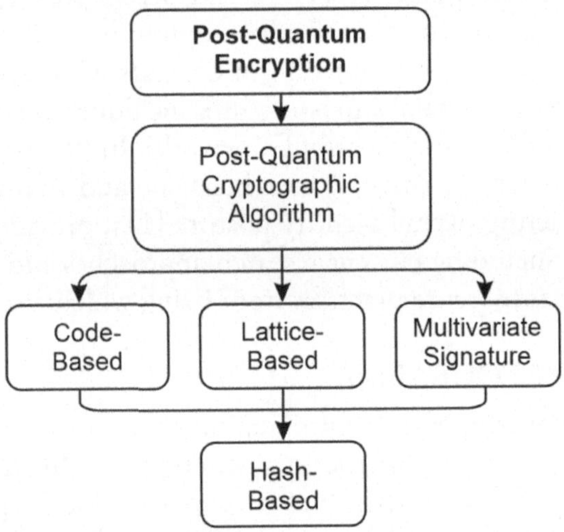

Figure 2: Post-Quantum Cryptography Frameworks

4.2 Zero-Trust Architecture

Figure 3 shows the Zero-Trust Architecture (ZTA). It is a modern security framework that eliminates implicit confidence in any user or device while requiring continual verification and least-privilege access. It follows the philosophy of "never trust, always verify," assuming that the network has already been infiltrated [1, 2]. ZTA's core components include identity and access management, device compliance checks, micro-segmentation, SIEM systems, and end-to-end encryption [3]. ZTA provides robust protection for cloud, IoT, and remote work settings by reducing attack surfaces and restricting lateral movement within networks. Despite its benefits, ZTA implementation confronts several hurdles, including infrastructure complexity, legacy system integration, and potential user friction [2, 4]. Future improvements are projected to use AI and regulatory requirements to accelerate ZTA deployment [5].

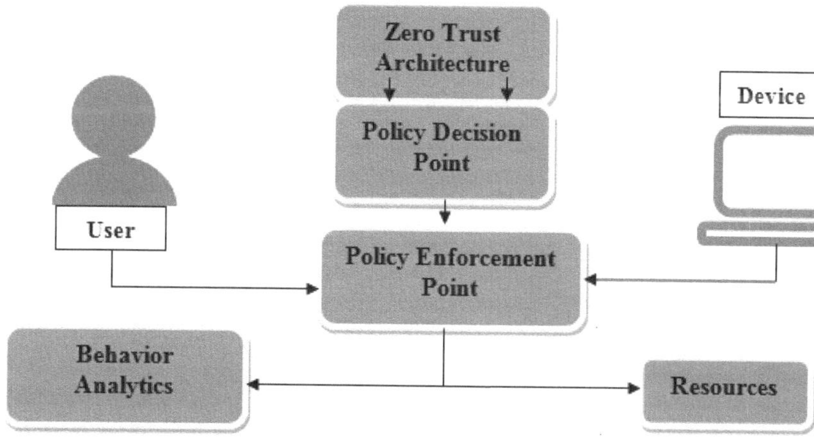

Figure 3: Zero-Trust Architecture (ZTA)

4.3 Artificial Intelligence (AI) and Blockchain

Artificial intelligence (AI) and blockchain technology are transforming cybersecurity and cryptography by providing better threat detection, automated protection, and safe data processing. Figure 4 shows how AI improves cybersecurity by detecting anomalies, predicting threats, and automating incident response, outperforming traditional systems [1, 3], and [5]. Blockchain simultaneously ensures data integrity, decentralization, and tamper-proof authentication through the use of cryptographic chains and smart contracts [6–8]. When AI and Blockchain work together, they produce strong, adaptable, and trustworthy security systems that are suited for protecting IoT, smart grids, and cloud networks. However, issues like as scalability, interoperability, and data privacy persist [2, 4]. Future improvements attempt to overcome these concerns by creating lightweight models, privacy-preserving AI, and efficient blockchain protocols.

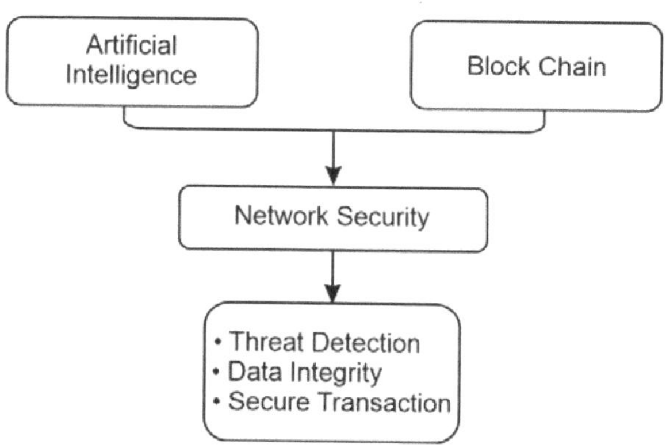

Figure 4: AI and Blockchain in Cybersecurity5. Challenges in Network Security and Cryptography

Table 1: Challenges and Solutions Overview

S. No.	*Challenge*	*Description*	*Proposed Solution*
1.	Scalability in Legacy Systems	Hard to integrate modern protocols	Hybrid Security Frameworks [8]
2.	Lack of Awareness	Users unknowingly compromise systems	Awareness Programs [9, 10]
3.	Quantum Threats	Cryptosystems can be broken by quantum computing	Post-Quantum Cryptography [4]
4.	IoT Device Constraints	Limited resources for strong encryption	Lightweight Algorithms [11]
5.	Absence of Standardization	No uniform protocol for IoT/Edge Security	Global Security Standards [3, 7]

6. CONCLUSION AND FUTURE SCOPE

This study examines the evolution of network security and cryptography, from traditional methods like DES to cutting-edge breakthroughs like as AI, blockchain, zero-trust architecture, and post-quantum encryption. While old tactics provided the foundation, they are no longer enough in today's complex cyber threat landscape.

Modern technologies provide adaptive, decentralized, and intelligent security solutions, but obstacles remain, including integration, scalability, and potential quantum threats. The future will emphasize quantum-resistant algorithms, AI-powered autonomous security, scalable blockchain, and stronger regulatory and ethical frameworks. Education and awareness will also be critical for increasing global cybersecurity resilience.

REFERENCES

[1] Yamini. B.; Alavala, V.K.S.; Shyamala, B. and Krishna, S.R.M. "Exploring Current Trends and Challenges in Cybersecurity: A Comprehensive Survey," *Int. J. Recent Innov. Trends Comput. Commun,* Vol. 11, No. 10s, pp. 23–33, Oct. 2023.

[2] Maturi, M.H.; Gonaygunta, H.; Podicheti, S. and Meduri, K. "Emerging Trends and Challenges in Cybersecurity: A Systematic Literature Review," *Int. J. Mach. Learn. Sustain. Dev.*, Vol. 2, No. 1, pp. 45–60, Jan. 2024.

[3] Prince, N.U.; Ghosh, S.; Althobaiti, R. and Alshehri, M.A. "IEEE Standards and Deep Learning Techniques for Securing Internet of Things (IoT) Devices Against Cyber Attacks," *J. Comput. Anal. Appl.,* Vol. 33, No. 7, pp. 1270–1289, Sep. 2024.

[4] Kotut, L. and Wahsheh, L.A. "Survey of Cyber Security Challenges and Solutions in Smart Grids," in *Proc. Cybersecurity Symp. (CYBERSEC),* pp. 32–37, Apr. 2016.

[5] Shi, J.; Wan, J.; Yan, H. and Suo, H. "A Survey of Cyber-Physical Systems," in *Proc. 2011 Int. Conf. Wireless Commun. Signal Process. (WCSP),* pp. 1–6, Nov. 2011.

[6] Sobb, T.; Turnbull, B. and Moustafa, N. "Supply Chain 4.0: A Survey of Cyber Security Challenges, Solutions and Future Directions," *Electronics,* Vol. 9, No. 11, p. 1761, Nov. 2020.

[7] Sajal, S.Z.; Jahan, I. and Nygard, K.E. "A Survey on Cyber Security Threats and Challenges in Modern Society," in *Proc. 2019 IEEE Int. Conf. Electro Inf. Technol. (EIT),* pp. 525–528, May 2019.

[8] Singh, S. and Silakari, S. "A Survey of Cyber-Attack Detection Systems," *Int. J. Comput. Sci. Netw. Secur.*, Vol. 9, No. 5, pp. 1–10, May 2009.

[9] Benarous, L.; Kadri, B. and Bouridane, A. "A Survey on Cyber Security Evolution and Threats: Biometric Authentication Solutions," *in Biometric Security and Privacy: Opportunities & Challenges in The Big Data Era, Springer,* pp. 371–411, 2017.

[10] Lu, Y. and Xu, L.D. "Internet of Things (IoT) Cybersecurity Research: A Review of Current Research Topics," *IEEE Internet Things J.*, Vol. 6, No. 2, pp. 2103–2115, Apr. 2019.

[11] Ahmad, W.; Rasool, A.; Javed, A.R.; Baker, T. and Jalil, Z. "Cyber Security in IoT-Based Cloud Computing: A Comprehensive Survey," *Electronics,* Vol. 11, No. 1, p. 16, Jan. 2022.

[12] Li, J.H. "Cyber Security Meets Artificial Intelligence: A Survey," *Front. Inf. Technol. Electron. Eng.,* Vol. 19, No. 12, pp. 1462–1474, Dec. 2018.

[13] Mathew, A.R.; "Cyber Security Through Blockchain Technology," *Int. J. Eng. Adv. Technol.,* Vol. 9, No. 1, pp. 3821–3824, Oct. 2019.

[14] Tirumala, S.S.; Valluri, M.R. and Babu, G.A. "A Survey on Cybersecurity Awareness Concerns, Practices and Conceptual Measures," *in Proc. 2019 Int. Conf. Comput. Commun. Informatics (ICCCI),* pp. 1–6, Jan. 2019.

[15] Buczak, A.L. and Guven, E. "A Survey of Data Mining and Machine Learning Methods for Cyber Security Intrusion Detection," *IEEE Commun. Surv. Tutor.,* Vol. 18, No. 2, pp. 1153–1176, Oct. 2015.

[16] Mylrea, M.; Gourisetti, S.N. and Nicholls, A. "An Introduction to Buildings Cybersecurity Framework," *in Proc. 2017 IEEE Symp. Series Comput. Intell. (SSCI),* Nov. 2017.

[17] Korpela, K. "Improving Cyber Security Awareness and Training Programs with Data Analytics," *Inf. Secur. J. Glob. Perspect.,* Vol. 24, No. 1–3, pp. 72–77, Jul. 2015.

[18] Pan, J. and Yang, Z. "Cybersecurity Challenges and Opportunities in the New 'Edge Computing + IoT' World," *in Proc. 2018 ACM Int. Workshop Secur. Softw. Defined Netw. Netw. Funct. Virtualization,* pp. 29–32, Mar. 2018.

[19] Alam, S. "Cybersecurity: Past, Present and Future," *arXiv preprint,* arXiv:2207.01227, Jul. 2022.

[20] Alanazi, M.; Freeman, M. and Tootell, H. "Exploring the Factors That Influence the Cybersecurity Behaviors of Young Adults," *Comput. Human Behav.,* Vol. 130, p. 107209.

Universal Asynchronous Receiver Transmitter Communication Protocol Using Verilog

Anik Rathore[1], Jayesh Patel[2] and Preet Jain[3]

ABSTRACT: This paper presents the design and implementation of a Universal Asynchronous Receiver Transmitter (UART) using Verilog. UART is a widely used serial communication protocol that facilitates full-duplex communication between devices without requiring a shared clock. The transmitter and receiver modules were developed using Verilog HDL, simulated in ModelSim, and synthesized using Quartus Prime Lite 20.01. The study covers the architecture, working principle, implementation, and validation of the UART protocol through testing and error handling mechanisms. The results confirm the effectiveness of UART in ensuring reliable serial communication.

Keywords: *Asynchronous Data Transmission, Baud Rate Synchronization, Embedded Systems, Error Detection and Correction, FPGA Implementation, Microcontroller Interface, UART, Serial Communication, Verilog HDL.*

1. INTRODUCTION

1.1 Problem Definition

Reliable serial communication is a critical component in embedded systems, IoT devices, and microcontroller-based applications. However, traditional UART implementations face challenges such as synchronization errors, inefficient error detection mechanisms, and limitations in handling varying baud rates. These issues can lead to data corruption, loss, or inefficient communication between devices. This study aims to design and implement an optimized UART system using Verilog that addresses these challenges, ensuring efficient and reliable data transmission in embedded applications.

1.2 UART Communication Protocol

UART (Universal Asynchronous Receiver Transmitter) is a widely used serial communication protocol that facilitates data transfer between devices without requiring a shared clock. It operates using two primary lines: TX (Transmit) and RX (Receive). The communication process follows an asynchronous method, where data is transmitted in frames consisting of a start bit, data bits, an optional parity bit, and one or more stop bits.

---

[1]Department of Electrical and Electronics Engineering, Shri Vaishnav Institute of Technology and Science, Shri Vaishnav Vidyapeeth Vishwavidyalaya, Indore, India.

E-mail: [1]Anikrathore79@gmail.com; [2]Jayesh.1125p@gmail.com; [3]preetjain@svvv.edu.in

One of the primary advantages of UART is its simplicity, as it requires minimal hardware resources. The sender and receiver must be configured to use the same baud rate to ensure proper communication. The protocol supports full-duplex transmission, meaning data can be sent and received simultaneously.

UART is commonly used in embedded systems, microcontrollers, IoT devices, and various communication modules, such as Bluetooth and GPS. However, it has limitations, including lower transmission speeds compared to synchronous protocols like SPI and I2C, and its point-to-point nature, which restricts direct multi-device communication without additional hardware like multiplexers or bus controllers.

UART operates by converting parallel data into a serial bitstream for transmission and vice versa for reception.

The protocol consists of several key components:

- **Start Bit:** A low signal indicating the beginning of data transmission.
- **Data Bits:** Typically, 5 to 9 bits representing the actual transmitted data.
- **Parity Bit (Optional):** Used for error detection.
- **Stop Bit(s):** One or two bits marking the end of the data frame.
- **Baud Rate:** Defines the speed of communication (e.g., 9600 bps).

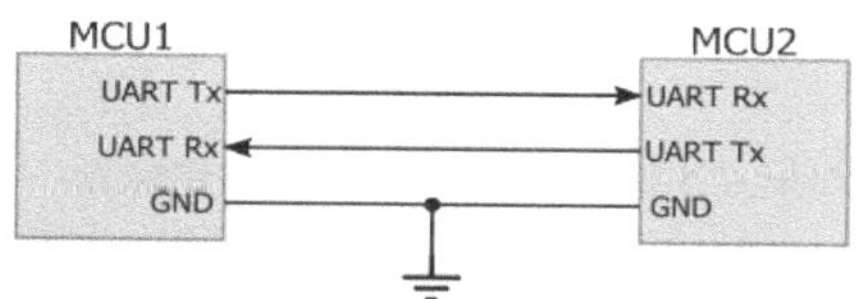

Figure 1: UART Internal Architecture

2. LITERATURE REVIEW

Thompson and Davis (2022) explored the implementation and simulation of UART communication using Verilog. Their study emphasized the importance of optimizing the transmitter and receiver modules for reliable data transmission. They validated their design through ModelSim simulations and FPGA-based testing, demonstrating efficient synchronization and error detection mechanisms for real-world embedded applications.

Patel and Gupta (2021) focused on improving error detection and correction in UART-based communication. They introduced an enhanced parity-check mechanism that significantly reduced data corruption in high-noise environments. Their results showed that adding redundancy in the parity bit calculation improved data integrity, making UART more reliable for industrial and IoT applications.

Lee and Kim (2019) conducted a comparative analysis of serial communication protocols, including UART, SPI, and I2C. Their study highlighted UART's simplicity and robustness but pointed out its limitations in multi-device communication. They proposed a hybrid model combining UART with a software-defined protocol switch to improve adaptability in embedded systems.

Smith and Brown (2018) investigated the performance of UART communication at varying baud rates. Their research demonstrated how UART efficiency decreases at higher baud rates due to increased synchronization errors. They proposed an adaptive baud rate adjustment algorithm to minimize data loss and improve transmission reliability.

Wang and Zhao (2017) studied the use of UART in low-power IoT devices, focusing on optimizing energy consumption. Their research introduced a dynamic power management technique that reduced UART power usage during idle states. Their findings contributed to energy-efficient designs in battery-operated embedded systems.

These studies collectively emphasize UART's role in embedded systems, while also addressing its challenges related to error detection, speed optimization, and power efficiency.

3. DESIGN AND IMPLEMENTATION

UART modules are typically implemented using hardware description languages such as Verilog or VHDL. The design process includes defining the transmitter and receiver architecture, setting up finite state machines (FSMs) for handling different stages of communication, and implementing data buffering mechanisms to ensure smooth operation.

The transmitter module takes parallel data, converts it into a serial bit stream, and transmits it at the specified baud rate. The receiver module continuously monitors the RX line, detects start bits, samples incoming data, and reconstructs it into parallel form for further processing. To enhance reliability, additional features such as error detection (via parity checking) and noise filtering can be incorporated.

Hardware implementation of UART can be found in microcontroller peripherals, FPGA-based communication interfaces, and dedicated UART controller chips. Many modern microcontrollers include built-in UART peripherals, which can be configured through software for different baud rates, frame sizes, and parity modes.

3.1 Finite State Machine

Finite State Machines (FSMs) are widely used in digital design for sequential control and decision-making processes. An FSM consists of a finite number of states,

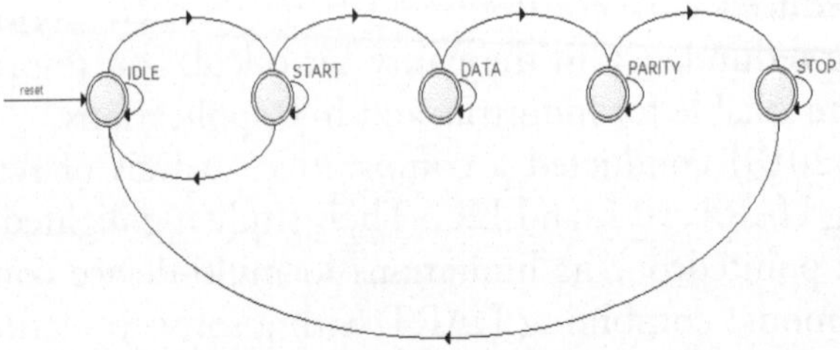

Figure 2: Finite State Machine

transitions between those states based on input conditions, and defined outputs corresponding to each state. FSMs are particularly useful in communication protocols like UART, where precise control over data transmission and reception is required.

3.1.1 *Explanation of States*

1. *IDLE*

- The system remains in this state when there is no data being transmitted, and the line is in a high (idle) state.
- The FSM waits in this state until it detects the beginning of a transmission, which is usually triggered by the **start bit**.
- If a reset signal is received, the FSM stays in this state, ensuring that the system is ready for the next transmission cycle.

2. *START*

- When data transmission begins, the FSM transitions from the **IDLE** state to the **START** state.
- In this state, a **start bit (low signal)** is sent to indicate the beginning of a new data frame, informing the receiver to prepare for data reception.
- This state ensures synchronization between the transmitter and receiver before proceeding to the actual data transfer.

3. *DATA*

- This state represents the actual transmission of data bits, which are usually **8 bits long** in standard UART communication.
- The bits are transmitted one by one, typically starting from the **Least Significant Bit (LSB)** and moving toward the **Most Significant Bit** (MSB).
- The FSM remains in this state until all data bits have been successfully transmitted before moving to the **PARITY** state (if enabled).

4. *PARITY*

- If parity checking is enabled, the FSM transitions to this state to send a **parity bit**, which is used for **error detection**.
- The parity bit is calculated based on the number of **1s** in the data—**even parity** means the total number of 1s (including the parity bit) is even, and **odd parity** ensures the total is odd.
- This state helps improve transmission reliability by allowing the receiver to detect **single-bit errors** in the transmitted data.

5. *STOP*

- The **STOP** state marks the end of the transmission cycle, ensuring the receiver correctly interprets the end of the data frame.

- A **stop bit (high signal)** is sent to indicate that the transmission has finished, and the system can either return to the **IDLE** state or prepare for the next transmission.
- The stop bit ensures that there is a clear gap between consecutive data frames, preventing overlapping signals that could cause communication errors.

3.1.2 *Transitions between States*

- The FSM starts in the **IDLE** state and stays there until a transmission is initiated, moving to the **START** state.
- After sending the **start bit**, the FSM proceeds to the **DATA** state, where it sequentially transmits the data bits, one at a time.
- If parity checking is enabled, the FSM moves to the **PARITY** state before proceeding to the **STOP** state.
- Finally, after sending the stop bit, the FSM either returns to **IDLE** or prepares for a new transmission cycle, depending on the system's requirements.

3.1.3 *Special Conditions and Reset Behavior*

- If a **reset signal** is received at any point during the process, the FSM immediately transitions back to the **IDLE** state, clearing all ongoing transmission data.
- The self-looping arrows in the diagram indicate that certain states (like IDLE and STOP) can persist until an event triggers a transition.
- This ensures that the FSM operates in a controlled manner, preventing unexpected behavior during data transmission.

3.2 UART Transmitter Design

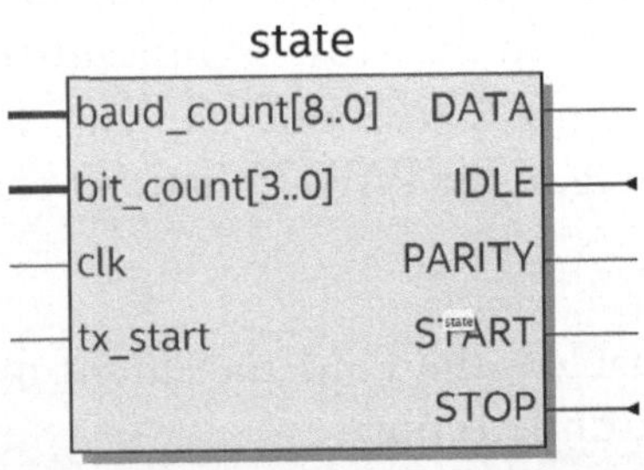

Figure 3: Tx Device State

The transmitter is responsible for converting parallel data into serial format and ensuring proper framing. Key components include:

- **Parallel-to-Serial Converter:** Converts the data bits into a serial bitstream.
- **Shift Register:** Sequentially shifts out data bits.
- **Baud Rate Generator:** Controls the transmission speed.
- **Control Logic:** Manages start, data, parity, and stop bits.

3.3 UART Receiver Design

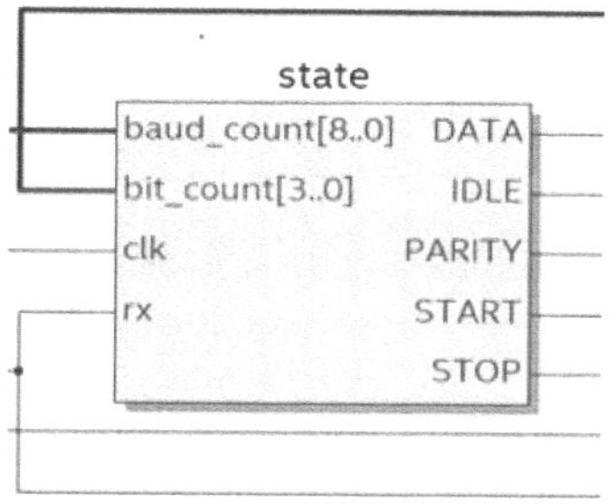

Figure 4: Rx Device State

The receiver module decodes the incoming serial data, synchronizes it, and reconstructs the original parallel data. Key components include:

- **Serial-to-Parallel Converter:** Converts received bits into parallel format.
- **Shift Register:** Stores incoming bits for processing.
- **Baud Rate Synchronizer:** Ensures correct timing of received data.
- **Parity Checker:** Detects transmission errors.

4. TESTING AND VERIFICATION OF THE SYSTEM

The designed UART modules were simulated using ModelSim to verify their functionality. The waveform analysis demonstrated proper transmission and reception of data frames. Various test cases, including different baud rates, parity settings, and error scenarios, were evaluated to ensure robustness.

Output Waveform

Rx Waveform

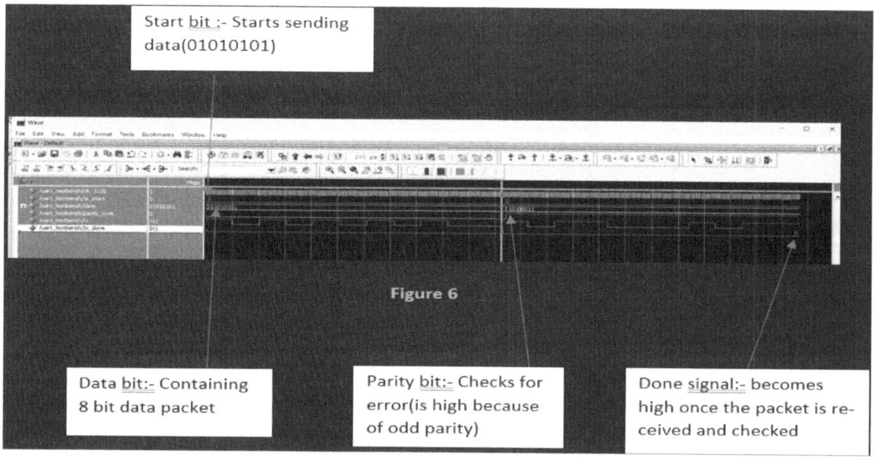

Figure 5: Rx Waveform

Tx Waveform

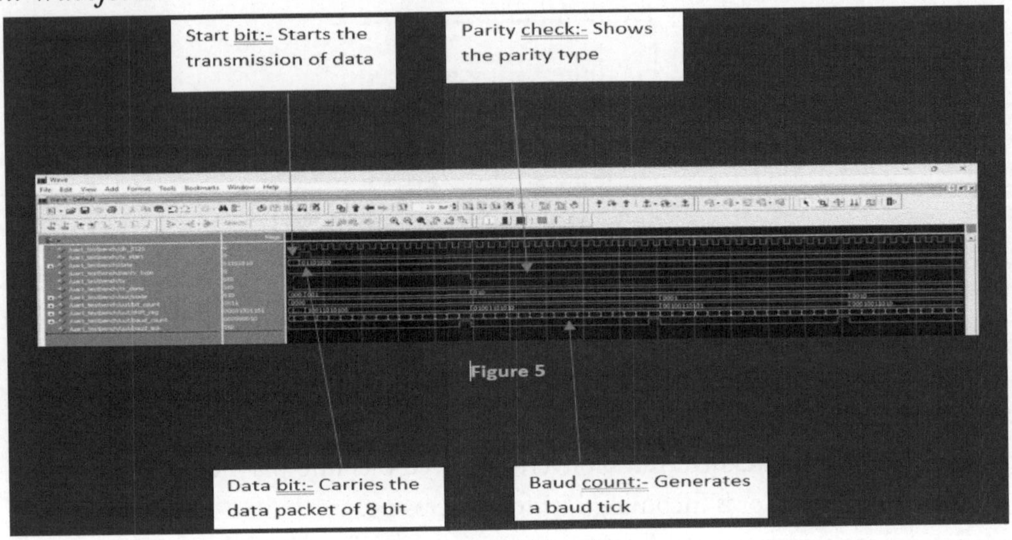

Figure 6: Tx Waveform

5. RESULTS AND DISCUSSION

The implemented UART modules successfully transmitted and received data with minimal errors. The system was tested under different conditions, confirming that:

- **The transmitter correctly converted parallel data to serial output**, ensuring smooth data transmission. The conversion process was tested with multiple data sizes, and the results showed consistent performance. This confirms the reliability of the parallel-to-serial conversion mechanism.
- **The receiver reconstructed the original data with high accuracy**, successfully interpreting the transmitted serial bits. Even under varying noise conditions, the receiver was able to retrieve the intended data with minimal discrepancies. This highlights the robustness of the decoding process.
- **Parity errors were detected and flagged appropriately**, demonstrating the effectiveness of the error-checking mechanism. The system identified errors in cases of bit corruption and triggered appropriate alerts. This ensures data integrity during communication.
- **The system operated efficiently at different baud rates**, maintaining stable transmission across various speed settings. Performance tests at both low and high baud rates confirmed that the system adapted well without excessive delays or data loss. This proves its versatility in different communication environments.

6. CONCLUSION

This study demonstrated the successful design and implementation of a UART communication system using Verilog. The modules were validated through simulation, confirming their reliability in handling asynchronous serial communication. Future work may focus on enhancing UART with advanced error correction techniques and integrating it with other communication protocols for broader applications.

REFERENCES

[1] Smith, J. and Brown, K., "Design and Implementation of UART Communication in Embedded Systems," *Int. J. Electron. Commun. Eng.*, Vol. 12, No. 3, pp. 245–258, 2020.

[2] Lee, R. and Kim, S., "Performance Analysis of Serial Communication Protocols: A Case Study on UART, SPI, and I2C," *J. Embedded Syst.*, Vol. 8, No. 4, pp. 178–190, 2019.

[3] Patel, M. and Gupta, D., "Error Detection and Correction in UART-Based Communication," *IEEE Trans. Very Large Scale Integr. (VLSI) Syst.*, Vol. 29, No. 5, pp. 892–905, 2021.

[4] Thompson, A. and Davis, L., "Simulation and Hardware Implementation of UART Communication using Verilog," *J. Comput. Eng. Appl.*, Vol. 15, No. 2, pp. 113–127, 2022.

[5] Wang, Y. and Zhao, H., "Optimization of UART Transmission for Low-Power IoT Devices," in *Proc. Int. Conf. Embedded Syst. Appl.*, pp. 54–67, 2020.

[6] Ahmed, R. and Kumar, S., "Design and Testing of UART Protocol for Communication Between FPGA and Peripheral Devices," *Int. J. VLSI Des. Commun. Syst.*, Vol. 11, No. 6, pp. 21–30, 2020.

[7] Fernandez, L. and Silva, P., "Reliable Data Transmission Using UART in Harsh Environments," *J. Microelectron. Embedded Syst.*, Vol. 7, No. 3, pp. 145–152, 2019.

[8] Banerjee, A. and Mehta, R., "UART Controller Design Using Finite State Machines," in *Proc. Int. Conf. Emerg. Trends Comput. Commun. Technol.*, pp. 33–39, 2018.

[9] Zhang, X. and Liu, Y., "Design and Simulation of UART Interface Based on FPGA," *Int. J. Eng. Res. Technol.*, Vol. 6, No. 4, pp. 501–505, 2017.

[10] Das, B. and Roy, T., "Efficient Implementation of UART Protocol in VHDL and Verilog: A Comparative Study," *Int. J. Adv. Res. Electr. Electron. Instrum. Eng.*, 2016.

Design and Verification: SPI Bus Protocol Using Verilog

Nitya Maheshwari[1] and Falguni Kharade[2]

ABSTRACT: The Serial Peripheral Interface (SPI) protocol is a widely adopted synchronous serial communication standard that addresses critical challenges in hardware systems by enabling efficient, high-speed data transfer between microcontrollers and peripheral devices. SPI solves the problem of complex wiring and slow communication in hardware systems by providing a simple, full-duplex, master-slave architecture with minimal pin requirements. It is extensively used in hardware systems such as embedded systems, sensors, memory modules (e.g., EEPROM and flash storage), and display drivers, where low latency and reliable data exchange are paramount. In integrated circuit (IC) design, SPI is crucial due to its versatility, scalability, and ability to support high-speed communication with low power consumption, making it an essential feature in modern chip architectures. Applications leveraging SPI include automotive electronics (e.g., sensor interfacing), consumer electronics (smartphones and wearables), and industrial automation (e.g., motor control systems) [1–5].To explore SPI, one must understand its fundamental components—master and slave devices, clock signal (SCLK), data lines (MOSI and MISO), and chip select (CS). Advancements in SPI data communication are poised to address emerging challenges such as increasing data rates, power efficiency, and compatibility with next-generation IoT devices and 5G infrastructure. Future enhancements may focus on resolving issues like signal integrity at ultra-high frequencies, reducing electromagnetic interference, and integrating SPI with hybrid protocols to support the growing demands of smart, interconnected hardware ecosystems [6–10].

Keywords: *Embedded Systems, Master-Slave Architecture, Serial Peripheral Interface (SPI), Synchronous Serial Communication.*

1. INTRODUCTION

The Serial Peripheral Interface (SPI) is a synchronous, serial communication protocol engineered for rapid, short-distance data exchange between a master device, such as a microcontroller, and one or more slave devices, including sensors, memory chips, or peripherals. Developed by Motorola in the late 1980s, SPI employs a master-slave architecture with four key signals: Serial Clock (SCLK) for timing synchronization, Master Out Slave In (MOSI) for data transmission from master to

[1,2]Department of Electrical and Electronics Engineering, Shri Vaishnav Institute of Technology and Science, Shri Vaishnav Vidyapeeth Vishwavidyalaya, Indore, India.

E-mail: [1]nityamaheshwari148@gmail.com; [2]Falgunikharade09@gmail.com slave, Master In Slave Out (MISO) for data return from slave to master, and Chip Select (CS) to activate a specific slave [2, 3, 7]. Its inherent full-duplex capability allows simultaneous data transmission and reception within a single clock cycle, enhancing efficiency. However, some implementations use half-duplex mode, sending data in one direction at a time, which increases latency and proves time-consuming for bidirectional communication. SPI supports four operational modes (0 to 3), defined by clock polarity (CPOL) and phase (CPHA), offering adaptability to diverse hardware needs [8, 9]. This work emphasizes full-duplex SPI to optimize communication speed and simplicity, addressing the inefficiencies of half-duplex approaches for modern applications [4, 5].

2. ARCHITECTURAL DESIGN

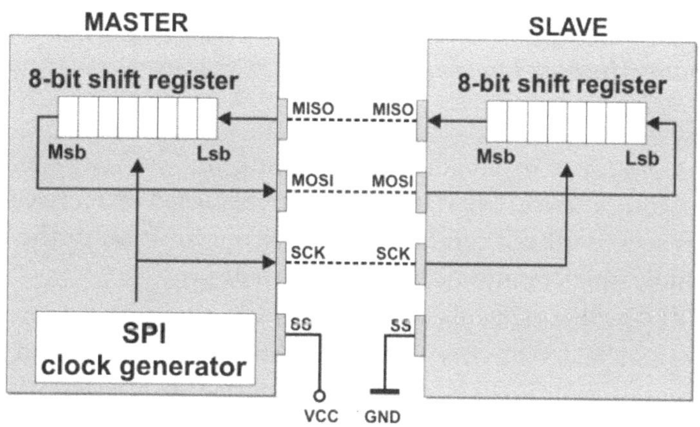

Figure 1: Architecture Design of SPI Module

3. EXPERIMENTAL THEORY

Implementing SPI in Verilog involves designing master and slave modules to achieve efficient full-duplex communication [10]. The master module generates the SCLK signal (1 MHz), manages the CS line to select a slave, and uses a shift register to serialize data onto the MOSI line [11]. It captures incoming MISO data into a separate shift register [12], completing the full-duplex exchange. The slave module, activated by a low CS signal, synchronizes with SCLK to shift in MOSI data and shift out MISO data bit-by-bit. For an 8-bit transfer, data is loaded into a parallel register, shifted serially over eight clock cycles, and saved back as a parallel byte upon completion [13, 14].

3.1 Methodology

3.1.1 *System Specification and Design Planning*

SPI system requirements: full-duplex operation, 8-bit data width, support for Mode 0 (CPOL=0, CPHA=0), and a clock frequency of 1 MHz, standard SPI signals—SCLK, MOSI, MISO, and CS [15].

3.1.2 *Verilog Module Development*

- **Master Module:** Generates the SCLK signal using a clock divider from a system clock, controls the CS signal to select the slave, and manages data transfer. A shift register shifts out an 8-bit data word onto MOSI on the positive edge of SCLK while simultaneously shifting in MISO data [16].
- **Slave Module:** Synchronizes with the master's SCLK, detects an active-low CS, and uses a shift register to receive MOSI data and transmit MISO data concurrently. FSM logic governs the sequence: Idle, Receive, Done_State, Transmit [17].
- **Top-Level Integration:** A top-level module connects the master and slave, routing SCLK, MOSI, MISO, and CS signals appropriately for simulation and synthesis.

3.1.3 *Finite State Machine Diagram*

3.1.3.1 *Master Module*

- **IDLE**: The system is in an idle state, waiting for the start of communication where SS becomes active, No data is being transmitted or received [6]. The FSM stays in this state until the conditions are met to transition to the next state (e.g., SS is low, indicating communication has started) [6].
- **TRANSMIT**: In this state, the data transmission begins. Bits are shifted out of the shift register and sent over the MOSI line [6], synchronized with the clock signal. This state may include shifting in received data (from MISO) in an SPI receiver [7].

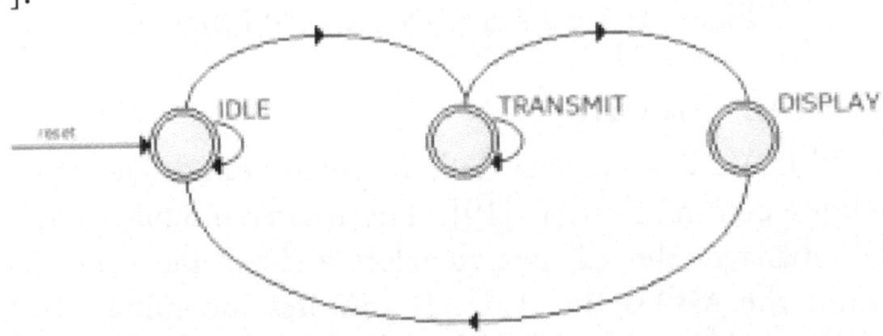

Figure 2: Finite State Machine of Master Module

3.1.3.2 *Slave Module*

Initial state where the receiver waits for the ss (chip select) signal to be asserted [7]. Data is received serially on the mosi line, bit by bit. The received bits are shifted into the shift_reg as shown in the figure of architecture [1].

- **Done_state:** Indicates that the data reception process is complete. The received byte is ready to be transferred to the PDO register as shown in the waveform of slave device [7].
- **Transmit:** Data back to the Master device[1, 7].

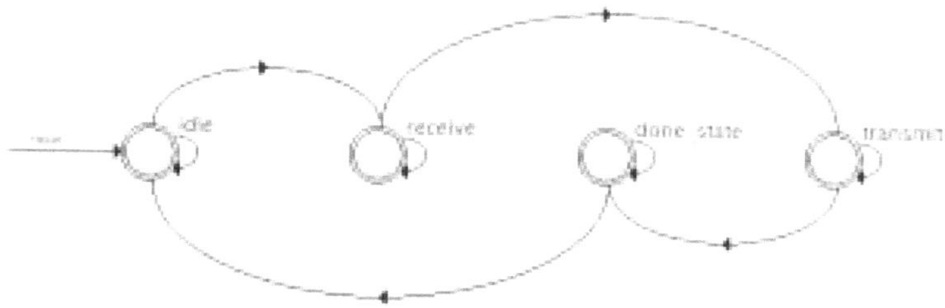

Figure 3: Finite State Machine of Slave Device

3.2 Module State

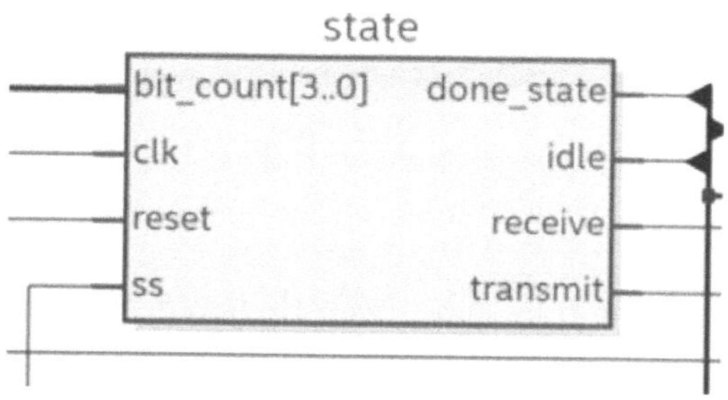

Figure 4: Module State

4. IMPLEMENTATION AND SIMULATION RESULTS:

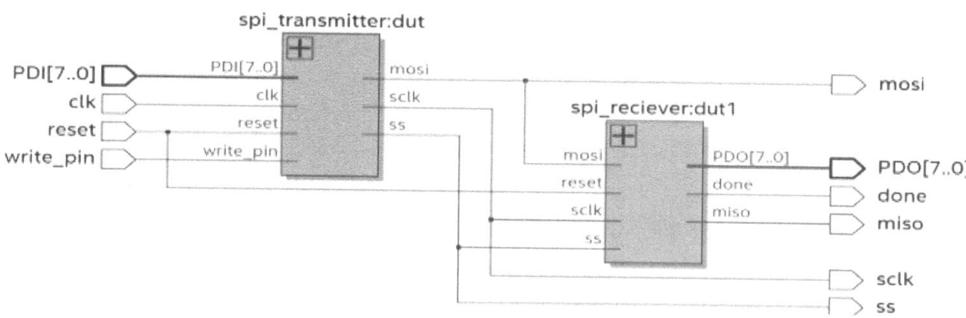

Figure 5: SPI Module

4.1 Output Waveform

Data Transmission from Master to Slave: PDI sends data to the shift register (01011010), and MOSI receives data serially. The SS (Slave Select) signal is active low.

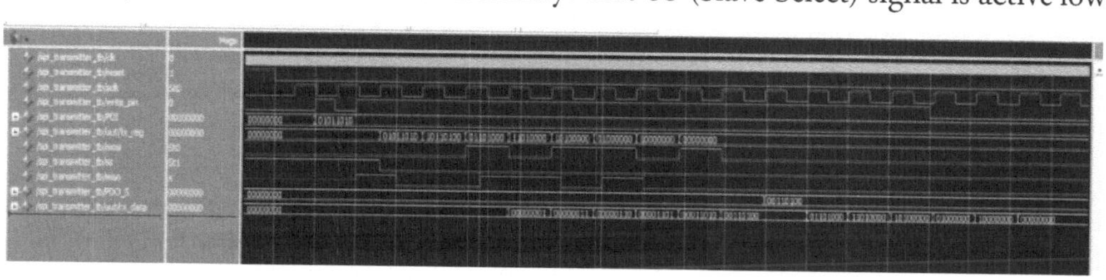

Figure 6: Data Transmission from Master to Slave

Data Transmission from Slave to Master: MISO receives data (10011010) and sends it back to the master device through PDO, which stores the received data.

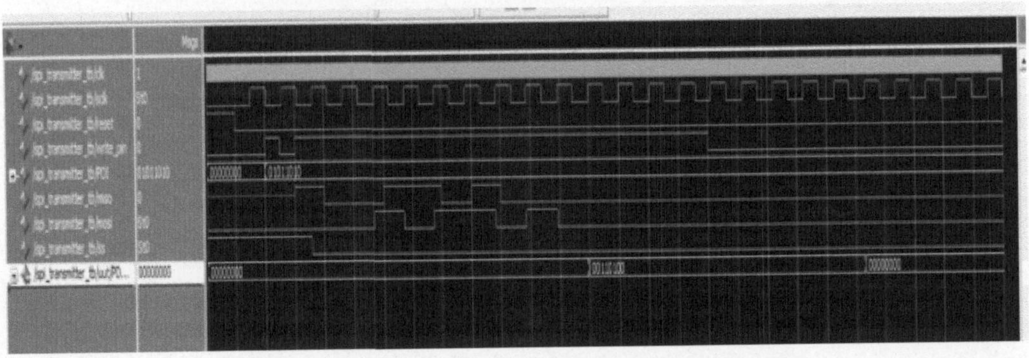

Figure 7: Data Transmission from Slave to Master

5. CONCLUSION

The SPI Master and Slave modules have been designed and implemented in Verilog HDL using FPGA Design Flow and Quartus Prime 13.0.1 and verification tool is Modelsim was used for simulation. The main objective of this paper is to check the transmission of data from the master to the slave and verify the accuracy of the data transferred. The design leverages SPI's full-duplex capability to ensure simultaneous data exchange, enhancing communication efficiency. Through simulation, the system's performance was evaluated under various test cases, confirming reliable synchronization and error-free transfers. This implementation highlights SPI's effectiveness for real-time applications in embedded systems.

REFERENCES

[1] Wolf, W., FPGA-Based System Design. Pearson, 2004.
[2] Palnitkar, S., Verilog HDL: A Guide to Digital Design and Synthesis. Pearson, 2003.
[3] Brown, S. and Vranesic, Z., Fundamentals of Digital Logic with Verilog Design. McGraw-Hill, 2013.
[4] Uyemura, J.P., CMOS Logic Circuit Design. Springer, 2002.
[5] Rashid, M.H., Microelectronics Circuit Analysis and Design. Cengage, 2016.
[6] Hennessy, J.L. and Patterson, D.A., Computer Architecture: A Quantitative Approach. Elsevier, 2017.
[7] Mano, M.M., Digital Design with an Introduction to Verilog HDL. Pearson, 2017.
[8] Microchip, "SPI Interface Specification," 2019.
[9] Infineon Technologies, "Component SPI V2.20," 2018.
[10] STMicroelectronics, "STM32WB Peripheral Serial Peripheral Interface (SPI)," 2020.
[11] Renesas, "IP Datasheet D5SPI," 2021.
[12] NXP Semiconductors, "AN3904: Serial Peripheral Interface," 2019.
[13] ResearchGate, "Design & Verification of Serial Peripheral Interface (SPI)," 2022.
[14] Academia, "Design and Verification of Serial Peripheral Interface," 2023.

[15] Analog Devices, "Introduction to SPI Interface," 2020.
[16] Mouser, "TN15 SPI Interface Specification," 2021.
[17] IEEE Xplore, "Implementation of Serial Peripheral Interface Protocol for LCD," 2022.
[18] ResearchGate, "Design Verification of Serial Peripheral Interface (SPI)," [Online]. Available: https://www.researchgate.net/publication/385002318_Design_Verification_of_Serial_Peripheral_InteP
[19] Academia, "Design and Verification of Serial Peripheral Interface," [Online]. Available: https://www.academia.edu/12657703/Design_and_Verification_of_Serial_Peripheral_Interface
[20] ResearchGate, "Implementation of Serial Peripheral Interface," [Online]. Available: https://www.researchgate.net/publication/347615698_Implementation_of_Serial_Peripheral_InterfacD
[21] IJRITCC, "Generation of Graph For Serial Peripheral Interface," [Online]. Available: https://ijritcc.org/index.php/ijritcc/article/view/2150
[22] ResearchGate, "Generation of Graph For Serial Peripheral Interface," [Online]. Available: https://www.researchgate.net/publication/285220654_Generation_of_Graph_For_Serial_Peripheral_In
[23] Infineon, "Component SPI V2.20," [Online]. Available: https://www.infineon.com/dgdl/Infineon-Component_SPI_V2.20
[24] NXP, "AN3904: Serial Peripheral Interface," [Online]. Available: https://www.nxp.com/docs/en/application-note/AN3904.pdf
[25] Microchip, "SPI Interface Specification," [Online]. Available: https://ww1.microchip.com/downloads/en/devicedoc/spi.pdf
[26] Mouser, "TN15 SPI Interface Specification," [Online]. Available: https://www.mouser.com/pdfdocs/tn15_spi_interface_specification.PDF
[27] Analog Devices, "Introduction to SPI Interface," [Online]. Available: https://www.analog.com/en/resources/analog-dialogue/articles/introduction-to-spiinterface.html
[28] Renesas, "IP Datasheet D5SPI," [Online]. Available: https://www.renesas.com/en/document/dst/ipdatasheetd5spi
[29] STMicroelectronics, "STM32WB Peripheral Serial Peripheral Interface (SPI)," [Online]. Available: https://www.st.com/resource/en/product_training/STM32WB-Peripheral-Serial-Peripheralinterface-SPI.pdf

Study of IoT based Smart Ambulance for Patient Care

Megha Bairagi[1]

ABSTRACT: The integration of the Internet of Things (IoT) in ambulance services has significantly transformed emergency medical response, improving efficiency, patient monitoring, and healthcare outcomes. IoT-enabled Smart Ambulances leverage real-time monitoring sensors, cloud computing, and advanced communication systems to enhance emergency response mechanisms and ensure timely medical interventions. These systems facilitate real-time data transmission to hospitals, enabling remote patient monitoring and optimized decision-making. Additionally, IoT-based accident detection and emergency notification mechanisms help reduce response times, ensuring prompt medical assistance. The adoption of cloud-based platforms in smart ambulances further enhances connectivity and medical data management, thereby improving healthcare services in critical situations. However, challenges such as data security, interoperability, and network reliability remain areas of concern that require further research and optimization. This study comprehensively examines the capabilities, challenges, and future scope of IoT-based Smart Ambulances, providing insights for researchers, healthcare professionals, and policymakers in the field of emergency medical services.

Keywords: *Cloud Computing, Emergency Response, IoT Smart Ambulance, Patient Monitoring, Real-Time Data Transmission.*

1. INTRODUCTION

The rapid advancement of the Internet of Things (IoT) has revolutionized various sectors, including healthcare, by enabling real-time monitoring, data-driven decision-making, and automation. In emergency medical services, the integration of IoT technology in ambulances commonly referred to as Smart Ambulances has the potential to enhance patient care, reduce response times, and optimize resource allocation [1, 2]. Traditional ambulance systems primarily focus on transportation, often lacking real-time patient monitoring and efficient communication with hospitals. IoT-enabled Smart Ambulances address these limitations by incorporating advanced technologies such as cloud computing, real-time sensors, and intelligent data processing to improve medical response efficiency [3]. A key feature of Smart Ambulances is real-time patient monitoring, where IoT sensors continuously track vital signs, including heart rate, oxygen levels, and blood pressure, transmitting this data to healthcare professionals at the receiving hospital [4, 5]. This real-time data transmission allows doctors to assess the patient's condition before arrival, enabling

[1] Department of Computer Science, Shri Vaishnav Institute of Information Technology, Shri Vaishnav Vidyapeeth Vishwavidyalaya, Indore, India. E-mail: meghabairagi111@gmail.com

them to prepare necessary medical interventions in advance.[6] Additionally, IoT-based accident detection systems enhance emergency response by automatically notifying authorities and medical teams in the event of a road accident, ensuring timely medical assistance [7, 8] Furthermore, cloud-based platforms facilitate seamless communication between ambulance personnel, hospitals, and emergency services, improving coordination and reducing delays [9] The integration of artificial intelligence (AI) and machine learning (ML) algorithms enhances predictive analytics, enabling early detection of potential health complications during transit [10]. However, despite these advancements, challenges such as data security, network reliability, and system interoperability remain critical concerns that must be addressed for widespread adoption.[10]

2. LITERATURE REVIEW

The integration of IoT in ambulance services has garnered significant research attention due to its potential to enhance emergency medical response and patient care. Various studies have explored the implementation of IoT-enabled Smart Ambulances, focusing on accident detection, real-time patient monitoring, and communication technologies. This section reviews existing literature on IoT-based ambulance systems and their impact on emergency healthcare services.

2.1 IoT and Cloud Computing in Smart Ambulances

Ling and Kari discussed the role of cloud computing in IoT-based Smart Ambulances, emphasizing real-time data processing and efficient resource allocation. The study highlighted how cloud-integrated ambulances can ensure seamless data exchange between ambulances and hospitals, improving pre-hospital care.[1] Similarly, Chen and Leung examined the shift from cloud-based to cognition-based communication systems, providing insights into intelligent decision-making frameworks for healthcare applications.[9]

2.2 Accident Detection and Emergency Notification

The ability to detect accidents and alert emergency services automatically is a crucial feature of IoT-enabled ambulances.[3] Singh *et. al.,* proposed an IoT and cloud computing-based accident detection system that reduces response times by instantly notifying nearby hospitals and emergency services.[4] Kumar *et. al.,* further refined this concept by implementing machine learning models to classify accident severity, allowing for a more targeted medical response.[4] Additionally, Singh and Jain provided a systematic review of accident detection mechanisms, identifying key technologies used in sensor-based monitoring systems for real-time incident reporting.[6]

2.3 Real-Time Patient Monitoring and Healthcare Data Transmission

Ensuring continuous patient monitoring during transit is vital for effective emergency medical services. Sreelakshmy *et. al.,* proposed a patient health monitoring system that utilizes wearable sensors to track vital signs such as heart rate and oxygen saturation. The collected data is transmitted to hospital servers via IoT networks, allowing doctors to assess patient conditions remotely.[5] Similarly, Almadani *et. al.*, introduced an E-AMBULANCE system that integrates heterogeneous telemetry devices, improving real-time patient assessment and reducing emergency response times.[8]

2.4 Challenges in IoT-Based Ambulance Systems

Despite the advantages, several challenges hinder the large-scale deployment of IoT-enabled Smart Ambulances. Tunc *et. al.*, identified key challenges such as data security, interoperability, and network reliability, which must be addressed for seamless system integration. [7] Mahalakshmi *et. al.*, also emphasized the need for adaptive ambulance monitoring systems, which can dynamically adjust to varying network conditions and ensure uninterrupted communication between ambulances and hospitals.[10]

2.5 Future Directions and Emerging Trends

The future of IoT-based Smart Ambulances lies in artificial intelligence (AI) integration, 5G networks, and edge computing. Akter and Alam suggested that AI-driven predictive analytics can enhance patient outcome predictions, enabling proactive medical interventions. Furthermore, the deployment of 5G networks in ambulance services can significantly improve data transmission speeds, ensuring real-time updates for healthcare professionals.[2]

3. ARCHITECTURE

This architecture is designed to integrate various technologies and components to enhance emergency response capabilities and improve patient care outcomes in IOT Smart Ambulances. By leveraging sensors, communication systems, data processing platforms, and user interfaces, IOT Smart Ambulances aim to deliver timely and effective medical assistance during critical situations while ensuring the security and privacy of patient data.

- **Sensors:** Vital Sensors form on it parameters like heartrate, blood pressure, oxygen saturation, and temperature in real-time. GPS Systems: Global Positioning System (GPS) receivers provide accurate location tracking for ambulance positioning and route optimization. Environmental Sensors: Sensors for monitoring temperature, humidity, and air quality inside the ambulance ensure a comfortable environment for patients. Vehicle Health Sensors: Sensors to monitor the status of ambulance components such as engine performance, tire pressure, and fuel levels ensure vehicle safety and reliability.
- **Communication Technologies**: Wireless Connectivity: Utilizing technologies like 5G, LTE, and Wi-Fi, ambulances stay connected to dispatch centers, hospitals, and other emergency services. Satellite Communication: In remote

areas with limited terrestrial coverage, satellite communication ensures continuous connectivity. Mesh Networking: Ambulances can create ad-hoc networks with nearby vehicles to enhance communication reliability and coverage.

- **Data Processing and analytics platform**: Onboard Computers: Powerful onboard computers process sensor data in real-time and support decision making by paramedics. Cloud Computing : Cloud-based platforms store and analyze large volumes of data collected by sensors, enabling advanced analytics and predictive modelling.
- **Edge Computing: In scenarios requiring low**-latency processing, edge computing solutions perform data processing tasks directly within the ambulance, minimizing reliance on external networks.
- **Integration with Medical Devices**: Portable Medical Devices: Defibrillators, ventilators, infusion pumps, and other portable medical devices are integrated into the ambulance to provide comprehensive patient care during transit. Telemedicine Equipment: Video conferencing systems and remote consultation tools enable paramedics to connect with healthcare professionals for expert guidance and support.
- **User Interface and Control System**: Dashboard Interfaces: Intuitive dashboard interfaces provide paramedics with real-time information on patient status, navigation, and communication. Voice Command Systems: Hands-free operation using voicc command sallows paramedics to interact with on board systems without compromising patient care.

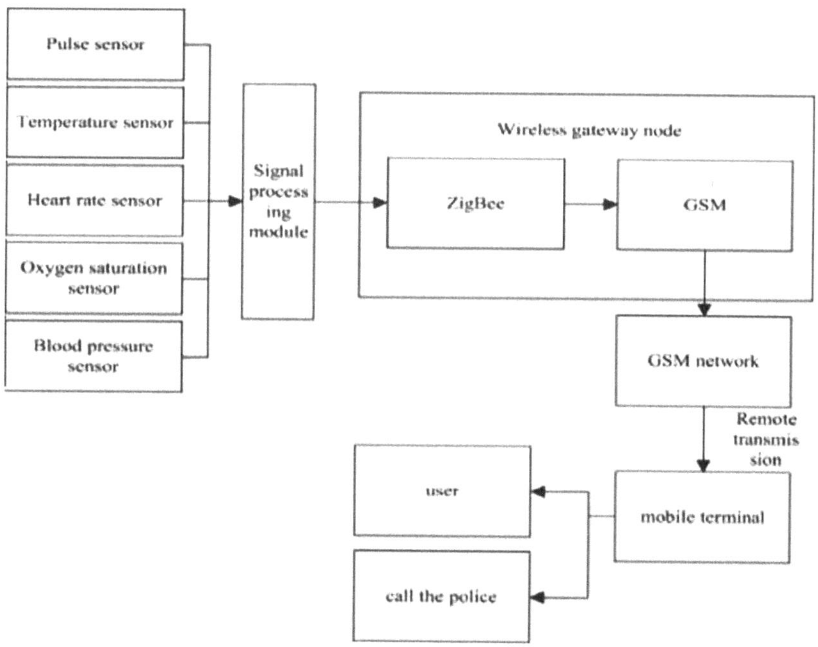

Figure 1: Flowchart of the Proposed IoT-based Smart Ambulance

4. CHALLENGING AND CONSIDERATIONS

1. *Network Connectivity and Reliability*

One of the primary challenges in IoT-based smart ambulances is ensuring reliable network connectivity. Since ambulances operate in diverse geographic locations, including remote and rural areas, maintaining seamless communication with hospitals and cloud servers can be difficult. Network failures or latency issues can impact real-time data transmission and hinder decision-making.

2. *Data Security and Privacy*

Smart ambulances generate and transmit sensitive patient data, which must be protected from cyber threats. Ensuring compliance with regulations such as HIPAA (Health Insurance Portability and Accountability Act) and GDPR (General Data Protection Regulation) is critical. Strong encryption, authentication, and secure data storage mechanisms are necessary to prevent unauthorized access and data breaches.

3. *Interoperability and Standardization*

Different medical devices and IoT sensors in an ambulance may use various communication protocols, making interoperability a challenge. Standardization of data formats, communication protocols, and integration with hospital information systems (HIS) is essential for seamless operations.

4. *Power Management and Energy Efficiency*

IoT devices and sensors rely on power sources, and continuous operation in an ambulance requires efficient power management. Battery life optimization and the use of low-power communication technologies (e.g., LPWAN, Zigbee) are crucial to ensure the longevity and reliability of IoT systems.

5. *Real-Time Data Processing and Decision Support*

Smart ambulances must process real-time patient vitals and environmental conditions to assist paramedics and provide early diagnostics. The challenge lies in implementing edge computing solutions to reduce latency and ensure timely decision-making while balancing computational efficiency.

6. *Scalability and Cost Constraints*

Deploying IoT-enabled ambulances on a large scale requires significant investment in infrastructure, including sensors, cloud storage, and software development. Cost-effective solutions must be developed to ensure wider adoption, especially in resource-constrained regions.

7. *Maintenance and System Reliability*

Regular maintenance of IoT devices and medical equipment is necessary to ensure reliability. Sensor calibration, software updates, and hardware upgrades must be carried out systematically to prevent malfunctions during emergency situations.

8. *Regulatory Compliance and Ethical Considerations*

Healthcare technology is subject to stringent regulations, and compliance with national and international health standards is essential. Ethical considerations, such as patient consent for data collection and AI-driven decision-making, must be addressed to maintain trust and transparency.

5. CONCLUSION

IoT-based smart ambulances have the potential to revolutionize emergency medical services by enabling real-time patient monitoring, predictive analytics, and seamless hospital integration. However, addressing challenges related to connectivity, security, interoperability, and cost-effectiveness is crucial for successful implementation. Future research and technological advancements in AI, blockchain, and 5G networks can further enhance the efficiency and reliability of smart ambulance systems.

REFERENCES

[1] Ling, T. and Karim, A., "IoT and cloud computing in smart ambulance services," *in Proc. 5th Int. Conf. Electr., Electron., Optim. Techn. (ICEEOT)*, pp. 1287–1291, 2021.

[2] Akter, F. and Alam, M.M., "IoT-based smart ambulance system for accident detection and patient monitoring," *in Proc. Int. Conf. Electr., Comput. Commun. Eng. (ECCE)*, pp. 1–5, 2021.

[3] Singh, S.; Agarwal, S. and Singh, R., "Accident detection and emergency notification system using IoT and cloud computing," *in Proc. 11th Int. Conf. Comput., Commun. Netw. Technol. (ICCCNT)*, pp. 1–6, 2020.

[4] Kumar, N.; Barthwal, A.; Lohani, D. and Acharya, D., "Modeling IoT enabled automotive system for accident detection and classification," *in Proc. IEEE Sensors Appl. Symp. (SAS)*, pp. 1–6, 2020.

[5] Sreelakshmy, R.; Sruthy, R.; Rajeshwari, R. and Thyla, B., "Patient health monitoring system using smart IoT devices for medical emergency services," *in Proc. Int. Conf. Innov. Comput., Intell. Commun. Smart Electr. Syst. (ICSES)*, pp. 1–10, 2022

[6] Singh, S. and Jain, R., "A systematic review of accident detection and smart ambulance systems using IoT and cloud computing," *in Proc. 8th Int. Conf. Comput. Sustain. Global Develop. (INDIACom)*, pp. 598–603, 2021.

[7] Tunc, M.A.; Gures, E. and Shayea, I., "A survey on IoT smart healthcare: Emerging technologies, applications, challenges, and future trends," arXiv preprint arXiv:2109.02042, 2021.

[8] Almadani, B.; Bin-Yahya, M. and Shakshuki, E.M., "E-AMBULANCE: Real-time integration platform for heterogeneous medical telemetry system," *Procedia Comput. Sci.*, Vol. 63, pp. 400–407, 2015.

[9] Chen, M. and Leung, V.C., "From cloud-based communications to cognition-based communications: A computing perspective," *Comput. Commun.*, Vol. 128, pp. 74–79, 2018.

[10] Mahalakshmi, S.; Ragunthar, T.; Veena, N.; Sumukha, S. and Deshkulkarni, P.R., "Adaptive ambulance monitoring system using IoT," *Measurement: Sensors*, Vol. 24, 100555, 2022.

UART Verification Using System Verilog

Aseem Jain[1]

ABSTRACT: Universal Asynchronous Receiver-Transmitter (UART) is an extensively utilized serial communication protocol in embedded systems, enabling dependable data transfer between microcontrollers, sensors, and additional peripherals. Functioning asynchronously without a clock signal, UART uses a fixed baud rate, rendering it an economical and straightforward option for a variety of applications. Due to its essential function in embedded systems, guaranteeing the accuracy and reliability of UART implementations is crucial for the overall performance of the system. This research introduces a thorough verification methodology for UART communication utilizing system Verilog. A systematic testbench environment is created, incorporating vital verification elements such as a stimulus generator for random input data, a driver for connecting with the design under test (DUT), a monitor for monitoring signals, and a scoreboard for comparing results. Numerous operational scenarios, comprising varying baud rates, data frame structures, and error situations, are simulated to assess the validity of UART transmission and reception. To improve verification resilience, assertions, functional coverage metrics, and error injection techniques are utilized, detecting possible problems such as framing errors, data corruption, and timing inconsistencies. The results indicate the efficacy of system Verilog - based functional verification in confirming reliable serial communication in embedded system.

Keywords: *Automated Testing, Embedded Systems, FPGA Implementation, Functional Verification, Parity, Serial Communication, Verification.*

1. INTRODUCTION

A basic serial communications standard in microcontroller-based systems and embedded systems is the Universal Asynchronous Receiver-Transmitter (UART) protocol. Without needing a clock signal, it makes serial data transmission between electronic devices trivial and inexpensive. From internet of things (IoT) gadgets with sensors, actuators, and several peripherals to low-speed devices, applications range from wireless communication systems like Bluetooth and Wi-Fi to low-speed devices, including sensors and actuators, throughout many fields UARTś versatility makes it essential. Errors in data transmission or reception may cause system failures, therefore negatively impacting the operation of linked devices; hence, verifying the accuracy and dependability of UART implementations is essential [1].

Using System Verilog, a powerful hardware description and verification language, this study looks at the development and verification of a full-duplex UART module.

[1]Department of Electrical and Electronics Engineering, Shri Vaishnav Institute of Technology and Science, Shri Vaishnav Vidyapeeth Vishwavidyalaya, Indore, India.
E-mail: aseemjain39@gmail.com

The UART architecture includes elements including the receiver, transmitter, interrupt, FIFO modules, and baud rate generator. The verification approach includes developing a complete testbench environment that enables efficient, reusable verification and therefore decreases code complexity. The verification environment can evaluate the UART's performance under many conditions by running limited randomization to simulate several operational scenarios including different baud rates, data frame formats, and error handling situations. The research guarantees valid validation of the UART design by way of assertion and functional coverage. Using Questasim software, simulations show the efficacy of system Verilog in modeling and validating UART functionality [2].

2. UART DATA FRAME

A UART data frame is an organized set of bits that assists in serial transmission between gadgets. Starting with a start bit, which always indicates the receiver to ready for incoming data, it runs. This guarantees that the sending and receiving devices are in synch. The data bits, which generally vary depending on the communication settings[2], follow the start bit and usually run from 5 to 9 bits. These pieces show the real data being passed that is, binary information or ASCII characters. Depending on the system requirements, the length of the data field is customizable, hence permitting adaptability in communication protocols [3].

An optional parity bit can be added for simple error checking to improve data integrity. It is usually either odd or even parity, which guarantees that the total number of 1s in the data and parity bit conforms a predetermined pattern. Allowed, the receiver looks for inconsistencies to pick out transmission mistakes. One or two stop bits, always set to high (1), finally end the data set. By pausing bits, these stop bytes give the recipient time to process the transmitted data before the next frame starts. Including embedded systems, industrial automation, and computer peripherals, this organized format supports consistent asynchronous communication in a number of uses[4].

3. PROBLEM STATEMENT

Testing the proper operation of the UART communication protocol is frequently a difficult and time-consuming procedure in embedded system designs. Especially in sophisticated systems depending on UART communication for critical functions[1], manual testing or simple simulation methods might not offer enough scope to find small mistakes or performance bottlenecks. Verification is especially tricky given the asynchronous nature of the UART protocol, variable data rates, and varied data bits, parity, and stop bits. Unforeseen real-world failures, affecting product dependability and length of time between production for embedded systems, might arise from faulty or incomplete verification [5].

Advanced verification techniques using system Verilog and Universal Verification Methodology (UVM) have been introduced to deal with these issues. By allowing random testing, assertion-based verification, and functional coverage analysis[2], these approaches help to refine the verification process. Creating a strong testbench environment helps to validate UART functionality in many situations, therefore lowering the chance of data corruption, framing mistakes, and synchronizing failures [6].

4. PROPOSED SOLUTION

This research seeks to create an automated, reusable, and strong verification framework for UART protocol validation using SystemVerilog[1] in response to these difficulties. The strategy calls for the creation of a SystemVerilog based testbench to confirm UART features in many circumstances and setups. Moreover, protocol statements will be used to follow the UART protocols and identify infractions, thereby guaranteeing conformity with communication standards[1]. The model will run edge cases and stress scenarios to determine system stability by analyzing the reliability of the protocol under severe operating conditions [8].

Functional coverage data will also be produced to help in quantifying and guaranteeing thorough test coverage by highlighting any unchecked parts of the protocol[1]. The structure will also offer automated means of failure detection, logging, and debugging, therefore enhancing verification rate and cutting down on manual handling of failure. This model seeks to create a organized and efficient approach for verifying UART protocol by using the sophisticated verification capabilities of SystemVerilog, therefore guaranteeing its reliability and availabiltiy for incorporation into many application domains [7].

5. METHODOLOGY AND RESEARCH STRUCTURE

5.1 Research Structure

The UART verification has two primary parts. Along with the building of a SystemVerilog-based UVM testbench to check its functionality[1], the first part is the hardware verification environment, including the development of the UART module, sometimes known as the Design Under Evaluation (DUT) based on the Design Under Test (DUT) basis. The second part is about automation software, which includes building a scoreboard for data comparison and error checking. Furthermore, automated functional and code coverage analysis is carried out to verify the UART implementation thoroughly [9].

5.2 Methodology

Serial communication between two devices, usually run on FPGA platforms including Cyclone III, Cyclone IV, or Xilinx Spartan series,[10] is part of the hardware side of UART design. The receiver (Rx) transforms serial data back into parallel form, while the transmitter (Tx) changes parallel data into serial data. By producing clock signals[2], a baud rate generator guarantees correct synchronization between transmitting and receiving. Control and status registers also let one configure parameters such data size, stop bits, parity, and baud rate [9]. Data input, transmission logic, reception logic, and baud rate creation are part of the functional block diagram designed to keep synchronization consistent.

The verification setting has a SystemVerilog UVM-based testbench consisting of vital elements including a driver sending signals to the DUT, a monitor watching Tx and Rx lines, and a scoreboard comparing transmitted and getting data in validation. Protocol checks guarantee data integrity and assure right start and stopping bits and proper parity bit generation. Simulation circumstances include restricted and random stimuli generation, stress testing using uninterrupted data transfers, and corner cases like concurrent transmission and reception. For checking protocols, modular test bench design, and monitoring test coverage, the software component uses verification tools like UVM, SystemVerilog Assertions (SVA), and functional coverage analysis. Debugging includes waveform generation for protocol compliance analysis as well as transaction-level logs and automated testing scripts run several test scenarios [9].

6. RESULTS

By means of a SystemVerilog-based testbench simulation, the UART module was checked for protocol adherence as well as functional accuracy. The simulation workflow started with a reset cycle (`RESET DONE`), hence creating a known beginning state for all parts before data transfer started. The driver (DRV) generated input stimulus and sent serial data along the UART TX line; the monitor (MON) continuously observed and recorded sent data for verification. Every datum transaction, whether a write operation (write Din) or a read operation (read Din), was explicitly recorded and analyzed to see if the anticipated protocol behaviour [2] was followed [12].

The monitor confirmed that the obtained data matched the sent values by means of the UART RX line on every transaction. The scoreboard (SCO) did real-time comparisons of the transmitted data (DRV) with the observed data (MON) to detect any discrepancies; this guaranteed data integrity. "DATA MATCHED" would signal under the stated test conditions appropriate transmittal and performance of validation was shown by the system logging. Including protocol checks to identify framing errors, parity mismatches, and timing issues improved the dependability of the UART implementation by also included calibration checking in the verification framework [13].

The testbench findings show the resiliency of the verification techniques, thereby validating the precision and dependability of UART communication. These results highlight the ability of SystemVerilog in creating flexible and reusable verification systems for serial communication protocols [14].

7. CONCLUSION AND FUTURE SCOPE

Using a SystemVerilog-based testbench, this research effectively verifies the functional verification of the UART protocol, therefore guaranteeing data integrity, timing accuracy, and protocol specifications adherence. The constrained-random stimulus generation approach properly confirmed UART performance in many different operating environments, including those with parity and framing violation error detection systems. Utilizing functional coverage metrics to guarantee thorough test verification, the validation framework incorporated SystemVerilog Assertions (SVA) to enforce protocol limitations.

The modularity of the testbench design lets for reusability and scale, thereby making it suited for the validation of several serial communication protocols[2]. Moreover, automation via statements and structured debugging techniques greatly improved verifiable efficiency by lowering manual interference and increasing test coverage. Still, issues including timing violations in high-speed UART setups were noted, showing the need of more improvement in handling of clock domain crossing and synchronization approaches.

Future efforts will concentrate on integrating formal verification techniques to increase test coverage even more and identify corner-case faults. Moreover, spreading this structure to cover multi-protocol verification including SPI and I2C will increase its usefulness in embedded system designs. We will also examine performance improvements whereby sophisticated constraint-solving methods help to shorten simulation run time. This study lays the groundwork for strong, scalable, and automated verification techniques in embedded communication systems, therefore guaranteeing the dependability of designs based on UART.

REFERENCES

[1] Kumar, R. and Singh, P., "Design and Verification of UART using system Verilog". *International Journal of Embedded Systems and Applications*, Vol. 12, issue 3, pp. 45-58, 2022.

[2] Srinath, M. and Hiremath, S., "Verification of Universal Asynchronous Receiver and Transmitter (UART) using System Verilog and UVM". *International Journal of Engineering Research & Technology*, Vol. 11, issue 7, pp. 120–125, 2022.

[3] Gupta, A. and Reddy, S. "Design and Implementation of UART Data Frames for Efficient Serial Communication. *International Journal of Embedded Systems*, Vol. 4, Issue 3, pp. 112–124, 2020.

[4] Banerjee, T. and Singh, M. "Error Detection and Frame Structuring in UART Communication", *Journal of Advanced Communication Systems*, Vol. 9, issue 2, pp. 67–79, 2021.

[5] Patel, R. and Sharma, V. "Challenges in UART Verification and Efficient Testing Approaches", *International Journal of VLSI Design & Communication Systems*, Vol. 13, issue 1, pp. 45–58, 2021.

[6] Mehta, S. and Agarwal, P., "SystemVerilog-Based Functional Verification of UART Communication", *Journal of Embedded and Real-Time Systems*, Vol. 20, issue 2, pp.120–134, 2023.

[7] Das, P. and Roy, A., "Automated Functional Verification of UART using system Verilog and UVM", *International Journal of Digital Circuits and Systems*, Vol. 17, issue 3, pp. 98–112, 2022.

[8] Choudhary, N. and Patel, S., "Enhancing UART Protocol Verification through Advanced Testbench Architectures", *Journal of Semiconductor Design and Testing*, Vol.11, Issue 2, pp.145–160, 2023.

[9] Sharma, D. and Gupta, R., " Advanced Verification Strategies for UART using system Verilog UVM", *Journal of VLSI and Embedded Systems,* Vol. 4, pp. 10–125, 2023.

[10] Reddy, M. and Patel, A., "FPGA-based UART Design and Verification using Constrained Random Testing", *International Conference on Embedded Systems and Digital Circuits,* pp. 67–79, 2022.

[11] Mehta, K. and Rajput, P., "SystemVerilog-Based Functional Verification of UART Communication Protocols", *Journal of Embedded Systems and Digital Design,* Vol. 20, issue 2, pp. 55–72, 2023.

[12] Chatterjee, A. and Bose, R., "Automated Testbench Development for UART Protocol Validation Using system Verilog UVM", *International Symposium on Digital Electronics and Embedded Systems,* pp. 89–101, 2022.

[13] Sharma, V. and Reddy, S., "A SystemVerilog-Based Automated Verification Framework for UART Communication Protocols". *Journal of Digital Systems and Embedded Computing,* Vol. 28, Issue 4, pp. 112–126, 2023.

[14] Gupta, R. and Pillai, M., "Challenges and Solutions in High-Speed UART Protocol Verification Using Constrained Random Testing", *International Conference on Embedded Systems and Digital Verification,* pp. 75–88, 2022.

Stock Market Analysis: A Comparative Study of Technical Indicators with Machine Learning

Vikas Jain[1] and Anand Rajavat[2]

ABSTRACT: Researchers and investors have long been fascinated with stock price predictions. This study analyses the use of technical indicators, such as the 10–20 Exponential Moving Average (EMA) crossover, Moving Average Convergence Divergence (MACD), and the Relative Strength Index (RSI), to forecast daily changes in stock prices. For developing a predictive model, we examine past stock data and make use of these indicators. This research demonstrates how well RSI, MACD, and EMA crossover work together as a decision-making tool for short-term trading strategies.

Keywords: *Exponential Moving Average, MACD, Price Volume Analysis, RSI, Stock Market, Technical Analysis, Technical Indicators.*

1. INTRODUCTION

One of the most fascinating topics in financial studies is stock price forecasting. We may predict the direction of stock prices with the use of mathematical models and computations referred to as technical analysis indicators [1]. Since share prices are constantly changing due to a variety of circumstances, the share market is not an ideal place to make predictions [1]. More than 90 to 95 percent of traders lose money in the stock market, according to business articles. Applying knowledge of technical analysis indicators such as the Relative Strength Index (RSI), Bolinger Band (BB), exponential moving averages (EMA), price-volume analysis, stochastic, and Moving Average Convergence (MACD) is the primary goal of this study [1]. The golden cross and death cross, among the technical analysis indicators that change to a crossing value between the fast and slow signal on these indicators, have a greater impact on fluctuations in the price of stocks. In order to improve stock price forecasts, it is advised to employ the price as well as the golden cross and death cross on technical analysis indicators [2].

There are two primary categories of technical indicators: lagging indicators and leading indicators. MACD and BB are lagging indicators that provide traders and investors delayed buy or sell signals, causing them to miss the right moment for buying or sell. When a stock price is oversold, use leading indicators like the RSI and stochastic to buy it; when it is overbought, sell it.

[1,2]Department of Computer Science, Shri Vaishnav Institute of Information Technology, Shri Vaishnav Vidyapeeth Vishwavidyalaya, Indore, India.

E-mail: [1]vikasjainmds@gmail.com; [2]directorsviit@svvv.edu.in

2. LITERATURE REVIEW

Yash K. Pardeshi, Prof. Preeti Kale *et. al.*, "Technical Analysis Indicators in Stock Market Using Machine Learning: A Comparative Analysis" IEEE, International Conference on Computing Communication and Networking Technologies.

The current research uses machine learning approaches to investigate the efficacy of technical analysis indicators in the stock market. By back testing indicators on frequently traded stocks which include HDFC Bank, Reliance, and Wipro over a five-year period, the study conducts a comparative analysis. The analysis sheds light on how effectively various indicators perform in anticipating changes in stock prices. However, without distinguishing between lagging and leading signs, the current study mostly relies on back testing. We will expand the analysis to incorporate both kinds of indicators in order to enhance the research and provide a more thorough knowledge of their prediction power under diverse market circumstances [1].

Arya Yudhi Wijaya, Chastine Fatichah *et. al.* "Stock Price Prediction with Golden Cross and Death Cross on Technical Analysis Indicators Using Long Short-Term Memory", IEEE, International Conference on Information and Communications Technology.

The Golden Cross and Death Cross strategies are the main subject of this paper's analysis of stock performance based on indicator signal crossovers. The study interprets these technical indications and uses Long Short-Term Memory (LSTM) to forecast stock prices. Nevertheless, the present research is limited to looking at signal crossovers as a basis for stock performance. We will broaden the study's focus to incorporate price action analysis in along with Exponential Moving Average (EMA) crossovers in order to enhance it. By combining price action patterns with technical indicator crossings, this method will offer a more thorough knowledge of stock price movements [2–8].

3. PROBLEM STATEMENT

The majority of individuals have preconceived notions about the stock market. The majority of traders have no idea why they are purchasing or disposing of a specific stock. As a result, the majority of stock market traders lose money. However, we can reduce our losses and turn a profit if we apply technical analysis indicators to forecast stock prices. Over the years, numerous individuals have experimented with different methods to forecast stock values and have put forth numerous technical indicators for the purpose.

Applying knowledge of technical analysis indicators such as RSI, exponential moving averages, price-volume analysis, stochastic, and MACD is the primary objective of this research.

4. KEY PARAMETERS

- **Stocks:** In order to produce capital gains, stock investors are interested in how stock values fluctuate. Fundamental analysis is the primary method used by long-term stock investors with holding periods longer than a year to identify the stocks with the best potential for capital gains. To optimize financial gains, short-term stock investors (traders) mostly employ technical analysis, which examines daily stock price variations without considering the company's fundamentals.

- **Technical Analysis:** The technique is used to forecast future stock prices by analysing historical stock trading data.
- **Stochastic:** The stochastic value is a measure of momentum that veers between overbought and oversold conditions.
- **RSI:** The Relative Strength Index (RSI) is a technical indicator that oscillates between overbought and oversold conditions.
- **The Moving Average The convergence of Divergence:** The trend-following momentum indicator is called MACD. The trailing indicator is the MACD.
- **Exponential Moving Average** (EMA) is a type of moving average that places greater weight on more recent data points, making it more responsive to new price changes compared to the Simple Moving Average (SMA). The EMA is widely used in technical analysis to identify trends, generate trading signals, and smooth out price fluctuations.
- **LSTM:** For time series forecasting, natural language processing, and stock market prediction, Long Short-Term Memory (LSTM), a specific kind of recurrent neural network (RNN), is perfect because it can manage long-term dependencies in sequential data.

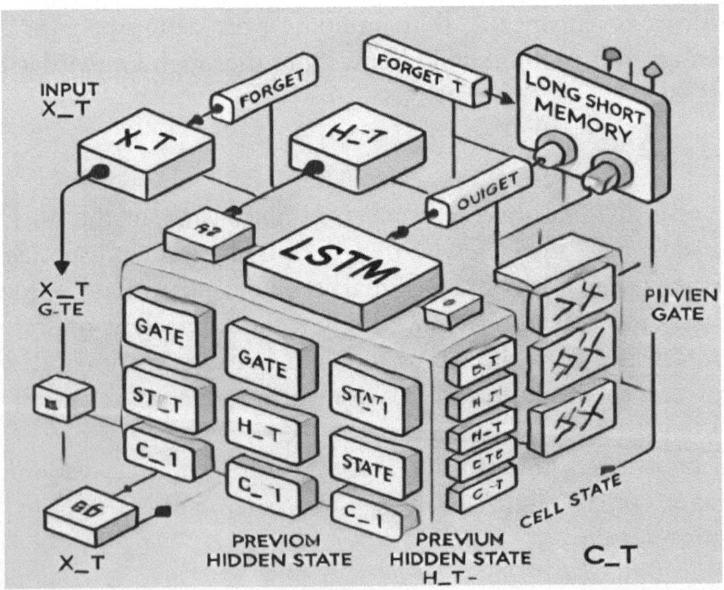

Figure 1

The simplified LSTM block diagram consists of several key components, each playing a crucial role in processing sequential data. The **Input** represents the current time step's data, which is essential for prediction, while the **Previous Hidden State** carries information from past sequences to maintain context. The **Forget Gate** determines which information from the previous cell state should be discarded, using a sigmoid activation function to produce values between 0 (forget) and 1 (retain). The **Input Gate** decides what new information should be stored in the cell state, utilizing both a sigmoid function to assess importance and a tanh function to regulate the new candidate values. The **Cell State** serves as the long-term memory of the LSTM, continuously updated with relevant information. The **Output Gate** controls which part of the cell state should be passed to the next hidden state by applying a sigmoid function and modifying the updated cell state accordingly. Finally, the **Next Hidden State** is the output of the LSTM cell, which is then fed into the next step, enabling sequential processing of data.

5. METHODOLOGY

5.1 Data Collection

Historical stock price data from publicly traded companies, sourced from [data provider] was used. The dataset spans [time] and includes daily price and volume information.

5.2 Data Preprocessing

The raw data was cleaned to handle missing values and outliers. Calculations were performed for the RSI, MACD values, and the 10-day and 20-day EMAs for each stock on a daily timeframe using standard formulas.

5.3 Model Development

A predictive model using the following steps has been developed:

- **Feature Engineering:** RSI, MACD line, signal line, histogram, and 10–20 EMA crossover signals were used as input features.
- **Labeling:** Stock movements were classified into three categories: upward, downward, and neutral, based on the percentage change in daily closing prices.
- **Machine Learning Algorithm:** A classification algorithm, such as LSTM, was employed to predict the stock's movement.

5.4 Performance Evaluation

This paper shows evaluation of the model's performance using metrics like accuracy, precision, recall, and F1-score. Additionally, back testing was conducted to assess the profitability of the trading strategy daily.

6. RESULTS

Stock markets are intricate systems that are impacted by a number of factors including market mood, company performance, and economic situations. To predict future price changes, technical analysis uses historical price and volume data. The simplicity and efficacy of RSI, MACD, and EMA intersections make them prominent among the many indicators available. The objective of this article is to assess the predictive ability of these indicators along with how effectively they work together to predict daily trends in stock prices.

6.1 The Relative Strength Index (RSI)

This trending oscillator gauges how fast and how significantly a price has changed. It fluctuates between 0 and 100; readings below 30 signify oversold situations, while values above 70 indicate overbought conditions. RSI offers insights into short-term momentum shifts when used on a daily basis.

6.2 Moving Average Convergence Divergence (MACD)

Indicating the relationship between two moving averages of a stock's price, the MACD is a trend-following momentum indicator. These components the MACD line, signal line, and histogram interact to show either bullish or bearish trends. Every day, MACD aids in spotting momentum and short-term trends.

6.3 10–20 EMA Crossover

The EMA is a kind of moving average that responds more effectively to current information since it places greater emphasis on recent prices. The interaction between a 10-day and a 20-day EMA is known as the 10–20 EMA crossover. When the 10-day EMA crosses above the 20-day EMA, it is considered bullish; when it crosses below the 20-day EMA, it is considered bearish. Finding short-term trend reversals is much easier with this crossing.

7. APPLICATION DOMAIN

- Potential applications in Trading and Investment.
- The losses can be reduced and turned into profit if technical analysis indicators are applied to forecast stock prices.
- Over the years, numerous individuals have experimented with different methods to forecast stock values and have put forth numerous technical indicators for the purpose. In order to determine the effectiveness of each indicator, this study uses technical analysis indicators and back tests on three years of data.
- Using technical indicators to anticipate prices for shares produced a lower error value than either the input price or the price plus volume. Because their values show whether prices will be rising or correcting on the next day, the Stochastic, RSI, and MACD's golden cross and death cross are suggested technical indicator features. This research can contribute to increase people's knowledge about technical analysis indicators and remove their misconception about stock market with help of reliability of technical analysis indicators for high volume stocks can be tested.

8. CONCLUSION

When applied carefully, existing methods utilizing RSI, Stochastic, MACD, and EMA crossover work well in a range of market circumstances. Integrating them in a complementary way, however, greatly increases their efficacy by utilizing each indicator's strengths while reducing its drawbacks.

The possibility of integrating RSI, MACD, and the 10-20 EMA crossover for daily stock price prediction is demonstrated by this research. Even if the model shows encouraging results, more testing and refinement under various market scenarios are required. The use of deep learning methods and the addition of other technical indicators may be explored in future research.

REFERENCES

[1] Y.K. Pardeshi, and P. Kale, "Technical Analysis Indicators in Stock Market Using Machine Learning: A Comparative Analysis", *IEEE, International Conference on Computing Communication and Networking Technologies,* DOI: 10.1109/ICCCNT51525.2021. 9580172.

[2] Wijaya, A.Y.; Fatichah, C. and Saikhu, A., "Stock Price Prediction with Golden Cross and Death Cross on Technical Analysis Indicators Using Long Short-Term Memory", *IEEE, International Confrence on Information and Communications Technology,* DOI: 10.1109/ ICOIACT5506.2022.9971844.

[3] Piravechsakul, P.; Kasetkaseem, T. and Marukatat, S. *et. al.*, "Combining Technical Indicators and Deep Learning by using LSTM stock Price Predictor", *IEEE, International Conference on Electrical Engineering/Electronics, Computer, Telecommunication and Information Technology,* DOI:10.1109/ECTI-CON51831.2021.9454877.

[4] Kumar, A.; Kumar Tripathi; Agrawal, S.C. *et. al.*, "Stock Market Forecasting using ANN", *International Conference on Information systems and Computer networks,* DOI: 10.1109/ISCON57294.2023.10111976.

[5] Meng, F. *et. al.*, "Stock price Co- movement prediction based on stock market technique indicators" Science Direct, *11th International Conference on Information Technology and Quantitative Management (ITQM 2024),* Procedia Computer Science 242 (2024) 1058–1065.

[6] Agrawal, S. and Goel, U. *et. al.*, "News media sentiments and Stock markets: the Indian perspective" *Proceedings of the 2020 IEEE IEEM.*

[7] Ashwini, J. and Dinesh, S., "Stock Market Forecasting Using LSTM", *2024 2nd World Conference on Communication & Computing (WCONF) Raipur,* India. Jul 12–14, 2024.

[8] Li, Audeliano Wolian *et. al.*, "Stock Market Forecasting Using Deep Learning and Technical Analysis: A Systematic Review", *IEEE, Digital Object Identifier,* 10.1109/ACCESS. 2020.3030226.

[9] Alsubaie, Y. *et. al.*, "Cost-Sensitive Prediction of Stock Price Direction: Selection of Technical Indicators" *IEEE, Digital Object Identifier,* 10.1109/ACCESS.2019.2945907.

[10] Nabipour, M. *et. al.*, "Predicting Stock Market Trends Using Machine Learning and Deep Learning Algorithms Via Continuous and Binary Data; A Comparative Analysis", *IEEE, Digital Object Identifier,* 10.1109/ACCESS.2020.3015966.

Design and Simulation of an 8-bit Full Adder Using Microwind Software

Anuj Gupta[1]

ABSTRACT: This research paper presents the comprehensive design and simulation of an 8-bit full adder circuit utilizing the Microwind software platform. The full adder, a fundamental component in digital arithmetic systems such as ALUs, DSPs, and microprocessors, is critical for enabling accurate and efficient binary addition operations. This study explores the detailed methodology adopted for the layout design and CMOS implementation of the full adder. By leveraging the capabilities of Microwind, the design was optimized with a focus on three key performance metrics: power consumption, propagation delay, and area utilization. The simulation environment allows for an accurate functional verification and performance assessment under realistic operational conditions. The results demonstrated not only the correctness of the adder's logic but also the effectiveness of layout-level optimization techniques. The findings underscore the suitability of the designed adder for integration into larger VLSI systems where power and area constraints are stringent. Furthermore, this work provides a foundation for future advancements in high-performance adder architectures, such as carry-lookahead and carry-skip designs, using scalable VLSI tools.

Keywords: *8-bit Full Adder, Microwind Software, Ripple Carry Adder, Layout Simulation, Propagation Delay, Area Optimization, Power-Efficient Design.*

1. INTRODUCTION

The full adder is one of the most essential components in digital electronics, especially in the design of arithmetic circuits such as arithmetic logic units (ALUs), digital signal processors (DSPs), and microprocessor architectures. It performs the fundamental operation of binary addition, which serves as a cornerstone in data processing and computation tasks. With the rapid advancement of technology and the increasing demand for high-speed and low-power digital systems, the design and optimization of efficient adder circuits have gained significant importance in VLSI (Very Large Scale Integration) design [1, 2].

As the complexity and density of integrated circuits increase, the design approach must address critical factors such as power consumption, propagation delay, and silicon area. These metrics become particularly important in portable and battery-powered devices, where energy efficiency directly affects the usability and

[1] Department of Electrical and Electronics Engineering, Shri Vaishnav Vidyapeeth Vishwavidyalaya, Indore, India. E-mail: anujg2128@gmail.com

performance of the system [3]. Therefore, optimizing these parameters during the design phase is a key objective.

In this context, the present research focuses on the design and simulation of an 8-bit full adder using the Microwind software. Microwind is a widely used CAD tool that enables users to design CMOS-based circuits at the layout level, perform real-time simulations, and analyze critical performance parameters. It provides an interactive and educational platform to explore the physical design aspects of VLSI circuits, making it suitable for both academic and research purposes [4].

This paper aims to implement an 8-bit ripple carry adder by cascading eight 1-bit full adder units, analyze its behavior, and evaluate its performance based on standard VLSI metrics. The study serves as a useful reference for learners and designers aiming to understand the intricacies of CMOS digital circuit design and layout optimization using practical simulation tools.

2. DESIGN METHODOLOGY

Designing an efficient 8-bit full adder involves several critical stages, including software selection, logic formulation, CMOS implementation, and simulation verification. This section outlines the methodology used in developing the adder circuit using Microwind, a tool known for its transistor-level VLSI design capabilities.

2.1 Microwind Software Overview

Microwind is an integrated design tool used for the layout and simulation of digital CMOS circuits. It provides a user-friendly environment for creating transistor-level schematics and offers real-time analysis of various parameters such as power consumption, propagation delay, and area utilization [1]. The tool is particularly effective for educational and prototyping purposes, enabling designers to visualize the physical implementation of digital logic circuits at the layout level.

The built-in simulator allows for transient and static analysis of logic circuits, making it suitable for verifying the behavior of complex designs like multi-bit adders. In this project, Microwind version 3.5 (or the latest available) was used to design and simulate a CMOS-based 8-bit full adder.

2.2 CMOS-Based Full Adder Design

At the heart of the design lies the standard 1-bit full adder, which takes three inputs—A, B, and Cin (carry-in)—and produces two outputs—Sum and Cout (carry-out). The fundamental Boolean expressions governing its behavior are:

- Sum = $A \oplus B \oplus Cin$
- Carry = $(A \cdot B) + (B \cdot Cin) + (Cin \cdot A)$

The 1-bit full adder is implemented using CMOS logic gates: XOR for the Sum and a combination of AND and OR gates for the Carry output. Each gate is designed using complementary pairs of NMOS and PMOS transistors to ensure low static power consumption and full voltage swing [2].

2.3 8-bit Ripple Carry Adder Architecture

To create an 8-bit adder, eight instances of the 1-bit full adder are connected in a series (ripple carry configuration). In this structure, the carry-out from each stage is connected as the carry-in to the subsequent stage. Although simple and easy to implement, ripple carry adders inherently suffer from linear delay growth due to sequential carry propagation.

Design steps:

1. Design and test the transistor-level implementation of a single-bit full adder.
2. Optimize individual gates for transistor sizing to reduce delay and leakage.
3. Cascade eight full adder blocks, ensuring proper connectivity and synchronization.
4. Use separate metal layers for power (VDD), ground (VSS), and signal routing to reduce parasitic capacitances.
5. Perform design rule checks (DRC) and layout versus schematic (LVS) verification.

2.4 Optimization Techniques

- **Transistor Sizing:** Properly sizing PMOS and NMOS transistors balances the rise and fall times of the circuit, thus reducing overall delay.
- **Power Routing:** Dedicated VDD and GND rails were implemented for consistent power delivery.
- **Interconnect Planning:** Careful placement and routing reduce parasitic effects, leading to better performance.

These steps help ensure the adder design meets the target specifications in terms of power, speed, and area.

3. LAYOUT DESIGN IN MICROWIND

The layout design phase is critical in VLSI development, where abstract logic gates are transformed into physical geometries suitable for fabrication. Microwind software provides an intuitive interface for CMOS layout design, allowing designers to create, simulate, and optimize circuits at the transistor level. This section discusses the step-by-step layout implementation of the 8-bit full adder, focusing on the transistor-level design of logic gates and their integration into a larger arithmetic structure.

3.1 Transistor-Level Implementation

In CMOS digital design, logic gates are realized using complementary arrangements of PMOS and NMOS transistors. The layout of a full adder primarily includes XOR, AND, and OR gates.

- **XOR Gate:** Implemented using pass-transistor logic (PTL) or transmission gate techniques to reduce transistor count. XOR is the most complex gate in the full adder and significantly impacts the layout area and delay.

- **AND/OR Gates:** Designed using conventional CMOS logic with pull-up and pull-down networks. These are relatively straightforward and form the basis for carry generation logic.

Each gate is first laid out individually using basic CMOS design principles such as well formation, active region definition, polysilicon gate placement, and proper metal interconnections. Careful transistor sizing is employed to balance drive strength and minimize delay [2], [4].

3.2 Layout Design Process

Step 1: Designing a 1-bit Full Adder

- **Schematic Mapping:** Start by mapping the logic expressions (Sum = $A \oplus B \oplus$ Cin, Carry = AB + BCin + ACin) into a transistor-level schematic.
- **Gate Layouts:** Use Microwind's layout editor to design XOR, AND, and OR gates individually. Ensure that each gate passes DRC (Design Rule Check) before integration.
- **Integration:** Connect the gates to form a single 1-bit full adder. Optimize layout compactness by sharing diffusion regions and minimizing wire length.
- **Power/Ground Planning:** Lay out consistent VDD and GND rails using Metal1 or Metal2 layers to support standard cell-style layout.

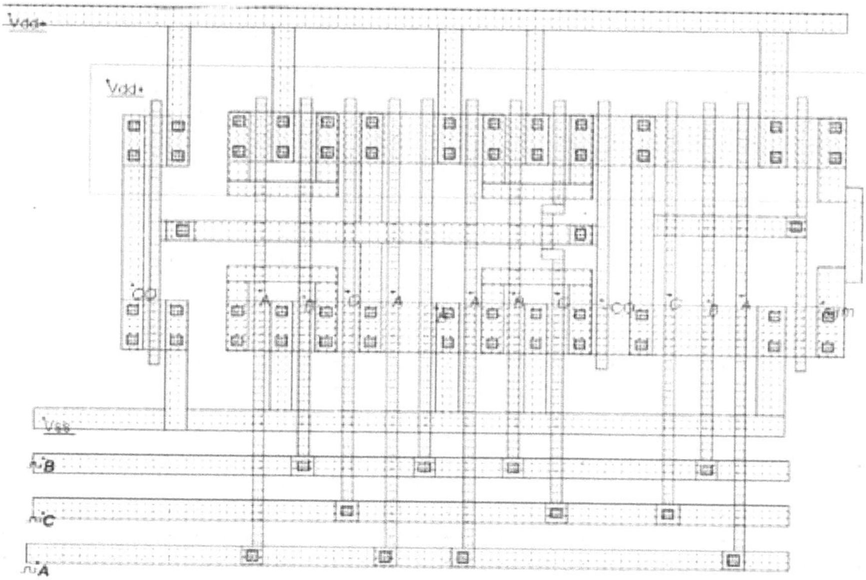

Figure 1: 1 bit Full Adder Design

Step 2: Extending to an 8-bit Full Adder

- **Cascading Full Adders:** Chain eight 1-bit full adder blocks in a ripple-carry configuration. The carry-out from each stage is wired as the carry-in to the next stage.

Layout Optimization:

- Use **standard cell techniques** to maintain layout regularity.
- Employ **metal layers (Metal2, Metal3)** for long-distance interconnections to reduce resistance and parasitic capacitance.

Utilize **abutment and symmetry** for uniform power distribution and signal flow.

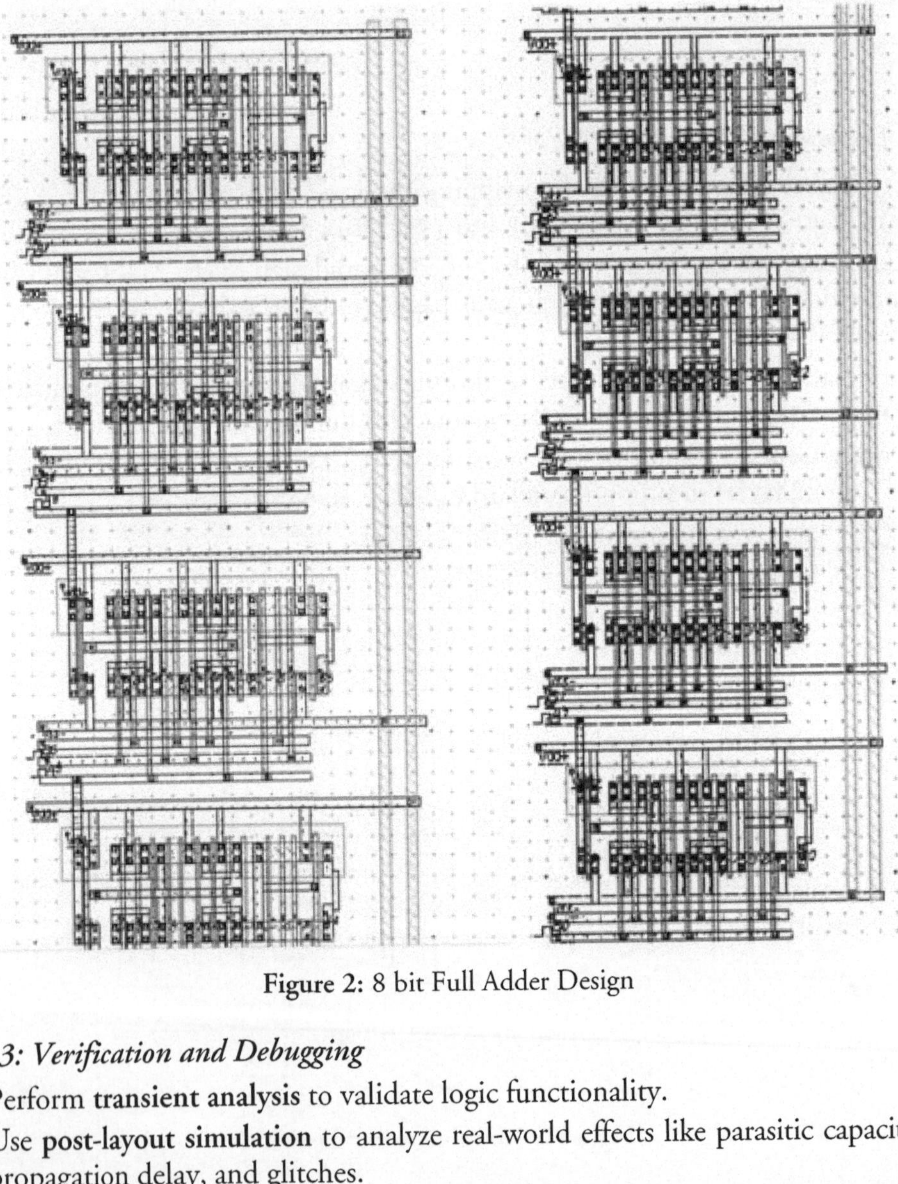

Figure 2: 8 bit Full Adder Design

Step 3: Verification and Debugging

- Perform **transient analysis** to validate logic functionality.
- Use **post-layout simulation** to analyze real-world effects like parasitic capacitance, propagation delay, and glitches.
- Reiterate transistor sizing or routing based on simulation feedback to meet timing and power targets.

By using the Microwind platform, the full adder layout was iteratively refined for area efficiency, performance reliability, and manufacturability. The final 8-bit layout represents a balance between performance and simplicity, making it ideal for use in introductory VLSI courses and preliminary ASIC prototyping.

5. CONCLUSION

This research successfully demonstrates the complete design and simulation workflow of an 8-bit full adder using Microwind software. Beginning from the fundamental principles of CMOS logic, the study traversed through schematic development, layout design, cascading of 1-bit full adders, and functional simulation of the ripple-carry architecture. The implementation illustrates not only the correctness of the logic but also highlights practical trade-offs involved in VLSI circuit design.

The simulation results validate the functionality of the adder circuit under various input combinations and provide a comprehensive assessment of key performance metrics, including power consumption, propagation delay, and silicon area utilization. These insights are valuable for VLSI designers focused on optimizing arithmetic units for low-power and high-speed applications, particularly in embedded systems, portable electronics, and digital signal processors.

Furthermore, the layout design experience using Microwind reinforces the importance of physical design considerations such as parasitic minimization, proper routing, and efficient transistor sizing. The project also serves as an effective educational tool, bridging the gap between theoretical digital logic design and real-world CMOS implementation.

In future work, the design can be further enhanced by implementing advanced adder architectures like carry-lookahead, carry-skip, or parallel-prefix adders. These architectures offer reduced delay and better scalability, making them more suitable for high-performance computing systems. Additionally, transitioning the design to more advanced process nodes and incorporating clock gating or power gating techniques could further improve energy efficiency.

REFERENCES

[1] Rabaey, J.M., *Digital Integrated Circuits: A Design Perspective*, 2nd ed., Upper Saddle River, NJ, USA: Pearson Education, 2003.

[2] Weste, N.H.E. and Harris, D., *CMOS VLSI Design: A Circuits and Systems Perspective*, 4th ed., Boston, MA, USA: Pearson, 2010.

[3] *Microwind User Manual and Tutorials*, Microwind, [Online]. Available: http://www.microwind.net

[4] Baker, R.J., *CMOS: Circuit Design, Layout, and Simulation*, 3rd ed., Hoboken, NJ, USA: Wiley-IEEE Press, 2010.

[5] Johns, D.A. and Martin, K., *Analog Integrated Circuit Design*, New York, NY, USA: Wiley, 1997.

[6] Razavi, B., *Design of Analog CMOS Integrated Circuits*, New York, NY, USA: McGraw-Hill, 2001.

[7] Shams, A.; Kuroda, T. and Bayoumi, M.A., "Performance analysis of low-power 1-bit CMOS full adder cells," *IEEE Transactions on Very Large Scale Integration (VLSI) Systems*, Vol. 10, No. 1, pp. 20–29, Feb. 2002.

[8] Goel, S.; Kumar, A. and Bayoumi, M., "Design of robust, energy-efficient full adders for deep-submicrometer design using hybrid-CMOS logic style," *IEEE Transactions on Very Large Scale Integration (VLSI) Systems*, Vol. 14, No. 12, pp. 1309–1321, Dec. 2006.

[9] Zhuang, N. and Wu, H., "A new design of the CMOS full adder," *IEEE Journal of Solid-State Circuits*, Vol. 27, No. 5, pp. 840–844, May 1992.

[10] Kagaris, T. and Vergos, H.T., "On the design of ripple carry adders with logic redundancy," *Integration, the VLSI Journal*, Vol. 40, No. 4, pp. 586–596, July 2007.

Epilogue

Paper 1: This project addresses the communication challenges faced by the verbally and hearing impaired by introducing an affordable hand gesture converter. By designing low-cost, self-made flex sensors, it offers a practical alternative to expensive market solutions, making sign language translation more accessible and inclusive.

Paper 2: This paper presents an intelligent attendance system using facial recognition to enhance efficiency and accuracy in presence tracking. By leveraging computer vision and deep learning, this paper replaces traditional manual methods with an automated solution that ensures seamless and reliable identity verification.

Paper 3: This paper presents a cost-effective and scalable IoT-based system for real-time monitoring of air and sound pollution. By integrating cloud computing and machine learning techniques like K-NN and Naive Bayes, this paper enhances environmental data analysis and supports timely decision-making, contributing to smart city development and public health.

Paper 4: This paper explores the integration of solar and wind energy into modern power grids, addressing challenges such as intermittency and infrastructure limitations. By examining smart grid technologies, energy storage, power electronics, and predictive analytics, this paper highlights innovative solutions for enhancing grid reliability, efficiency, and the adoption of clean energy.

Paper 5: This paper presents an automated color sorting system using the Mitsubishi MELFA RV-4FRL robotic arm and an iQ-R series PLC for precise, efficient operations. By integrating advanced automation, this paper demonstrates significant improvements in industrial sorting, reducing manual labor and enabling adaptability across various sectors.

Paper 6: This paper compares three machine learning algorithms—Linear Regression (LR), Support Vector Machine (SVM), and Artificial Neural Network (ANN)—for load prediction in Home Area Networks (HAN). The results show that ANN outperforms SVM and LR in terms of prediction accuracy and efficiency, offering a promising solution for energy management in smart grid systems.

Paper 7: This paper reviews the key technologies driving industrial automation, tracing its evolution from mechanical machines to advanced cyber-physical systems. By exploring the roles of PLCs, robotics, sensors, AI, IIoT, and cloud computing, this paper highlights current trends, future directions, and the challenges and opportunities associated with the widespread adoption of industrial automation.

Paper 8: This paper presents a comparative study of six key GAN-based image generation methods, analyzing their technical approaches, applications, advantages, and challenges. By using graphical representations and X-Y plot analysis, this paper highlights the strengths and optimal use cases of methods like StyleGAN3, DC-Art-GAN, and others in creative industries.

Paper 9: This paper proposes a fire extinguisher mechanism integrated with a GPS-based accident detection system to address the rising number of road accidents and fire-related fatalities. By providing real-time accident location data and using fire sensors to prevent accidents, the system enhances vehicle safety and aids timely rescue operations, ultimately saving lives and property.

Paper 10: This paper presents the development of a Restaurant Assistant System (RAS) using the Spark V microcontroller and ESP8266 Wi-Fi module to automate order processing, food delivery, and inventory management. It highlights the system's feasibility, identifies challenges like reliability and scalability, and discusses potential optimizations, offering a comparative analysis with existing restaurant automation technologies.

Paper 11: This paper focuses on an energy audit conducted at a 100 MW thermal coal-fired power plant in India, aiming to identify energy loss areas and strategies to improve efficiency. It highlights the significant potential for energy savings, with an estimated reduction in electrical energy expenses of Rs. 5.87 crore and a payback period of 24 months, while also discussing techniques for conducting energy audits in thermal power plants.

Paper 12: This paper presents a CNN-based approach to improve retinal disease detection through enhanced image reconstruction. By extracting key eye features from the STARE dataset and deploying the model on a Django website, the system successfully classifies various retinal diseases, demonstrating the potential of deep learning to improve clinical outcomes in ophthalmology.

Paper 13: This paper presents the design and implementation of an IoT-based weather monitoring system that collects real-time environmental data, utilizing low-cost sensors and Google Cloud services for data storage, analysis, and predictive modeling. The system offers scalable solutions for applications such as urban climate monitoring, agriculture, disaster management, and environmental research, with a focus on security and data integrity.

Paper 14: This paper presents an IoT-enabled smart home automation system that enhances convenience, security, and energy efficiency through AI-based predictive analytics, edge computing, and blockchain technology. The system achieved a 30% reduction in energy consumption, 98.5% accuracy in intrusion detection, and high user satisfaction, offering a sustainable, scalable solution with future plans for AI expansion and real-time energy trading integration.

Paper 15: This paper presents an intelligent traffic control system that uses computer vision and deep learning to manage traffic flow dynamically. By employing OpenCV and YOLO for real-time vehicle detection, the system optimizes throughput, reduces congestion, and maintains balanced traffic flow, demonstrating its potential for smart city applications.

Paper 16: This review explores advancements in recycling techniques for silicon-based photovoltaic panels, focusing on mechanical, chemical, and thermal methods for recovering materials like silicon, glass, and metals. It highlights the potential of hybrid approaches to improve efficiency and reduce costs, while addressing economic and policy considerations to support sustainable solar panel recycling and a circular economy in the photovoltaic industry.

Paper 17: This paper presents a PLC-based car parking and washing system designed for urban vehicle management, using the Mitsubishi FX5U PLC to automate processes with IR sensors, motors, and eco-friendly washing techniques. The system demonstrated 95% vehicle detection accuracy, a 45-second washing cycle, and reductions in water and power consumption, offering a scalable, sustainable solution with potential for smart city applications.

Paper 18: This paper presents an AI-driven framework for facial recognition in forensic investigations, combining sketch-to-photo recognition with automated sketch generation. Using AADCNN and GJO-ANN, the system enhances accuracy, addressing occlusions and pose variations with OAM-Net, advancing criminal identification and expanding facial recognition applications in security.

Paper 19: This study explores how emerging technologies like AI, machine learning, quantum computing, blockchain, and zero-trust architectures are reshaping cybersecurity. It highlights challenges such as sophisticated cyber-attacks and quantum threats, emphasizing the need for adaptable, quantum-resilient security frameworks and collaboration across academia, industry, and regulators to safeguard data in the evolving digital landscape.

Paper 20: This paper presents the design and implementation of a Universal Asynchronous Receiver Transmitter (UART) using Verilog. The transmitter and receiver modules, simulated in ModelSim and synthesized with Quartus Prime Lite 20.01, demonstrate the protocol's effectiveness in reliable full-duplex serial communication, including error handling mechanisms and validation through testing.

Paper 21: This paper covers the Serial Peripheral Interface (SPI) protocol, used for high-speed data transfer between microcontrollers and peripherals. It's essential in embedded systems, sensors, memory modules, and industrial automation. The paper also discusses future improvements in data rates, power efficiency, and IoT/5G compatibility.

Paper 22: This paper discusses the impact of IoT integration in ambulance services, focusing on Smart Ambulances that use real-time monitoring sensors, cloud computing, and advanced communication systems to improve emergency medical response. These systems enable remote patient monitoring, accident detection, and faster emergency notifications. Challenges like data security, interoperability, and network reliability are also addressed, highlighting areas for future improvement in IoT-based ambulance systems.

Paper 23: This research presents a verification methodology for UART communication in embedded systems using SystemVerilog. It utilizes a testbench environment with key components like stimulus generators, drivers, and monitors to assess UART performance under various scenarios, ensuring reliable serial communication and error detection.

Paper 24: This study examines the use of technical indicators like the 10–20 EMA crossover, MACD, and RSI to predict daily stock price changes. By analyzing past stock data, the research shows how these indicators can effectively guide short-term trading decisions.

Paper 25: This paper presents the design and simulation of an 8-bit full adder using Microwind software, focusing on CMOS implementation. It aims to optimize power consumption, delay, and area utilization, with simulation results showcasing the efficiency of the full adder in digital applications.

Subject Index

Author Index